7.50 EEE

Sixteenth-Century Germany

Sixteenth-Century Germany

Its Topography and Topographers

by Gerald Strauss

The University of Wisconsin Press

Madison   1959

Published by The University of Wisconsin Press
430 Sterling Court, Madison 6, Wisconsin

Copyright © 1959 by the Regents of the University of Wisconsin
Distributed in Canada by Burns and MacEachern, Toronto

Printed in the United States of America
by Cushing-Malloy, Inc., Ann Arbor, Michigan

Library of Congress Catalog Card Number 59-14648

Contents

1 Introduction: Motives, Inspirations, and Impulses   3

2 The Search for the German Past   29

3 The Formation of the Topographical-Historical Genre   45

4 The Regional Chorographies I: Germany   60

5 The Regional Chorographies II: Switzerland   86

6 The Great Cosmographies   111

7 The Chorographies and their Readers   135

Abbreviations   152

Appendix   153

Notes   159

Bibliographical Remarks   189

Index   192

Illustrations

	Between Pages
Raetia, Vindelicia, Noricum, Pannonia from Ptolemy's Geography	7–8
Magna Germania from Ptolemy's Geography	8–9
"Geography" and "Chorography," from Peter Apianus' Cosmographia	55–56
The city of Nuremberg	65–66
Detail of Philip Apianus' map of Bavaria	76–77
A schematic outline of the divisions of Raetia	93–94
The city of Würzburg	123–24
Title page of Johann Rauw's Cosmographia	136–37

Preface

This book is not so much concerned with topography itself,
as with a phase in the history of the humanist movement in
Germany in the sixteenth century. It deals with the successful
attempt of a group of men of learning and of letters to write a
comprehensive description of their country and its people. The
gripping political events of the time, to which the humanists
were for the most part spectators, as well as the exigencies
of the rapidly developing interests and techniques of scholarship, of which they were the principal practitioners, made such
an ambitious undertaking necessary and natural. Their idea
was to "illustrate" the German past and its passage into the
present, and to "display" the land and its inhabitants as they
appeared in their own time. Descriptive geography and narrative history were brought together to accomplish this purpose,
and the resulting volumes, though they bore many individual
titles, were generally spoken of as topographies, or chorographies.

I became aware of the bulk of this descriptive literature some
years ago, while occupying myself with one of the favorite enterprises of the older German humanists, the <u>Germania</u> <u>Illustrata</u>
of Konrad Celtis and his friends (discussed in Chapter 1). I
soon realized that individual studies of the various antiquarian,
historical, and ethno-geographical projects of these busy scholars could be made meaningful only by relating them to the German humanists' general concern with the traditions of their
nation and its progress in modern times. I was rather surprised
to discover that such a larger study had not been made. The out-
come was a doctoral thesis, done for Columbia University,* of

---

*<u>Germania</u> <u>Illustrata</u>: <u>Topographical-Historical</u> <u>Descriptions</u>
<u>of</u> <u>Germany</u> <u>in</u> <u>the</u> <u>Sixteenth</u> <u>Century</u> (Columbia University Dis-
sertation, 1957).

which the present book is a considerably altered version. Readers interested in more extensive documentation than the format
of this volume permits may consult my dissertation, which has
the critical apparatus customary with such studies.

It is a pleasure to be able to record here my gratitude to
Professors Garrett Mattingly and Paul Oskar Kristeller, both
of Columbia University, whose suggestions and criticism have
helped me much. I must also thank the editors of Studies in the
Renaissance and The Germanic Review for permission to include here portions of Chapters 2 and 3 which first appeared
in these journals.

Sixteenth-Century Germany

1

Introduction: Motives, Inspirations, and Impulses

TO STATE, as Michelet did, that the Renaissance "discovered" the world is to tempt exaggeration. To say, on the other hand, that the men of the late fifteenth and sixteenth centuries found much in their world that was different, new, and fresh to them is merely to repeat an observation which they themselves frequently made. The sixteenth century was an age of transformations of the most far-reaching kind and of a spectacular nature. The great voyages of discovery and exploration, the political and military struggles centered about Italy, the constitutional reform movement in the Germany of Maximilian I, the devastating plagues, the religious disputes, the peasant uprising, and, most disturbingly, the progress of the Turks into eastern and central Europe—all these must have appeared to men then living as tugging at their world, shaking its stability, turning it into a different place. It must have been a world that compelled attention, a world that called the active and the thoughtful to participation. A reflective person, as he sat down to compile a record of his life's adventures, could well begin by asking:

> Who is not aware from his own experience that the wars which occur every day, the terrible plagues and epidemics, are causing great changes in kingdoms, lands, towns, and villages? Places we used to call magnificent and beautiful are now devastated and useless; on the other hand, regions once despised as undesirable and barren have turned, in our age, into blooming and fruitful gardens. He who realizes this will admit that our time has much to learn and to find out that was not recorded by the ancients. Our world is such a big book that we can never read through all of it. [1]

Views differed, of course, on the meaning of observed
changes. Some saw the destructive blows of enemy and disease as clear evidence of the running down of time. Hartmann
Schedel left in his Chronicle of 1493 only a few blank pages
between his last entries and his vision of Judgment Day,
enough space for the events of two or three generations; and
a short time later Johann Carion, a widely read Protestant
chronicler, wrote: "Since in this year of our Lord 1532 about
five thousand four hundred and seventy-four years have
passed since the beginning of the world, we may hope that
its end is now near at hand."[2] But an expectation of Doomsday was perhaps a trait of temperament rather than a conclusion drawn from events. A more earth-bound voyager
through the sixteenth century could observe much to justify
a conviction that his world was actually gaining in vitality.
Plague and Turks and internecine European wars may well
have been the death agonies of an epoch which was passing;
at the same time there were portents which to those who
marveled at them were assurance that they were entering
the spring of a new age.

The Portuguese and Spanish voyages were the surest sign
of this awakening. They pushed back in a palpable way the
limits of the world and of the present and opened new ranges
of investigation and speculation. German printers were quick
to see in the reports of these voyages the stuff of a popular
literature. From the year 1497, when the first report of the
New World reached the reading public through a German version of the Columbus letter,[3] the feats of travel, discovery,
and conquest on the other side of the Atlantic were received
with eager curiosity. Not only were the important documents
of these exploits edited and translated for German readers—
the Vespucci letters, the reports of Cortes to Charles V—
but hair-raising tales of German adventurers who had braved
the dangers of unknown climes became favorite reading. The
memoirs of one such vagabond, Hans Staden's Truthful
History and Description of the Wild, Naked, Ferocious Cannibals in the New World,[4] went through four editions in its
first year of publication and frequently saw print thereafter,
alone or in company with other yarns. The source of such
popularity is not hard to find. Staden's detailed description
of native customs, including an eye-witness report of a
ghastly cannibalistic feast, held high excitement for the arm-
chair traveler. To this impressionable customer all the many
anthologies of voyages which appeared throughout the century
were addressed.[5] Their editors, men like Sigmund Feyerabend,
Theodor de Bry, and Levinus Hulsius, were not in any sense

men of learning. They were publishers and booksellers, and they aimed their anthologies at the broad reading public, not at the academic profession. This explains the titillating titles, the sensational details, the ample illustrations and maps.

But the implications of such astounding tales of new worlds were not lost on the learned. Their impact on the professional community may be traced in the letters of the humanists, its most articulate citizens. These men, whose virtue was learning and whose ideal was the productive scholarly life, reacted instinctively to every stirring of the intellectual atmosphere. From their classrooms in universities and princely courts, from monasteries and wayside inns where they stopped in pursuit of their studies, they began to exchange views on the import of the discoveries. Excitedly they compared what information they had been able to collect. [6] One major reorientation was in store for them: the reports from America conflicted with the testimony of the authorities. In 1503, Konrad Celtis, the most active member of the humanist community and its undisputed leader at the time, was told by a correspondent in Antwerp that the marvelous tales of Portuguese sailors who landed there cast doubt on the reliability of all ancient writers. [7] By 1518, Joachim Vadian, an earnest and creative student of geography, had made up his mind that on questions of geography living writers are to be preferred to dead ones. [8] Sebastian Franck, who had written a cosmographical book in which he surveyed the entire world, stated in its preface that if there was a conflict, the first-hand experience of contemporaries must be trusted, not the authorities. [9] Where the ancients failed to provide guidance, modern scholars had to be audacious enough to step independently. Geographical studies flourished in the sixteenth century because the voyages showed that the largely Mediterranean world of the classical authors was not the whole world, and because many of the discoveries to be made might in fact turn out to be not so far from home.

No obstacles of conscience stood in the way of a new examination of the earth. "The Lord God," explained the theological faculty of the University of Marburg in its recommendation of a bulky geographical volume, [10] "placed man in this world as in a beautiful showcase and endowed him with sense and reason so that he need not, like a beast, live only for his stomach and for material goods, but may direct his gaze outward to observe the skies, the air, and the waters, and stroll about the surface of the earth." Beyond this approval by spiritual mentors, however, the study of geography and its skills was sanctioned by necessity. The new and

better maps which came off the drawing boards of German
cartographers called for descriptions of the charted regions.
Even before the turn of the sixteenth century a well-traveled
Dominican-friar, Felix Fabri, had noted that the new maps
of his day offered an altogether different picture of the European world, and that fresh descriptions of its countries were
very much to be desired. [11] After 1500, Fabri's voice was
sustained by a chorus of similar observations.

The sort of descriptive geographical narrative that Fabri
had had in mind was especially attractive to the humanists.
A leisurely, rambling style and wide-open structure offered
their roaming minds a vehicle for the generalizations and
comparisons they loved to make. Few among the German
humanists professed the skills that would have enabled them
to make solid contributions to scientific geography, but they
possessed unbounded enthusiasm, and all had formulated
strong views on the role of geography in the quest for general
knowledge. Celtis regarded the science as indispensable to
the philosopher, [12] and Peter Apianus, a professional geographer and astronomer, thought it essential to the poet and
theologian as well. [13] The Swiss humanist Heinrich Glareanus
enthroned geography amid the liberal arts. [14] Others asserted
that geography is rightly called "the eye of history" [15] because
"we grasp the customs, arts, laws, practices, and characteristics of the various peoples more clearly when we are able
to see them before our eyes." [16] The new geographical awareness demanded that a historian locate a country's civilization
not only in time, but in space; and towards the end of the century all humanists would have agreed with Peter Albinus, the
writer of a territorial chronicle, that "when we plan to write
the story of a land we must begin by giving a clear outline of
its position in the world and on its continent, of the countries
and peoples that surround it, and of the mountains, rivers,
and forests within it—in short of all the features that constitute what the Romans called the situs." [17]

The age of discoveries, then, may be said to have stimulated
geographical description. But for most of the German humanists the form into which their geographical writings were
cast was not determined by the great voyages or by the
achievements of the mapmakers, but by a new-found zeal to
depict their own country. The decline of imperial authority
had brought much scorn upon the empire which was now,
under Maximilian, eager for an assertion of itself as a state.
Still echoing in German ears were the words of a distinguished
visitor of a former time. "More widespread is your nation

than ever before, and so mighty that it is second to no other people," Enea Silvio, the future Pope Pius II, had written in 1457,[18] and to the German humanists of the century that followed Enea's honeyed flattery, these words were both laurel and spur. Gratified as they were at the approbation of the discriminating Italian, they regarded his words as an admonition to employ their pens to draw images of the splendors of their land, and to dispel for all time the lingering notion that Germany was a wasteland peopled by oafs and ruffians.

Much has been written on the subject of the patriotism of the German humanists,[19] and while recent approaches are far less emotional in their recognition of nationalistic trends than earlier studies, they corroborate a general impression that the humanists of the sixteenth century gave voice to a sincerely felt, if somewhat contrived, patriotic fervor. In its constructive political phase this national consciousness sounded the call for unification under the imperial crown, as when Heinrich Bebel, in an oration delivered in 1501 in Innsbruck in the presence of Maximilian (who then crowned him poeta laureatus), pronounced a long diatribe against the inner dissension which fragmented the empire.[20] What makes German patriotism so difficult to identify is its refusal to depart from the axioms of medieval universalism. While in Italy Bruni and Biondo dated the rise of an independent Italy from the decline of the Holy Roman Empire, German thinkers continued to adhere to the imperial dream. Bebel pleaded with the Swiss to return to the fold.[21] Jakob Wimpheling, the Alsatian humanist and patriot, similarly urged the citizens of the Confederation to remember their duty to the crown from which so much good had come to them.[22] Vadian of St. Gall, in an address to Maximilian in 1515, saw the empire held together not by homogeneity of territories or language but by the common German qualities of fidelity and courage,[23] and in a scholarly work published three years later he made a special point of identifying the Swiss as Germans.[24] The emperor is always the rallying point, and the humanists express themselves on the efficacy of the imperial crown not only when they adulate Maximilian but also when they venerate Charles the Great and when they recount, usually in painstaking detail, the tragedy of Henry IV, which became, with many of them, an epic of national betrayal and its hero a major figure of self-identification.

In the Middle Ages the German humanists recognized the Time of Troubles of their own past, and the struggle of emperors against popes was portrayed as a timeless conflict against the Wälsche. In the same way, the revolt of the princes against Henry was projected onto the scene of their own time

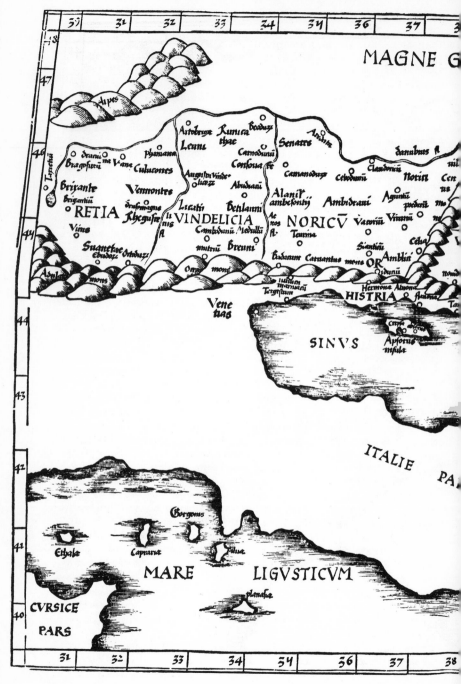

Raetia, Vindelicia, Noricum, Pannonia from Ptolemy's Geography,

in Willibald Pirckheimer's edition (Strassburg, 1525).

and the plea for unity made once again. The haughty eagle, he-
raldic symbol of a former unity, was no more, and the pitiful
naked bird pictured by one writer, feathers and wings in the
clutches of the princes,[25] was to many humanists the sad image
of the empire as they knew it. The danger of complete breakup
was acute, and the Swiss chronicler Johann Stumpf seems to
have seen it as such when he exclaimed in the words of Christ:
"Every kingdom divided against itself is brought to desolation,
and every city or house divided against itself shall not stand."[26]

But the most fearful prophecy was uttered by one who knew
the foibles of his fellow men better than most, Sebastian Brant.
"I have no tears left," Brant wrote to Konrad Peutinger in 1504:

> I see now that it all happens according to an inexorable ne-
> cessity.... Everywhere dissension, no law, no friendship
> is left in the world!... Destiny may yet deprive us of our
> scepter and the empire will crumble into dust. Many por-
> tents now point to this but no one will believe that the time
> is near.... And better times will not come; no, worse days
> are ahead. Philosophers know it and signs indicate it: man-
> kind will become more and more corrupt. For does not
> everything mortal bear in it the seeds of decay? And the
> end of our German might will be no different than the de-
> struction that engulfed all the other great empires of his-
> tory. There will be left only dust and ashes, a rubble heap,
> a mere name![27]

Not all Germans, to be sure, faced the future with such stark
pessimism. The topographical writers especially, because
they knew the strength of German regional culture, maintained
their good cheer. Brant himself was more hopeful at other moments. But everyone who could interpret the symptoms of dissension saw danger ahead and listened with apprehension to the
voice of gloom.

If Germany was a house divided she was also a house besieged. In the opinions of the humanists at least, Germany was
surrounded by hostile, jealous, and malicious neighbors bent
on impugning German honor and wit[28] and on suppressing the
fame of German accomplishments.[29] It was especially by Italy
that Germany felt herself betrayed and threatened. The Italians,
more than any other people, were held responsible for the ignorance of German deeds which prevailed in the world. A common charge was that Italy had destroyed those records of antiquity which were thought to have documented the excellence
of the ancient Germans. "Let them give back to us the entire
History of Tacitus which they have hidden away," challenges
Albert Krantz, a Saxon chronicler, "let them return Pliny's

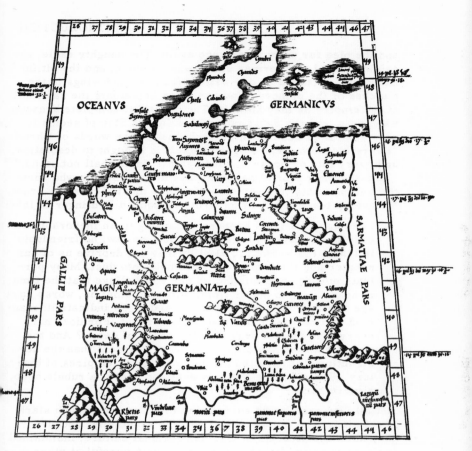

<u>Magna</u> <u>Germania</u> from Ptolemy's <u>Geography</u>,
in Willibald Pirckheimer's edition (Strassburg, 1525).

twenty books on Germany!"[30] If Europe has a false picture of
the Germans it is because their history has been wholly written by foreigners whose off-hand treatment, full of "falsifications and lying inventions,"[31] hardly constitutes unbiased historical writing.

Nor was such resentment altogether unjustified. A German
who, around 1500, looked into Zacharias Lilius' Orbis breviarium, an otherwise useful geographical dictionary, would have
learned to his surprise that his country was bounded by the
Rhine and the Danube, that the land, where not swampy, was
overgrown with immense forests and overrun by wild oxen the
size of elephants, and that he himself was of a warlike disposition and especially noted for his ability to go about nude in
freezing weather.[32] Was this refusal to recognize that things
had changed in Germany motivated by ignorance or by malice?
Probably by the latter, because Wälsche attributes, as seen by
German humanists, were not qualifications of objective historians. Krantz refers to Italians as poisoners, masters in the
art of shortening lives, faithless, discordant among themselves![33] generally they were considered shrewd, crafty, cun-
ning, and ruthless,[34] as opposed to the Germans who recognized
their distinction in their moral traits.

What the sophisticated Renaissance Italian thought of Germany may be seen in the letters of Giovanni Antonio Campano,
an intimate of Enea Silvio and later Bishop of Teramo. In 1471,
Campano was at the diet of German princes at Regensburg,
which had been called to explore ways to stem the Turkish advance. Campano had composed an oration for this occasion
which was full of graciously turned compliments to the Germans, emperor and nation. But more honest and more interesting are his observations on German customs and manners
as he recorded them in personal communications to his friends
in Italy. These letters from Germany fill the sixth book of his
epistolary, which is part of his published work.[35]

The very name of the country sickens him, he writes,[36] and
the climate makes him miserable.[37] Everything he sees repels
his sensitive nature: "O! What a chasm separates the Danube
from the Tiber!" he calls out. At night he dreams of Italy and
in the daytime he can speak of nothing but Italy. His delicate
stomach and urbane palate revolt at the coarse food served
him.[38] Germany is a land of the dead; even the smell is of de-
caying bodies. The letters go on and on; there is only ridicule
and abuse for Germany, while each thought of his homeland
brings on elegiac feelings:

> Italia, Italia est: resonat mihi dulcis in ore
> Italia, Italia fixa mihi est animo.[39]

The sighs for the day of his reunion with the land of sunshine
and laughter occur more frequently as his stay in Germany is
prolonged:

> Quando erit illa dies? quando erit illa dies?[40]

The reaction of German humanists to such sentiments may
be imagined. It was not merely that they resented the Italians'
air of superiority. They deplored their own inability to state
the case for Germany effectively. Germans still lacked the
verbal facility and rhetorical polish to enter the debate.[41]
Moreover, how could Italian slanders be exposed and the true
splendor of Germany be illuminated if the country was unknown even to the Germans themselves? "We would be ignorant of our own antiquity," it was said, "if Cornelius Tacitus
(though a Roman) had not recorded it."[42] And while we "want
to see and describe the whole wide world, about Germany, our
fatherland, we know nothing,"[43] so little, in fact, "that many a
German can hardly tell an island in India from the valley of
his next-door neighbor."[44] How could Germans express surprise and anger that ancient writers like Ptolemy erred in
mapping Germany "when we see that our own countrymen, in
describing German lands, make such clumsy mistakes that an
Egyptian could hardly do worse."[45]

The study of history and descriptive geography was thus not
only a response to public interest in these arts but also an expression of the urge to portray country and people so that Germany's place among the nations might be re-established. This
patriotic feeling was most genuine in the territories of the German Stämme, for the patriotism of the German humanists was
really regional. And while the loudest expressions of regional
loyalty came from the border lands—from Switzerland, Alsace,
Flanders, the Rhenish cities, and Bohemia[46]—the native sons
of all German territories reveal in their utterances a warm
attachment to their Stamm and their locality. To this fidelity,
in fact, we owe most of the topographical-historical literature.
The description of all of Germany was too formidable an enterprise for one individual to undertake, but a territory or a city
might well be surveyed by a single person.

But it was not merely the disdain of haughtly aliens which
had to be overcome. The indifference of their compatriots ir-
ritated the sensibilities of the humanists even more. As the
topographical-historical works were to be addressed to German readers, they might become effective instruments of instruction. The combination of history and geography was surely more than a formal coupling. It grew out of the humanist
urge to depict, illustrate, portray, and at the same time to in-

struct, preach, and reform. Historiography was, of course,
conceived in a thoroughly Tacitean sense. Its function was
"to laud the honest deeds and virtues of good men and to illustrate the vices so that they may be avoided."[47] If humanist
writing was to bring about the hoped for enlightenment, it had
to chide as well as praise.

And there were shortcomings and faults enough for which
to rebuke the Germans. Not only was the physical and intellectual coarseness which alienated Italians resented, but also
the moral blemishes and that gross sensuality which is the
principal vice against which Sebastian Brant thrusts his pen
in his Ship of Fools. Johann Boemus, an eager student of comparative customs and institutions, could draw on a wealth of
material to illustrate the vices of each Stamm, and he cites a
contemporary proverb to the effect that Germany was enviably
self-sufficient in her needs since Swabia furnished her whores,
Franconia her thieves and beggars, Bohemia her heretics,
Switzerland her pimps and fornicators, Saxony her drunkards,
the Palatinate her gluttons, and Frisia her perjurers.[48] Such
self-reproaches are common in the literature and in no way do
they impugn the German's pride in Stamm and country. The
primarily ethical position from which German humanists
viewed the world made them especially sensitive to deviation
from the norm of moral uprightness which they regarded as
the characteristic attribute of a German, the ideal expression
of which they found in the tribal customs of Germanic antiquity.
The reforming impulse in German humanism saw it as a duty
to restore the uncomplicated decency of ancestral times, and
not merely to bring elegance to Germany. The humanist as
historiographer found no difficulty in culling from the record
of the past a series of warning examples, and as reformer he
could not always refrain from moralizing. Since the topographical-historical genre offered the opportunity to examine the
feats of man along with the works of nature, it proved an ideal
vehicle for this as for all other efforts of German humanism.

But this form had first to be created, and the early German
humanists were a long way from it. They had before them,
however, some excellent models. If the German attitude towards Italy had been one of simple dislike and distrust, this
new source of inspiration would never have had its effect. But
the psychological relationship of the German humanists to the
land beyond the Alps was one of great ambivalence. If the Italians were feared and envied it was because their intellectual
superiority was recognized and their traditional role as mentors resented, though accepted. Few German humanists could

or would deny that they had much to learn, and most of them
went to Italy for the final touch to their education, for that
subtle gloss which could be added only there. Sebastian Brant
might taunt that

> Some fools have let it swell their heads
> That they've slept in Italian beds,[49]

referring to those of his countrymen who went to Italy to study
and for the remainder of their lives gave themselves airs, but
it was still the Italians who set the tone for humanist pursuits.
And the prince of these Italians, as far as Germany was concerned, was Enea Silvio Piccolomini, humanist par excellence,
traveler, man of letters and of affairs, diplomat, cardinal, and,
in 1458, Pope Pius II.

Enea Silvio's role as a cultural prime mover in Germany
is too well known to call for comment.[50] His presence at the
court of Frederick III and his travels across Germany in the
service of the Church left the imprint of his personality on a
host of intellectual matters. His close acquaintance with country and people had made him a kind of honorary German. "As
we have lived in Germany more than twenty-four years," he
was quoted, "we do not believe that we should be regarded as
a stranger here. Moreover, since we have served the emperor
and his subjects with long and devoted labors ... we act in such
a way that we may be believed to be as German as we are
Italian."[51] An occasional irate voice might be raised against
one or the other of his allegations,[52] but in general his authority was not questioned.

This acceptance was not due merely to his official kinship
with Germany but to the sheer excellence of his literary accomplishments. German writers who were eager to find suit-
able expression for their ambition to describe their own country drew close to Enea's fine cosmographical studies. These
works, with their easy fusion of geographical description and
historical characterization, must have suggested to them an
ideal approach. When Hartmann Schedel incorporated a con-
densed version of Enea's Europa, a geography and history of
the whole continent, into the great chronicle which he completed in 1493,[53] he still felt obliged to justify the inclusion of
an Italian work by quoting Enea on his elective affinity for Germany.[54] Not long afterwards there was hardly a paragraph of
Enea's Asia which had not been incorporated in the cosmographies of Franck and Münster, nor a passage of his Bohemian history that had not found its way into a dozen German
volumes. Albert Krantz appropriated nearly the whole description of Bohemian geography,[55] Johann Boemus accepted

him as a major source for folklore along with Strabo and
Pliny,[56] and a conscientious historian of Basel thought it un-
necessary, in 1580, to offer any description of the city other
than the fine sketch which Enea had written in 1434.[57] But it
would be tedious to pursue in detail the passage of Enea's
observations into German topographical-historical writing.
Wherever one turns, one is likely to find that the influence of
this Italian humanist has been at work.

The volumes with which Enea so impressed Germany were
the History of Frederick III, the German emperor whose
chancellery he had entered in 1442, and the History of Bohemia,
which Jean Bodin's catalogue of historians still lists as the
only satisfactory treatise on that country.[58] More important
was the so-called Germania, that long open letter of August,
1457, written by Enea, then a cardinal, to Martin Mayr, the
chancellor of the Archbishop of Mainz, to counter Mayr's allegations of curial extortion and arrogance in Germany.[59] The
papacy had impoverished Germany, Mayr declared. "Our nation, once of such great fame, that acquired with her courage
and blood the Roman Empire and was mistress and queen of
the world, has become poor and a tribute-paying maid!"[60]
Not at all, retorted Enea, and he went on, in the second of the
three parts of his treatise, to sketch a glowing image of German culture in the fifteenth century, the result of the civilizing
mission of the Roman Church which had lifted the tribes from
barbarism to proud and prosperous civilization. Enea's Germania became one of the foundations of German patriotism
but, beyond that, it remained the archetype of the kind of cultural history that was soon to be produced in Germany. It
proved that a true literary portrait of a country could be fashioned out of a study of its situation, its history, institutions,
and ethnic traits.

Enea's most impressive piece of scholarship was his Cosmographia. In form and purpose this work foreshadowed much
that was later accomplished in Germany, and its various editions were models for German workers in the genre. The Cosmographia takes up Asia and Europe; for a projected third
section on Africa the busy Enea never found time. While Asia
is mainly geographical in its sweeping survey of countries
and peoples, their customs and government, and the flora and
fauna amidst which they lived, Europa concentrates on the political events leading up to Enea's own time.[61] The two sections are preceded by seven chapters on the earth in the universe, the sort of scientific introduction which later on became almost mandatory in cosmographical writing. The aim
of the whole work is clearly stated at the outset: to describe

the regions and peoples of our world and, on this basis, to understand the histories of the various countries.[62] Sources were Strabo, Ptolemy, and Herodotus, and these guarantee a stimulating survey of the eastern world. But for the European countries they hardly suffice, and that is why Enea, in the second part, places the accent on the contemporary scene.[63]

But here, too, the description is lively, and comments are placed in a geographical frame of reference. Enea outlines the physical boundaries of a region, names important rivers and cities, comments on products of the soil and on commerce, traces the origin of the population, and relates its character, language, institutions, and system of laws. The description is hardly ever systematic —it was all jotted down in the high spirit of a carefree traveler, one critic observes[64]—but the quick daubs of color with which Enea works, the sudden illuminations, create sharp aperçus. He is, of course, fascinated by curious customs, by the punishment of theft in the Carinthian town of Klagenfurt, for example, where all suspects were hanged before the trial commenced and those who were subsequently proven guilty were left hanging while the innocent were given religious burial;[65] or by the primitive custom which survived in Halberstadt in Thuringia of loading all the sins of the community on one unfortunate wretch who had to carry them, barefoot, around the town for forty days.[66] When he comes to Italy in the final section of his book, Enea gives detailed treatment to the great cities of Genoa, Milan, Venice, Florence, and Rome. Here the Germans learned much from his expert intertwining of the strands of history, geography, folklore, and current politics. Even more gratifying, and no less seminal, were the fully twenty chapters which Enea devoted to Germany, "because the ancient authors wrote so little about this country that you would think the German people lived outside the world."[67] These were magic words, and they quickly gained currency in Germany.

But if one examines Enea's works for the source of their great influence on German topographical writing, one has to look beyond his major historical and geographical volumes. Geography and topography were not formal pursuits to Enea. He did not urge their study on his readers, nor did he lay claim to scientific standards in his own writing. Notes on position and location of places, inferences from the historical past to present actualities, glosses on the behavior of individuals and groups were Enea's natural mode of observation. They were the way in which he looked about him in life and the manner in which he recorded impressions. The germ of his method of presentation may no doubt be found in Strabo, who was

available in Guarino's translation when Enea worked on his
Cosmographia.[68] But to the breadth of Strabo's interests he
added his own unique gusto and charm of style, both expressions of a full and warm personality. That is why the brightest gems of his descriptive talent are to be found among his
shorter pieces. His letters and his Commentaries received
the unrestrained flow of his experiences and recollections.
There his style is most sparkling, his approach to historiography
least pedantic, and his re-creation of the scene around him
altogether successful:

> A rocky mountain about six stades high rises in the mid-
> dle of the valley. On its summit is a plateau three miles
> in circumference. Precipitous cliffs nowhere less than
> twenty ells high take the place of walls. Here were once
> splendid private houses and great palaces built of hewn
> stone. Age has destroyed much, civil strife has burned
> and ravaged more. Half ruined towers and crumbling
> churches are still to be seen, but the Church of the Bless-
> ed Virgin, which is inferior to none in Italy, stands intact
> in the middle of the city. It is remarkable for size, mate-
> rial, workmanship and design. The walls and floor are of
> varicolored marble; the façade is very high and wide and
> filled with statues by the best sculptors, chiefly Sienese,
> who are not inferior to Pheidias and Praxiteles. The faces
> stand out from the white marble as if alive and the bodies
> of men and beasts are so well rendered that art seems to
> have equaled nature. Only speech is lacking to make them
> live.[69]

The Commentaries are filled with such sketches as this one of
Orvieto with its magnificent black-and-white marble cathedral.
Their rapid, often breathless, phrases hold much keenly ob-
served and informative detail.

> The roofs of the churches [of Basel] are made of many-
> colored glazed tiles, and when the sun strikes these they
> sparkle brilliantly. Since a good many private dwellings
> are also tiled, a beautiful spectacle rewards one who views
> the city from a nearby eminence. These roofs are very
> steep because the great weight of the winter snow would
> cave them in if they were not. The roof tops are inhabited
> by storks who build their nests there. People do not molest
> them because they have a superstition that if the birds are
> deprived of their young they will set fire to the houses.

> The interiors of the homes are exceedingly well appointed,
> much like Florentine apartments. They quite gleam with

cleanliness. Each house has its garden, also a well and a
courtyard. Each has a chamber which may be heated, and
in this one room they are accustomed to eat, live, and often sleep. The windows in these rooms are of glass and
the walls and floors of pine. Caged birds add their trills
to the general merriment. Walls are papered, and carpets
cushion the floors. The boards sparkle with precious silver.[70]

Government and law are matters of absorbing interest to him:

Basel is governed democratically. There are two Councils,
the Large Council which has 200 members and a Council
of Elders which has 12. Commoners as well as the nobility
are eligible to sit in these. But the third branch of the government, the executive, is in the hands of the aristocracy.
There are many governmental departments, but the highest
authority is the mayor who must be a noble....

The Baseler live without a definite legal code and are
guided more by usage than by the letter of the law. There
is no jurisprudence and no knowledge of Roman law among
them. If a novel situation arises, a judge resolves it according to his lights: "Thus and so this business appears
to me," he says. But they are strict with themselves and
have great respect for equity and right.

But above all Enea can make us see the charm of life, for he
was inimitably adept at evoking nature in all its freshness.
His talent would have been rare in any age; in his century it
was unique:

Mount Amiata is in the Sienese territory. It is as high as
the Apennines and in all Italy only the Pistoian Alps and
two other mountains are said to be higher. It is clothed to
the very summit with forests. The upper part, which is often cloud-capped, is covered with beeches; below are
chestnuts and below them oak and cork trees. The lowest
slopes are covered with vines and cultivated trees, tilled
fields and meadows....

In the center of this region there was a natural plain about
eight stades long covered all over with chestnuts. There
the ancients built a town protected on one side by precipitous crags and on the other by a wall and a moat kept full
by running streams. In it they constructed very comfortable houses of squared stone with roofs of material that
would resist the snow. In front of the town the woods were
cut away for about a stade to make room for gardens and

a little pasture land. There is an ancient monastery here
with an extremely well-built church and monks' quarters.
... It owned precious sacred vessels and a splendid library, of which only a few volumes remain. Among them
is a large and admirable copy of the Old and New Testa-
ments in Majuscules which Pius beheld with envy....

In July the cherries there were not yet ripe. Nearby an a-
bundant spring gushes from the rock, and after he had
lunched beside it, Pius heard embassies and petitions
there.[71]

No wonder Enea's style attracted those among the German humanists who were eager to sing the praises of their own lovely country. "Of all the ancient and modern writers," confesses
one of his earliest followers in the German lands, "it is that
sweet Enea Silvio who has nursed me with the sugar of his
words and has given me of the honeycomb of his art to nourish me on my way."[72]

Enea had drawn much of his own sustenance from a contemporary who was to be only slightly less compelling a master in Germany than he himself, Flavio Biondo.[73] Biondo was
born in 1388, a native of Forlì in the Romagna. All his life he
was a faithful papal man of letters, but he died in neglect and
poverty in 1463, missed by few except Enea, who mourned him
as a fine historian and a savant.[74]

A greater contrast between two writers can hardly be imagined. Biondo was a collector of forgotten facts, a researcher
whose aim was erudition, not elegant statement, but Enea esteemed in him his patience and the painstaking precision of
his scholarship. Enea criticized the winding sentences of
Biondo's History of Italy from the Decline of the Roman Empire[75] but his Epitome of the first two parts of this work[76]
was not made to revise the original's style but to avail himself of its solid exposition of medieval Italian history. Biondo
was never exclusively antiquarian, however. His books on Roman antiquities contain innumerable references to modern
institutions, topography, and customs. In the Roma instaurata
he compares the streets and squares and buildings of classical Rome with the city in his own time, and at the conclusion
of the Roma triumphans he establishes the connection between
ancient institutions and the modern age: now the pope is the
consul, the emperor the magister militum, the cardinals constitute the Senate, and the Christian kings, princes, dukes,
and counts are the legates, tribunes, quaestors, and centuri-
ons. In his day as in antiquity, Rome unifies and civilizes the
nations.[77]

This is rhetorical flourish, but the attempt to link the old and the present worlds motivates all Biondo's writings. And it is this purpose which drew attention to his works in Germany. There the desire to bridge the gap between modern Germany and the tribal past created a scholarly climate in which Biondo was accepted as an authority. He pointed a way for the German humanists to take. It was a harder way than the path along which Enea strolled; it stayed close to the ground, near the rubble of bygone ages, the inscriptions, the ruined foundations, the fragments of classical letters. It never scaled the cool, beech-covered summits of Enea's Italy or reached a shady spot from where the sun's fireworks on distant tiled roofs could be seen. But its tortuous windings promised to lead to an understanding of the past and its lessons for the present day.

In Germany, Biondo's Italia illustrata was regarded as his most important work. Here he restores to life, as he says himself, the ancient places and inhabitants of his homeland.[78] When the barbarian tribes put an end to the Roman might,

> the cultivation of literature came to a standstill and historical writing was entirely extinguished because, everything having been torn up by the barbarians,[79] not only was there no one left to transmit current events to posterity, but the very identity of the regions of Italy—the cities, lakes, rivers, mountains—was lost, even though they are mentioned in the writings of the ancients; and even more lamentable is the fact that no information has come down to us on the founders and the dates of foundation of many new towns which were erected in Italy during this age. But since this present century has seen the rise of all the arts, notably the arts of eloquence and literature, and as these studies have created in us an ardent desire to understand the past, I have determined to make an attempt, within the limits of my knowledge, to restore to life the names of the ancient places and peoples, to rediscover the origin of cities still standing and give to those now ruined that life which remembrance can bestow, in other words, to shed light on what is obscure in the history of Italy.[80]

These sentences made a deep impression on Biondo's German readers, and his intention and method were followed closely. Again it was Hartmann Schedel, that diligent compiler of historical miscellany, who transmitted the accomplishments of this Italian master. Large chunks of the Italia illustrata are to be found in his Chronicle,[81] and the History of Italy was a veritable mine of information for him. As Biondo had surveyed

the Italian peninsula, describing the boundaries, mountain con-
tours, cities, and towns of each area, listing individuals whose
births had brought honor to a region or town, narrating noteworthy local history, and stopping everywhere to establish the
correct ancient and modern names of topographical features,
so the German humanists were to examine their country. As
always, they were annoyed that Biondo had taken so little notice of Germanic civilization in its own right and wrote Italian
history "as though nothing worth the telling had happened in
other parts of the world."[82] But Schedel, who always spoke up
for his authors, regarded him as "a most learned man...who
tells us the lost history of a thousand years, not alone of Italian lands, but of all the provinces in the Roman empire."[83] In
any case, the German humanists followed the direction he had
taken. One of the finest of the topographical-historical volumes produced in the German lands, Johann Stumpf's Description of the Swiss Confederation, was plainly an imitation of the
Italia illustrata. But it is also clear that with such works as
Stumpf's, the Germans succeeded in going beyond their models
to an art which was uniquely their own.

Still, little might have come of all this had not the final im-
petus to action been given by the most elusive and, at the same
time, the most determining figure in German humanism, Konrad
Celtis.[84] In the spring of 1492 we find Celtis in the Bavarian
town of Ingolstadt whose young university, established only
twenty years before, had offered him a chair of rhetoric. Celtis
was thirty-three years old that year. Like most of the German
humanists he had been born in humble circumstances. He had
studied at the universities of Cologne and Heidelberg, then
turned to the itinerant life he loved so well, lecturing on Platon-
ic philosophy, Ciceronian rhetoric, and the poetry of Horace.
An educational journey to Italy came next, and association,
though not intimacy, with Pomponius Laetus, Beroaldus, Aldus
Manutius, and a few other distinguished persons. In the year of
his return to Germany he was crowned with the poet's silver
laurel by Frederick III. Disciples gathered around him and admirers sent praise and invitations. Excursions and visits took
him to all parts of the Empire. Everywhere his name was held
synonymous with learning and scholarship.

In May of 1492, Celtis temporarily settled[85] in Ingolstadt. At
the end of the first semester the university asked him to stay
on,[86] and, to open the new term, he delivered the customary
oration on the dignity of his subject. But this Oratio in Gymnasio
in Ingolstadio publice recitata is more than a routine perform-
ance. It is an outline of his entire teaching program. More, it
is a plan for nothing less than a thoroughgoing reform of the

entire intellectual life of Germany, and the prominent place
here given by Celtis to historical and geographical studies indicates the importance these arts had assumed in the schemes
of the German humanists. The speech deserves close attention.
Celtis begins[87] with an apology that he, a native German,
"born in the midst of barbarians and drunkards," should address them in his halting way. But, he goes on, "I have decided that I cannot address you more worthily or more pleasantly, or choose any topic better suited to myself and you my
audience than by encouraging your minds in virtue and the
study of the liberal arts." For only a quest for wisdom can
make life meaningful; only knowledge is a worthwhile pursuit.
Let us therefore, he admonishes, turn aside from our hunt for
material possessions and try to win renown through the cultivation of wisdom:

> I shall be satisfied—and more than satisfied, O German
> men and illustrious German youths—if anything I may say
> today...succeeds in adding and inculcating and, as it were,
> branding into your minds some incentive to fame and vir-
> tue, so that you may have immortality above all things ...
> that immortality which can only be sought at the fountain-
> head of philosophy and eloquence.

Only poets and philosophers teach us to live wisely and vir-
tuously and happily "and have set before us Nature, the par-
ent of the human race...as an example and mirror of life for
us to imitate." The words of the poet and orator must be employed in order to "enjoy that unique element in human happiness, the power to transmit one's thoughts to posterity." On
this point especially he wishes to address his German listen-
ers, "to whom by virtue of the courage of your ancestors and
the unconquerable strength of Germany the Italian empire has
passed." Our object, he says, must be to

> do away with that old disrepute of the Germans in Greek,
> Latin, and Hebrew writers who ascribe to us drunkenness,
> cruelty, savagery and every other vice bordering on bes-
> tiality and excess. Consider it...the height of shame to
> know nothing about the topography, the climate, the rivers,
> the mountains, the antiquities, and the peoples of our re-
> gions and our own country.

And then he sounds the cry which was to be repeated throughout the course of humanist historiography in Germany:

> I am greatly astonished to reflect on the painstaking ex-
> actitude and subtle learning with which the Greeks and Ro-

mans have surveyed our country; ... they have expressed
our customs, our emotions and our spirits as graphically
as a painter might delineate our bodies.[88] Cast away, noble
gentlemen, cast away and wipe out those acts of robbery
which those authorities declare to have been held as proof of
courage amongst us. It is astonishing that this hereditary
disease should have persisted still in certain parts of Germany for some fifteen hundred years, for even now when,
after the draining of marshes and the cutting down of vast
forests, our climate is more cheerful and our land populated with famous cities, we still fail to dislodge the leaders of that robber crew. ... Let us be ashamed, noble gentlemen, that certain modern historians (who, publishing
new Decades, boast that they have equalled the ancient Roman empire)[89] should speak of our most famous leaders
merely as "the barbarians" ... in order to ... disparage
the reputation of us Germans. ... Let us be ashamed, I
pray, that ... not one of you should be found today to hand
down to posterity the deeds performed by German courage.
Yet many foreigners will be found who, in their historical
works and contrary to all historical truth, will hiss like
vipers against our courage with all the pretentious cajol-
ery of their style and seek with falsifications and lying inventions ... to belittle our glorious achievements.

This is a forceful statement of the arguments for topographical-historical writing, and Celtis' allegations were soon accepted as axiomatic. But at this occasion he conceived of the
genesis of a German school of historiography only within a
broad program of enlightenment and educational reform,[90] and
to this matter he then drew the attention of his audience. In
the most general sense, it is the study of philosophy which he
advocates: "For philosophy indeed is like a school which teaches
most liberally the knowledge of matters human and divine and
their respective spheres." More specifically, he urges pene-
tration into the "secrets of literature," by which he means
those aesthetic and psychological appreciations of the classics
which had not been within the ken of the schoolmen who expounded the texts in the universities. The reference calls for
a digression and a little diatribe against the bigotry and nar-
row-mindedness of the academicians who, "neglecting all teaching in philosophy and rhetoric, strain every nerve of their intellect to achieve an empty loquacity," and purvey learning which
is "mortar without lime and a voice without blood." We can
hear his voice rising in pitch as he charges the entrenchments
of the universities. Again he turns to the unheeding attitude of

the Germany of his day. "But we do not perceive our own rot-
tenness." We pursue, at best, "minor aims," and lose sight of
the true goals of life because of our occupation with material
cares. From these let us turn our attention to "higher concerns, which only philosophy can teach." The ancients sought
to unite wisdom with eloquence, and their success in bringing
about this union accounts for the grandeur of their civilization.
Let our young men imitate them, he concludes, let them study
poetry, oratory, eloquence, and the secrets of letters, and
"from these they may then rise to original composition and to
the sublimity of the art of poetry, finally to achieve the reputation of illustrious writers by composing histories and poems
and to win thereafter immortality for themselves and glory
and renown for their native land."

Since Celtis lectured on rhetoric at Ingolstadt, an enthusiastic endorsement of poetry and letters was indicated. But his
vigorous acclaim, at this occasion, of the role of history, topography, and related studies, must have sprung from an eager
acceptance of the concerns of his generation with the depiction
of Germany. Emulation of Italy[91] and the creation, in Germany
of a polished, literate society were his immediate projects;
these were not new, for Rudolf Agricola had already urged
such a program in his treatise on education.[92] Celtis only gav
greater force to the utterance. Apollo, he said, had to be
brought to Germany.[93] But such aims were preliminary to the
accomplishment of a graver object: Germany was to become
conscious of her proud heritage, and this awareness must be
made concrete through historical and geographical treatises
whose purpose it should be to draw a faithful likeness of the
land, catch the image of its past, and reflect the spirit of its
culture.

This is the genesis of Celtis' great historical project, the
Germania illustrata.[94] Taking his cue from Biondo's more mo
est Italia illustrata, Celtis set about to work out a parallel des
cription of ancient and modern Germany, depicting her territories, drawing up a comparative table of localities, cities,
rivers, and peoples, and uniting the whole project with a con-
necting thread of dynastic history from the tribal chiefs to the
reigning Habsburg. First the correct nomenclature of the phys
ical features would have to be worked out, then the pertinence
of ancient references to country and inhabitants tested. The
starting point in the works of the classical writers was a natural one for Celtis and his group. Their antiquarian orientatic
demanded that at the outset of the undertaking the testimony o
ancient authors be reconciled with the evidence of observed
facts. The resulting catalogue of transformations would enabl

them to engage in favorite speculations on time, the nature of
change, and the fickleness of fortune. Part of the Germania
illustrata might be in verse,[95] most of it in prose.[96] For the
Germany of antiquity the classical writers were to be studied,
for the history of the medieval empire the sources had first
to be found and published. In the meantime, other scholars
were to work on genealogical and dynastic studies, and topographical descriptions were to be procured from all the cor-
ners of the German land.

It is evident that Celtis could never have conceived such a
sweeping plan had he not been able to rely on the immediate
interest and unstinted support of his colleagues in all parts of
Germany. The quickness with which they responded to his call
is the measure of the widespread enthusiasm for topographical-
historical activities. It also reveals to us something about
Celtis' own driving energy. At once he set to work preparing
a number of classical and medieval sources.[97] Among these
were two editions of Tacitus' Germania, the first in Germany,
and two medieval texts, the works of the tenth-century nun
Roswitha and a twelfth-century epic on Frederick Barbarossa,
the Ligurinus. In all his work as poet, commentator, and editor a strongly marked bent for geographical and ethnological
description appears. A reader who comes upon the innumerable topographical references in his Odes and Amores[98] will
be puzzled by the ingenuousness with which personal and often
erotic thoughts are blended with precise geographical detail.
But German geography was on Celtis' mind:

> Some boast of having traveled in Gaul and Spain, both
> Sarmathias and Pannonia, and even transoceanic coun-
> tries. I however, regard as no less worthy the scholar
> who observes the regions of his mother tongue and the
> people who live there, their customs, tongues, religions,
> also their conduct and their passions, and the shapes of
> their bodies,

he wrote in the Amores in 1502,[99] and he himself could boast that
he had seen Germany. In his years of wandering, before going
to Ingolstadt, he had journeyed not only in his native Main and
Rhine country, but had walked through much of Austria, Tirol,
Swabia, Bavaria, Poland, Silesia, Bohemia and Moravia, Saxony, and the Baltic seaboard. His impressions of the scenery,
of popular traits, of climate, language, and customs found their
way into every one of his poetic works. He had an eye for the
characteristic and a sense of the unique; his sketches are vivid
and his descriptions, though impressionistic, have substance.

As a foretaste of the planned Germania illustrata, Celtis

published in 1502, along with the <u>Amores</u>, a poetic description
of Germany, the <u>Germania generalis</u>.[100] It begins, character-
istically, with the creation of the world "ex ventre Demogor-
gonis," but then proceeds to what is for Celtis an exact description of German geography and customs. He speaks of the
position of Germany in the temperate zone where, with hard
work, the soil can be made to yield rich fruits. He lauds the
aptitude of Germans in war as well as in the peaceful arts of
commerce, agriculture, letters, and especially printing. He
compares Gutenberg to Daedalus. The four great rivers, Vistula, Elbe, Rhine, and Danube, are described; also the three
mountain systems, the Alps, Carpathians, and the "Hercynian"
range. Lastly, he describes the quality of the German soil,
making a proud comparison between the barrenness of ancient
times, as it was recorded by Tacitus and Strabo, and the pres-
ent-day fertility so pleasing to every observer. Each of these
points was later taken up and developed by Celtis' spiritual
descendants.

Far more significant than Celtis' individual labors was the
zeal for coöperative action that he excited among his contemporaries. While he lived he presided over the scholarly collaboration of German humanists, and the persistence of this
group effort shows how effective a heritage he left. The ma-
chinery for concerted action which he attempted to set up, the
sodalities modeled after the Italian academies and dedicated
to the furtherance of the humanistic disciplines and the search
for manuscript material, did not long survive his driving geniu
But the germs of the ideas he had scattered began to sprout, a
the sort of individual studies he had advocated as leading to a
<u>Germania illustrata</u> materialized.

Celtis himself kept the plan alive by means of occasional ref
erences in the works that, in quick succession, flowed from hi
pen. At the end of the first chapter of his little book on Nurem
berg he speaks of the "Germania illustrata on which we are
now at work."[101] The reference was retained in the second edi
tion and it turns up again in the letter to the Elector Frederick
of Saxony which accompanies the Roswitha publication,[102] and
in the dedication to Maximilian of the <u>Amores</u> in the spring of
1502.[103] In 1504 he had another opportunity to call the project
to the emperor's attention and to remind him of the value of
his high patronage.[104] Meanwhile, correspondence had been in-
itiated with scholars in other parts of the Empire, all member
of that eager circle of humanists who were either personal acquaintances or distant admirers of Celtis. One furnished a des
cription of the Adige valley,[105] another contributed an account
of the castle fortresses of southern Tirol,[106] a third surveyed

the town of Nonsberg.[107] In 1505, Celtis discussed with Peutinger the possible incorporation of the latter's history of the
Roman emperors from Caesar to Maximilian in the Germania
illustrata.[108] After that year his interest seems to have waned,
but at the time of his death in 1508 his contemporaries regarded the project as a concrete achievement. In a woodcut
of Celtis done by Hans Burgkmair, the Germania illustrata appears, with the Amores, the Odes, and the Epigrams, as one
of the four works on which Celtis' immortality rests.[109]

If Celtis had lived longer the force of his personality might
well have brought the great project to completion. After 1508
only its memory lingered. The ideals of the Germania illustrata were accepted by the humanist community, but the strands
of the Germania's subsequent history lose themselves in the
efforts of individual scholarship.

We can still trace them for a while. Four years after Celtis'
death the Nuremberg schoolmaster Johann Cochlaeus published
his little Germaniae descriptio as an appendix to his textbook
edition of the Chorography of the first-century Roman epitomizer Pomponius Mela.[110] It was faithful to the character of
the Germania illustrata studies, but the ambitious project,
Cochlaeus realized, was still far from finished, and contributions were needed.[111] In 1525 the Bavarian historian Johann
Aventinus, disciple and close friend of the deceased Celtis,
suggested to his colleague Beatus Rhenanus a common program of travel through Germany with the object of describing
the country, recording inscriptions, and collecting manuscripts.[112] "The history of Germany," he stated "can be written only if a number of scholars with official support search
in every corner of every territory for traces of vanished cities,
if they exploit libraries, peruse documents, and then compare
the results of their researches with the tradition of antiquity.
At the end of their labors these men must gather in conference
to pool the results of their exploration." Rhenanus was impressed,[113] and the two men continued to correspond about
matters relating to the Germania illustrata, chiefly the problem of coördinating the ancient and contemporary nomenclature of German geography.[114] Meanwhile, to make a definite
beginning, Aventinus was at work on a Germania illustrata of
his own. It remained fragmentary, but the Indiculus to it, completed about 1531,[115] outlines a list of topics that a work of this
kind must take up,[116] while the preface to the body of the work
is instructive on the preliminary studies and activities which
Aventinus regarded as essential.[117] The fragment itself[118] is
disappointing, however, and in no way constitutes a topographical-historical study, an enterprise Aventinus conceived in

theory but lacked the discipline to carry out.

Little more, perhaps, could be done with the plan. A change in the nature of the <u>Germania</u> <u>illustrata</u> becomes evident with the growing interest of Sebastian Münster, that versatile and attractive cosmographer of whom much will be said later. For eighteen years, Münster writes in the preface to his great <u>Cos</u> <u>mographia</u> of 1544, he had been trying to obtain precise information about German cities and territories by enlisting the aid of other learned and experienced men;[119] and how he went about this inquiry may be seen from a little work of thirty quarto pages on the subject of sun dials which he published in 1528.[120] Its second part is entitled "Exhortation and Plea of Sebastian Münster to all Practitioners of the Gentle Art of Geography, to Aid him in the Truthful and Rightful Description of the German Nation," and what Münster proposes here to his fellow geographers is most interesting:

> It is plain and obvious that the maps of Germany which have been appearing of late have been drawn with erroneous longitudes, as is clearly indicated by the wide arc which they attribute to the Rhine between Strassburg and Mainz, not at all like the actual course of the river as I have observed it. One map maker copies the other, right or wrong.

> It is true that it would be too heavy and costly a burden for one man to observe and describe Germany properly. Not many lords and princes are nowadays inclined to support such descriptions, although in the old days even Kings and Emperors paused in their affairs of state to show interest in matters of learning. Notwithstanding this difficulty, we must seek support in our plan to describe Germany's territories, cities, towns, villages, distinguished castles and monasteries, its mountains, forests, rivers, lakes, and its products, as well as the characteristics and customs of its people, the noteworthy events that have happened, and the antiquities which are still found in many places.

> I shall now begin this undertaking, hoping that many of you will come to my assistance; indeed, I have no doubt that Georgius Tannstetter or Johann Vögelin in Vienna, Johann Aventinus in Bavaria, Johann Schöner and Sebastian Rotenhan in Franconia, Peter Apianus in Meissen, Matthäus Aurigallus in Saxony, Konrad Peutinger in Augsburg, Johann Stöffler in Württemberg, Johann Huttichius and Lorenz Friess in Alsace, Heinrich Glareanus in the Confederation all of them highly learned men and lovers of knowledge—wi

help and sustain me in my enterprise, along with many other erudite men of whose names I am ignorant, else I should
ask them too to be of help to me.

Now, I think we should attack the project in this way: Herr
Konrad Peutinger shall be responsible for the description
of Augsburg and surroundings to a distance of six to eight
miles from the city. Johann Aventinus shall undertake to
describe Regensburg or Landshut and their environs in a
circumference of as many miles.... And all others do likewise and send the descriptions on to me or to Jakob Kobel,
municipal secretary at Oppenheim. I shall gather them all
together and have them printed; then we shall see what
kind of a land our ancestors conquered for their home: not
a crude, uncivilized country but a paradise and pleasure
garden in which everything necessary to man's happiness
is found.

Therefore, good Germans, help me to bring honor to our
country and place its beauties in the clear light of day. Do
this, and your descendants shall hold us in honor and affection. Scholars and artists! Do not hesitate to goad the lords
of our lands into action to have their domains described.
Pass the word to other learned men whom my little work
may not reach; you shall be esteemed for it. Cities of the
German nation! Do not regret the Gulden or two you might
spend on a description of your region. Let everyone lend a
helping hand to complete a work in which shall be reflected,
as in a mirror, the entire land of Germany with all its peoples, its cities, its customs.

As we shall see, Münster's notion of describing Germany
differed in many essentials from Celtis', and though we hear
the echo of the Ingolstadt address in Münster's plea, the attack is not the same. The collaborative scheme he suggests
here is the plan for his own <u>Cosmographia</u> which was the fruit
of this and similar[121] entreaties as well as of the travels and
investigations Münster undertook himself. In their approach
to the material and to the reader, Münster's intentions went
far beyond the imagination of Celtis and his disciples. But
Münster's proposal of action again reveals the striking harmony of mind and closeness of association that must have prevailed among men of learning in Germany, and the reality of
the idea of a humanist community. Indeed, but for the vigor of
this body the project would have been stillborn.

In the preface to the <u>Cosmographia</u> Münster reports on the
results of his quest.[122] It appears that the response was en-

couraging. Contributions came not only from Germany, but
from Italy, France, England, Poland, and Denmark, though
many regions did not answer or were not able to find a skilled
person to describe, chart, or draw their cities. His inquiry
has taught him, Münster notes, that not every artist can portray a town nor every literate person describe it. Whether
Münster's plea was responsible for the many pertinent works
which soon began to appear in print we are not able to say.
But Sebastian Franck, writing in the preface to his <u>Chronicon
Germaniae</u> in 1538, expressed his great satisfaction that so
many of his contemporaries were at work "to raise Germany
from the dust of neglect." [123]

The <u>Germania</u> <u>illustrata</u>, then, remained an idea, but it left
its imprint on the development of the topographical-historical
genre. It established it as a goal that could be reached only
through a concerted effort, and it made pre-eminent for a time
the antiquarianism of Celtis and his group. Morever, it was
directly responsible for a number of investigations which were
in their own right important preliminary studies on which later
writers could and did base their work. If Celtis' project remained a fragment, it was because its creative energy merged
with the forces which were then developing a more universal
type than that of the <u>patria</u> <u>illustrata</u>, and because those works
which were produced under Celtis' inspiration soon found their
logical place in the larger venture of the topographical-histori
cal literature.

The Search for the German Past

EAGER AS the German humanists were to describe the contemporary scene, their most insistent questions concerned the past. Before the likeness of their land could be established for posterity, questions about the identity and traits of their forebears had to be formulated and, if possible, answered. The central idea of the <u>Germania illustrata</u>, to relate the Germany of antiquity to the Germany of the sixteenth century, was therefore most consistently developed in the erudite works on ancient Germany of which the century was so productive, and which have won for their authors a place in the history of German scholarship. The reasons for concentration on the German past are plain. Humanism exalted antiquity. Roman antiquity was admittedly glorious, establishing a noble foundation for Italian claims to cultural supremacy. German antiquity had been altogether neglected as a subject devoid of order and dignity. But sources for its history existed, many of them newly brought to light during the lifetime of German humanism. If read without prejudice they might reveal a tradition as deeply rooted, as venerable as that of the Latins. The special studies accumulated this source material and settled scholarly disputes. They unlocked the past and made ancient Germany a living reality to an age for which antiquity had little more depth than the thickness of a folio volume. They opened the German lands to exact observation. Although these scholarly writings were indispensable to the authors of the descriptive topographical-historical volumes, they were not mere preliminary spadework. Long after the great cosmographies of the mid-century had become popular reading, they continued to appear. They form a distinct type, but in purpose and subject they are part of the topographical-historical literature.

There could be no question about one point: the ancients had slighted the Germans by the scantness of their historical references.[1] That the scope of the works of Polybius, Livy, Pliny, Strabo, and Ptolemy should not have permitted a thorough investigation of the civilization of the Germanic tribes seemed inexplicable and shameful. Some writers saw downright malice in this neglect, blaming the ancients for the avidity with which they "appropriated to themselves all antiquity by means of spurious histories"[2] and suppressed all facts not directly conducive to their own greater glory.[3] "Therefore I shall indicate in this chronicle of mine," writes Sebastian Franck, a moderate man whose words ordinarily lack the rancor which so often disfigures German humanist writing, "that Germany, no less than the Greeks and Latins, had its share of wise, brave, and otherwise distinguished men. But because none of them recorded their history, Greeks and Romans wrote about Germany according to their fancies, partly because of lack of knowledge, partly out of a desire to increase the fame of their own lands and folk by suppressing the just glory of other peoples."[4]

More usually, however, ancient neglect was attributed to mere ignorance. The ancient writers never saw Germany, explains Münster,[5] and since they had no first-hand knowledge they were led "by their imagination and whims" to write all kinds of nonsense about the country.[6] They could not have penetrated into the heart of Germany because "at that time the approaches to its interior were blocked by raging rivers, dense forests, and vast lakes,"[7] and since Germans had no fixed habitations and were constantly on the move, the ancient writers could hardly have gathered much information about individual tribes.[8] But because these authors lay claim to almost infallible authority in matters of which they treat, their silence, or near silence, on Germany has been interpreted to mean the absence of things worthy of mention. Thus, charges Franz Irenicus, historian of ancient Germany and one of its most vociferous defenders, "Ptolemy's account, or rather his neglect, has diverted men... from showing interest in Germany, although Ptolemy claims to have shed light on the entire world. In truth, he darkens the veritable light (which, through the bounty of nature, Germany enjoys) as he, with his digressive and far-fetched arguments, plunges Germany into obscurity."[9]

From such acrimony one writer was excepted: Tacitus, whose Germania was the most abundant source for ethnological and cultural studies of ancient Germany as well as the historical foundation of humanist patriotism. Tacitus' little work was of paramount importance in fixing an authoritative image of Germany and the Germans in the first century of the Christian era which, when seen in the frame of the cultural conditions of the sixteenth century, became an irresistible theme for comment,

comparison, and exhortation. No other classical source had so
much influence.

The manuscript of the Germania had been discovered in the
monastic library at Hersfeld by Poggio and was brought to
Rome sometime between 1429 and 1455.[10] It was first printed
at Venice in 1470, and three years later again at Nuremberg.
The discovery and these first editions of the document seem,
however, to have made little impression in Germany. It was
Enea Silvio's open letter to Martin Mayr that brought the value
of Tacitus' study home to the German humanists. This letter,
it will be recalled, was written in 1458, first circulated in manuscript, and printed in Leipzig in 1496. What it has to say on the
country and people is based on Tacitus,[11] and because it was
also provocative it indicated for the first time what might be
done with the source which had come into German hands. "Let
us see," writes Enea at the beginning of his discourse, "what
Germany was like in the old days, and how it looks today."[12]
No investigation could be more appropriate for the German humanists to undertake.

In 1500 and 1505 appeared the first editions of the Germania
by Celtis, neither of them a substantial work of learning, but
of significance in further apprising the German humanists of
the possibilities of the treatise. Celtis also lectured on Tacitus,
again the first to do so in Germany. But most exhaustive in its
treatment of the text, at least until the appearance of Philip
Clüver's Germania antiqua at the beginning of the seventeenth
century, was a commentary upon the Germania by Andreas
Althamer. The author was a priest turned Protestant, active in
Lutheran theology at Wittenberg after 1525.[13] His glosses on
the Germania were originally published as Scholia in Cornelium
Tacitum (Nuremberg, 1529), but a greatly expanded version was
turned out seven years later.[14] This revision is a model of humanist scholarship, dedicated in its treatment of the source and
its interpretive problems and conscious of all the interests of
the humanists' world.

The portion of the book most pertinent here occurs at its beginning.[15] It is a geographical comparison of the Germania of
Tacitus' day with modern Germany in the form of elaborations
on the first sentence of the text: "Germany is separated from the
Galli, the Rhaeti, and Pannonii by the rivers Rhine and Danube;
mountain ranges, or the fear which each feels for the other,
divide it from the Sarmatae and Daci." Althamer releases his
learning upon every geographical word in the passage. He delineates the ancient and modern boundaries of Germany, for
things had changed so since the first century that the confines
of tribal Germany were but a portion of the modern country.[16]

He draws the topographical distinctions between upper and lower Germany and discusses the <u>nationes</u> resident in each. He
takes up Raetia and the other territorial divisions, consider-
ing again boundaries and nature of terrain, and giving a complete list of cities both in ancient and present times, with their
Latin and German names, the composition of the soil on which
they stand, products raised and made, and whatever else might
interest an intelligent reader. He compares Rhine and Danube
for length and navigability, even for clarity of water. He traces
each river from its source to its mouth by enumerating the
towns located on its banks. This geographical section is succeeded by a variety of comments on historical and cultural
matters. We are instructed on the great eponymous hero Tuisco,
fourth son of Noah, and how he came to Germany to be the ancestor of all Germans, as related by Berosus.[17] We hear about
the tongues of the tribes and their songs and hymns which contained their history. The evidence for Hercules' travels in Germany is presented, the physical attributes of the people enumerated. Then comes a discussion of climate and environment,
especially as these influence the German character, and this
leads to a topography of all Germany, territory by territory,
in which products, mineral deposits, and other sources of
wealth are examined.

There **follow** discourses on military tactics employed by the
warring tribes, their governments, religious usages, family
associations. There is a catalogue of German cities and towns,
arranged according to their endings: -<u>dorf</u>, -<u>weyler</u>, -<u>mark</u>,
and so on. Another section takes up Tacitus' allegation that
the Germans were entirely ignorant of letters. Things have
changed now, Althamer assures the Roman rhetorically, and
he marshals an impressive list of scholars, poets, theologians,
inventors, and men of affairs of his own time. Here and there
in the text we come across geographical word pictures—a view
of the Hercynian forest, glimpses of cities, descriptions of Holland, Hessia, and Swabia.[18]

As fruitful a source for elaboration as Tacitus' <u>Germania</u>
was the geography of the first-century epitomizer Pomponius
Mela, which the Swiss humanist Joachim Vadian selected for
comment. Pomponius' <u>Chorographia</u> is a digest of Strabo and
a popular summary of the geographical notions of his time.
Written in the form of a periegesis, that is, a consecutive description of countries and regions as though author and reader
were journeying along roads and coasts lines, it covers briefly the areas of the three continents as they were known in Strabo's day. There was a section on Germany,[19] and this may have
attracted Vadian's interest since Pomponius was one of the

many classical observers who had held the lands beyond the
Rhine and Danube in disdain.

Pomponius' scheme presented Vadian with an opportunity
to roam leisurely over the fields of geography and history,
commenting, filling in, digressing. "How can one speak more
clearly about geographical principles and problems than in
connection with an ancient writer?" he asked,[20] and the answer, which might have been given by any one of his colleagues,
was that one could not. The text to be expounded gave to a rambling discussion a thread of unity and a point of return, while
in his comments the modern writer matched wits with an ancient author. Vadian had little interest in mere exegesis, however. His treatise was not to be a commentary, he said, but
rather scholia, and by that he meant an analytical, illustrative,
and interpretive unfolding of the meaning of his source, at
once critical and speculative.[21] He rarely takes up a matter
without examining its relevance to his age, and Pomponius'
obvious geographical limitations call for a full review of the
geographical knowledge of Vadian's time. In preparation for
his scholia he had undertaken travels to many parts of Europe,
and his voluminous correspondence is replete with references
to maps, descriptions, and documents which he asked his colleagues to procure and abstract for him. Vadian had an acute
eye for new developments in the geographical fields. He was
one of the first men of his time to utilize the discoveries of
the Portuguese and Spanish in his geographical writings,[22] and
he had only derision for the kind of scholar who closes his
eyes to the world and clings to auctores and other founts of
authority.[23] Knowledge depends on observation and critical
reasoning, and geographical study, he was convinced, sharpens
these faculties.

The scholia on Pomponius' sparse account of ancient Germany occupy seven folio pages of very fine print[24] and take up
matters close to the interest of German humanism, such as
boundaries and extent of territories, the physical appearance
of the Germans, and the problem of establishing their ethnic,
linguistic, and geographical identity. There is some discussion
of special subjects arising from Pomponius' handling of the
description, the truth of the severe coldness he attributes to
the climate, for example, and the allegedly delayed maturity
of German males. One slighting reference elicits a comment
on the German legal system. Vadian observes that cruelty of
punishment and other judicial barbarities have disappeared;
duels, for instance, are restrained by the law of the Church,
and no man may be killed whatever the circumstances.[25] Vadian,
like his colleagues, emphasizes the great changes that had taken

place since ancient times; no longer may Germans be ridiculed for their gross food habits,[26] and the present state of cultivation in Germany offers a pleasing contrast to the cheerless land pictured by Pomponius.

Vadian's work won fervent praise in the humanist community. All of his regular correspondents, and a great many who wrote on that one occasion only, sent well-turned compliments. He was urged to prepare a second version, and printers communicated with him to suggest that he publish subsequent editions with them.[27] Some proposed the inclusion of maps and other illustrative material. And a good many years later Münster remembered the work when he was planning his edition of Ptolemy's Geography and suggested to Vadian that they collaborate on the project and produce it "in the form of your annotationes to Mela."[28]

The year of the first printing of Vadian's commentary, 1518, also saw the appearance of the most singular work of humanist scholarship on the subject of ancient Germany, Irenicus' Germaniae exegeseos volumina duodecim or, as it is more often called, Exegesis Germaniae.[29] Franz Friedlieb, or Irenicus, was a Swabian, born in 1495 in Ettlingen, who was trained at Pforzheim and Tübingen in the philological sciences, and eventually became a Lutheran minister after a brief and unsuccessful diplomatic career.[30] Of the extraordinary precocity of his talent the Exegesis, published in his twenty-third year, is convincing evidence. It is a stormy, unrestrained, impulsive confession of his faith in the excellence and honorable antiquity of his country. No sense of proportion guided the rush of the material he had accumulated, no feeling for style cleared his crabbed composition of denseness and ambiguity. In its achievements as well as in its failures the Exegesis reveals both the "youthfully awkward desire for knowledge that characterized German humanism"[31] and its patriotic mood.

Irenicus cast his work in that form, so much in favor among the German humanists, which is a blend of exegetical, narrative, and hortatory writing. He explicates the text of all the ancient authors who referred to Germany, he appraises modern writers, he criticizes or encourages his contemporaries on matters of current import. And all the while he describes and relates. He knew the historian's responsibility: "I promise to bind the reader to no opinion which I believe to be that of a vain person. However, as I confirm the judgment of one or the other writer, I would incur the derision of the reader if I did not also report the persuasive arguments of authors who hold differing views."[32] But he was not able to bring to

his endeavors the discipline of an Althamer or the imaginative
grasp of a Vadian. His historical and geographical investigations remained textbound and took little but zeal from the new
learning.

Irenicus' labored and digressive style could be illustrated
by a passage chosen at random, but most interesting from this
as well as from a conceptual point of view is the <u>Oratio</u> <u>Pro-
treptica</u>, a sort of epilogue on the proper function of history
and geography, which stands near the end of the volume. I quote
some of the most revealing passages:[33]

> Chorography concerns itself with particular spots which
> it treats singly and separately, depicting each down to the
> smallest detail, such as harbors, estates, people, deltas,
> and such like things. The purpose of geography, on the oth-
> er hand, is to investigate and set forth each and every hab-
> itable place on earth, describing its situation and its nat-
> ural endowments, as well as furnishing a general impres-
> sion of such features of its environment as the larger
> towns, the mountains, and the better known rivers, along
> with some pertinent information about each of these.[34] Too
> minute a description, however, prevents rather than helps
> the realization of the plan of a geographical work. To take
> an example from medicine: how often does the mention of
> a German herb remind us of something, from there we go
> on to discuss its origins, and soon our work has grown <u>ad
> infinitum</u>. We see, moreover, how our volumes take on
> such weight and bulk that if ever an even greater creative
> desire should come over us, to which we add an excessive
> liberality with words and subjects, Heaven only knows in-
> to what kind of colossus the work will swell, regardless
> of what it is about.

> But I have gone too far.... We have spread our sails to the
> wind, driven on by youthful enthusiasm, without any thought
> of return, and now we have nearly sailed beyond the limits.
> We have not been cautious enough to keep our sails furled.
> While far from the coast, in the middle of the sea, we have
> lost sight of the shore for which we were bound. Coming
> back, at last, to our original purpose, then, and giving
> thought to the difficulty of our task, let us pray for the
> safety of our voyage....

> No geographer has exceeded Strabo in skill and knowledge.
> However even his most comprehensive work, intended to
> describe the whole world, fails to do justice to our Ger-
> many which, because of its size and distance, has been

beyond the range of the most learned ancient geographers.
Hearsay, and things which pertain only to individuals, we
have deliberately omitted from the scheme of our work.
For it is useless to drag the reader through lengthy arguments (as the famous orator says) to follow the developments of each event, and to trace the cause of every object. Such practices lead to attacks on customs, to wrangling about usages which have given rise to bad habits, and
to catering to special interests. I myself consider it among
the first of a historian's virtues to be somewhat ignorant
of a few things and not to want to pursue everything, but
rather to try to know what is most important and most significant. . . .

Therefore it is the duty of a historian, in giving an account
of events, to pass over remote and irrelevant details, and
also, for the sake of the attractiveness of his work, occasionally to do a bit of sugarcoating [suco illinire], as far
as the seriousness of his subject permits him. This, however, is to be done with moderation. It is more a matter
of omitting than of inventing material. For which reason
I do not agree with those who hold that all things that have
happened should be told as they happened. Events ought to
be related not as they occurred, but as it is expedient to
tell them, therefore the basic and hidden meaning inherent
in things must be sought. Thus, the essential task of geography consists not alone in the investigation of occurrences
but in their evaluation and this, being the furthest removed
from the power of sight, springs from the mind and reason
rather than from the senses. For the mind is shaped by con-
templating the truth as it is found in history and other records of the past, and this contemplation is, in all disciplines, more important than the acquisition of empirical
knowledge.

Consistency and method, it is clear, are not Irenicus' strong
points, and his argument for historical selection sounds strange
from one who is always upbraiding the ancients for not following the strict facts of matters. But Irenicus was single-minded
in the pursuit of his real aim: to create an ideal image of ancient Germany as a source of inspiration and a model of conduct for the present.

It would lead too far to follow Irenicus through all the many
chapters in his heavy folio. There is astounding variety: the
entire history of historical and geographical writing on Germany, an exhaustive list of the ancient tribes, a long rhapsody
on the theme of the ancestors' excellence in every quality and

every pursuit, 117 genealogical chapters on German princely
houses, a detailed exposition of the military history of each
of the tribes. But there is concentration too. The entire second half of his work—Books Seven to Twelve—is devoted to a
demonstration of the physical characteristics of the German
lands, though one must not expect anything in the way of scenic description from Irenicus. Just as the historical sections
of the first part were predominantly an anthology of literary
references, the geographical half is a synthesis of what has
been written on the subject in ancient, medieval, and modern
times.

Thus, when Irenicus comes to the Hercynian forest,[35] a subject on which the German humanists are generally fervent, he
merely cites Strabo on the trees, Herodian of Syria on the
density of vegetation, Pliny on the hills and mountains, and
Tacitus on forest products. He makes reference to his own
time only when he quotes Enea Silvio and Konrad Celtis. In
the same way he describes the Rhine by quoting or paraphras-
ing Herodian, Claudian, Caesar, Plutarch, Nauclerus, Pomponius Mela, Tacitus, Leonardo Bruni, Strabo, Celtis, the
Suidas, Ammianus Marcellinus, Dracontius, Pliny, Otto of
Freysing, Dionysius Periegetes, Appianus, Boccaccio, Enea
Silvio, Virgil, and Hegesippus.[36] Here as everywhere the account is statistical and philological, and he clearly feels most
at home in the concluding sections of the work, Books Eleven
and Twelve, which comprise a gazetteer of German cities,
towns, regions, monasteries, and other places of note. These
are taken alphabetically, and since "Germany" as a geographical term was broadly construed, Irenicus ranges widely
through Belgium, France, Poland, and Hungary as well as
Germany itself. Here is an example of his method:

> Magdeburg is the capital of Saxony. It is called "Dmoadum
> Pirgum" by Johann Capnio [Reuchlin], that scholar learned
> in all things, in his letter to Johann Wolf of Hermesgrün.
> This is from the Greek dmoades [sic], that is, "maid ser-
> vants," of which, by dropping the first letter, we make
> "Magd," and πύργον, "pyrgum," which we turn into "Bur-
> gum," as in πύξος, which becomes "Buxus." So much for
> that. You can see how the two languages agree in rendering
> this name δμωή δμωῆς "ancilla," or δμωΐs δμωΐδοs χοὺ
> [καὶ οὐ?] δμωάδες [sic; δμωΐαδες?].Enea Silvio refers to
> Magdeburg as "Virginopolis" and calls it the most distin-
> guished city of Saxony by virtue of its learned men and
> their works.

Magdeburg was originally founded by Otto at the instiga-
tion of his wife Edith, the daughter of King Echtmund of
the Angles. She lies buried there. Lupold, in his thirteenth
chapter, speaks of Magdeburg as "Virginopolis," from
Venus (because that Virgin was worshiped there) and calls
it a Saxon city, located on the Elbe, and built by Otto who
reposes there. Likewise Otto of Freysing, Book VI, Chapter 20. The Ligurinus calls it Virginis urbs ἀπὸ τῆς
παρθενικῆς ἡ παρθένου, that is, from the Virgin, ἡ ἀπὸ
τῆς παρθενῶνος, city of the Virgin, i. e., τῆς πόλιος, of
the city. Ptolemy, in Book II, if the text is not corrupt,
calls the city ηοεουιον or Moevium, the capital seat founded by Charles the Great.[37]

The Exegesis draws to a close with a careful index and then,
in an appendix, the Norimberga of Celtis is given in full as a
sample of the kind of writing Irenicus regarded as the logical
extension of his own work, the next chapter in the full description of Germany.

Irenicus' treatise is a characteristic product of the age of
humanism and points directly to some of its tendencies in Germany. Much of it could still be read with profit, and no one
comes away from the text without having learned a good deal.
But Irenicus attempted too much. The confidence of youth, perhaps, led him to reach out for more than he could control.

Of German folk, their deeds and cities you wrote, Irenicus,
When only a boy. What have you done since then?

ran a current epigram.[38] His contemporaries pronounced
the work disappointing, some challenging its reliability, others
criticizing its glaring lack of unity and elegance.[39] Perhaps
the cruelest verdict was the condescension with which some
of the men of the second half of the century regarded it. "I
see that our good Irenicus has copied much from older com-
mentators, some of them liars," wrote Kaspar Brusch to a
colleague, "but we must not judge him too harshly. He lived
in a time when men were still unlettered. Let us praise at
least his good will."[40] There was no demand for a second edition, and Irenicus seems not to have published anything else.

But the importance of the Exegesis to the history of topographical-historical literature would not have been in any case
its charm of form or style. Its significance is that Irenicus,
early in the century, stated exhaustively the point of departure of every topographical-historical work: Germany as seen
by the classical and medieval authorities. There was no need
for later scholars to burden themselves with this basic pre-

liminary study. They may not have enjoyed reading the Exegesis, but as a repository of references it remained unsur-
passed for a century. It became customary to send the reader
to pertinent chapters in Irenicus,[41] and in spite of the cavils
of the aesthetes, the Exegesis, soon after 1518, became itself
an authority.

Other volumes were written in the decades following the
publication of Irenicus' work which, while not nearly so comprehensive in scope, treated even more exhaustively some
single aspect of his subject. Most important of these is a little work of sixty-five octavo pages, issued in 1530 by Willibald
Pirckheimer, that may be regarded as the final word on the
comparative nomenclature of ancient and modern German geography. It is called Germaniae ex variis scriptoribus perbrevis explicatio,[42] and it identifies ancient place names with
modern localities. It also reveals the precise and consistent
effort of which sixteenth-century scholarship at its best was
capable. A Nuremberg patrician by birth, by training a jurist,
Pirckheimer was above all a humanist who put both wealth
and natural endowment at the service of learning. It was to
Pirckheimer and his circle of friends in Nuremberg that the
heritage of Celtis had fallen. The Germania illustrata project
would surely have succumbed with Celtis had not Pirckheimer
continued to develop its central theme, the historical and geographic comparison of ancient and modern Germany. The work
in question here grew out of Pirckheimer's occupation with
Ptolemy's Geography, which he had translated and printed in
1525 with the annotations of Regiomontanus.[43] The knowledge
gained in his editorial labors was placed at the disposal of his
desire to furnish more information about ancient Germany
than he found in the sources.[44] The Explicatio is therefore
more than a by-product of his Ptolemaic studies; both purpose and subject link it with the other learned volumes on German antiquity.
   The ancient material in the Explicatio is taken largely from
Ptolemy, though occasional references to Tacitus and Strabo
broaden the scope. His method remains constant throughout:
proceeding across Germany region by region, Pirckheimer
first discusses the physical boundaries of a territory as a
Roman province, then lists the important cities, setting Latin
and German names in parallel columns. Where definite information was lacking, a parenthetical coniectura indicates as
much.[45] In cases where the absence of a continuous historical
tradition made the establishment of the nomenclature well-
nigh impossible he proceeded as follows: when he could be

certain of the site of an ancient locality he searched the map
for a modern place whose name retained a remnant of the
classical designation, for example, Campodunum—Kempten,
Parthanum—Partenkirchen; when such precise information
was lacking he might take from his classical source that the
town was located at, say, the juncture of two streams, in which
case the connection could be made, for example, Bojodurum—
Passau; or he might learn about ruins still existing near a
modern town. [46] By using one of these methods he was able to
establish a large number of connections.

Pirckheimer's work is as valuable to the modern student
as it must have been to the humanist scholar trying to orient
himself on a map still conceived in the geographical terms of
the Roman administrative system of the second century. The
question of the boundaries and divisions of Germany was indeed a vexing one in the time of the humanists. Ancient Germania was easily enough tucked into the Rhine-Danube rectangle, but what determined modern Germany? The Flemish
mapmaker Abraham Ortelius tried, in the first edition of his
atlas of 1570, to fix the German borders with accuracy;[47] in
the subsequent versions he withdrew the attempt, stating merely that "her boundaries have been given differently by the various authors."[48] It was realized, of course, that Germany had
acquired since antiquity "more new territory from foreign nations than was formerly contained within her borders,"[49] but
whether geographical limits or other considerations should
determine the extent of this new Greater Germany was an open
question. The Swiss chronicler Johann Stumpf, in his map of
Germany, disregarded the description of the ancients "who
enclosed Germany between the Rhine and Danube," and determined "rather to indicate her extent by examining customs,
character, and language," and these showed that "we Germans
have spread far beyond the Rhine and Danube." [50] Ulrich
Hugwald, or, as he preferred, Mutius, similarly felt that in
his day Germany embraced any area in which the German language or any of its dialects were spoken.[51] Vadian's conviction that traits of character and not territorial borders distinguish the German people has already been mentioned. [52] On
the other hand, it seemed to some that territorial Germany
had far outgrown ethnic and linguistic Germany, and that a
more comprehensive criterion than race or language had to
be employed. "There is no country in all Christendom," declared Matthias Quad, a popularizer of geographical facts and
figures, "which under one name embraces so many lands as
Germany."[53] The Rhine and the Danube now flow through the
center of the country, writes Stumpf, [54] and Albert Krantz dis-

tinguishes between a territorial <u>Germania</u> in which many peoples and languages have their home, and a <u>Teutonia</u>, the German language domain.[55]

It is instructive to glance for a moment at a contemporary attempt to make sense out of the German boundary maze. Johann Rauw's great <u>Cosmographia</u> of 1597, a work written for the interested layman, in German and in the form of a dialogue, tries valiantly to come to grips with the problem. Rauw differentiates between the language domain of present Germany—"an unstable and uncertain thing, increasing or decreasing according to the temper of the time and to chance"[56] —and the "permanent" Rhine-Danube rectangle that defined ancient Germany. He goes on:

> In sum, the German landscape makes me think of a great and splendid city with its suburbs, the city itself located within its walls and fortifications, the suburbs without.... Thus all countries that use the German language are called German Countries, and you find German land on the far as well as on the near side of the Rhine and Danube. But the old and true and real Germany remains within the walls, that is, within her ancient boundaries. The other German regions, however, which are located beyond the Danube and the Rhine, are like suburbs in that they became attached to the real and old Germany, but are not by rights a part of it.[57]

When the interlocutor, who is not quite satisfied with this analogy—Rauw is exceedingly fond of analogies—wants to pursue the matter, Rauw puts him off: "You must know that our geographers do not hold just one opinion in their descriptions of Germany, nor do they make use of but one method to determine her divisions." But the questioner persists. In spite of the difficulties that beset any such endeavor, may he not have at least a suggestion of the outer limits of the regions where the German language is spoken? Rauw at last agrees to supply a sketch:

> If you would walk the circumference of Germany, as far as the German language is spoken, you would have to set out from Chur in Switzerland and go from there to Alsace at Metz, then to Brussels in Flanders, from there to Ghent, Maastricht, Groningen, Aldenburg, Hamburg, Rostock, Kammin, Dantzig, Königsberg in Prussia, Gilgenburg, Breslau, Vienna, Graz·in Styria, Kernten, Brixen, and thence again to Chur. According to the reckoning of Pantaleon,[58] such a journey around all of Germany would take

ninety-three days, provided that you travel five miles each day.[59]

As much debated as boundaries were the name and the origin of the German people. The first of these matters posed relatively little difficulty. Most humanists, after displaying their etymological adroitness for a bit, agreed that the ancient Germans called each other "Bruder" just as Germans in their own time said "Landsmann,"[60] or that "the name was given to them because during wartime, in calamity and success, each shared the other's lot in a brotherly spirit, while those who remained behind, tending flocks and fields, supported the wives and children of men at war for the sake of the common weal."[61] The question of indigenousness was a harder one, but the answer was really a foregone conclusion. Celtis had already established the autochthony of the Germans, relying on the authority of Tacitus,[62] and though none of his followers went so far as his poetic extravagance that the Germans had been created with the first living things by the Demogorgon, most of Celtis' successors accepted autochthony and racial purity as axioms. Only Philip Clüver, with the more powerful critical scholarship at his command, succeeded in demonstrating the Celtic and Germanic migrations from Asia.[63]

It is no wonder that such unsettled questions as these stamped nearly all humanist works on German antiquity with a polemical character. There is one, however, which may fairly be styled a synthesis, being both comprehensive in viewpoint and dispassionate in tone. This is Beatus Rhenanus' splendid study on ancient Germany, published at Basel in 1531, the Rerum Germanicarum Libri Tres.[64] Like all the works of its kind Rhenanus' volume proceeds directly from the Germania of Tacitus. In 1519, while reading proof for Froben, who was then printing an edition of Tacitus, Rhenanus had composed a little register of those proper names occurring in the Annals and the Histories that relate to German affairs. At the same time he was engaged on a somewhat more extensive treatise published that year as Commentarii in Tacitum.[65] These two were small booklets which concerned themselves only with isolated points; Rhenanus' major work, however, reveals the fruit of his occupation with the Roman historian. The three books on Germany show us how a first-rate mind was able to assimilate and utilize the ethnological and cultural material offered by Tacitus and how the balanced genius of a keen historical observer could extend it without getting bogged down in irrelevancies.

Rhenanus' two main topics of investigation are familiar ones:

the whereabouts and names of the German Stämme in early
Roman times, and the paths of their migration into the empire. Here too we find much space given to a consideration of
the boundaries of Roman and modern Germany, to a summary
of Tacitus on tribal mores, to earnest praise of Germanic
ideas of freedom.[66] But where Irenicus rambled, Rhenanus is
concise and direct. Chronological points of reference are exact. The course of the Völkerwanderung is clarified by a useful distinction between emigrationes, that is, the movement
of the tribes from their original homes in Germany[67] to the
Roman frontiers, and the immigrationes, the incursions into
the interior of the crumbling empire. He makes a lucid transition from ancient to medieval history by observing the effects of the invasions on tribal organization and on that of the
empire. He is convincing on the significance, as a historical
turning point, of the Battle of Zülpich in 501 in which the Franks
defeated the Alemanni. Though the local patriotism of the native Schlettstädter colors the narrative here, his tone elsewhere is cool and objective. There is greater detail for Alsace
than for any other single region, but the balance is not upset.
Above all, Rhenanus brings discrimination to massive historical material whose sheer bulk had overwhelmed less assured
writers.

To Rhenanus' rule of conciseness there are two significant
exceptions, the descriptions of Basel and of Schlettstadt in the
third of his books. They occur in the course of an attempt to
sketch a comparative topography of southwestern Germany,
the region he knew best, and their detail sets them apart from
the rest of the book. In the depiction of Basel, Rhenanus elaborates on the topography with some municipal history, but of
his native town he offers a comprehensive description.[68] He
suggests the position of the city on the banks of the Ill, cradled
in hills and forests. He pictures walls, towers, and moats. We
walk with him through the gates and along roads leading to and
from the city, observing vehicular and river traffic and learning that "about 2,600 people who go to mass" live here, all
humble, forthright folk. A little lecture on the history of the
city in ancient and medieval times follows; next comes a catalogue of distinguished citizens. There is time to glance at some
points of interest—churches and public buildings, monumental
fountains, monasteries. Most of all, we are made to admire
Schlettstadt's renowned school, "which has brought so much
fame to the city." This description comprises the liveliest section in Rhenanus' book. Warm affection for his native town ani-
mates the impression he creates, but it is the only extended
departure from his essentially antiquarian concerns.

But the point is that antiquarian scholarship on the subject of Germany reaches a summit with Rhenanus. The Alsatian part of his work was not superseded until the publication, more than two hundred years afterwards, of Daniel Schöpflin's <u>Alsatia illustrata</u>. Wolfgang Lazius, who in his monograph on the migrations[69] produced a most detailed summary of the period, did not attain Rhenanus' sense of form and balance. Rhenanus' scholarly calm, his unwillingness to be diverted, and above all his critical acumen refine and illumine every page of his work. They endow his book with an authority that we are not accustomed to find in the tomes of other writers of the age. Only Philip Clüver exceeded him in range of learning and devotion to the craft of scholarship, but Clüver belongs to a new age with fresh interests and different demands.[70]

3

The Formation of the Topographical-Historical Genre

> "Ich hab wöllen den Gelerten ein weg anzeigen,
> wie man nach so vil Teutschen Chronographien
> auch gar nützliche Cosmographien und Topo-
> graphien schreiben möchte...."[1]

AMONG the learned disciplines through which the German
humanists attempted to understand their past, the art of
geography had a prominent place. This was due not so much
to a scholarly ambition to know the geography of ancient Germania, as to a desire to see in the appearance of contemporary
Germany a reflection of her material growth from distant prim-
itiveness to wealth and honor. The image of ancient Germany
and her denizens served as the underpainting on which the
bright hues of the present were spread by writers whose eyes
were sensitive indeed to the light and shade around them. One
observer put into homespun German verse sentiments such as
must have been in the hearts of many:

> O Germany, when long ago
>   You were neglected, poor and low
> How you were rough and overgrown,
>   Uncultivated, nothing sown,
> And an unlettered, simple race
>   Peopled your country in those days.
> But when today I look at you,
>   Happy you are, and bright and new,
> And prosperous with honest gain
>   And fertile with much fruit and grain.
> Of men of wit and learning rare
>   You have today a goodly share,
> And mighty towns and cities stand

>   In your once bare and savage land.
>   How has, O Germany, your state
>   Been raised by a benevolent fate! [2]

The German scene gladdened the hearts of all who beheld it,
but the humanists were prepared to do more than look. They
wished to display Germany's likeness and preserve it for all
time. To accomplish this aim, to depict country and people
with a knowledge of their heritage and a sense of their destiny, the geographical-historical genre was developed out of a
multiplicity of disciplines which, in the hands of the German
humanists, united into a universal descriptive form. The catalyst of that form was geography.

This was natural in a country whose geographers had won
more unstinted acclaim than any of its other scholars. And it
is, no doubt, due to this "geographical renaissance" in Germany and to the presence of so many distinguished professional geographers that the topographical-historical works were
built on a sound basis of academic geography. This was hardly
a requirement for the fulfillment of their real purpose, which
was to describe. To know about zones and parallels, the sequence of spheres and the cause of eclipses, to be able to determine one's exact position on the surface of the earth, could
not have been considered generally desirable except in a time
of lively geographical curiosity. In such a time the descriptive works demanded not only a tone of severe accuracy, but
more than a modicum of scientific substance. Matters that
were close to the hearts of all German humanists could be pur-
sued properly only with some reference to mathematics and
astronomy:

>   How broad the earth, how long and wide,
>   How deep and large the seas expand,
>   What holds the ultimate sphere of land,
>   And how at ends of earth the sea
>   Clings tight to its extremity;
>   If 'round the earth a man can fare,
>   What men live here, what men live there. [3]

And the reply to Sebastian Brant's jibe,

>   Into these problems each would delve
>   Yet can he understand himself? [4]

which, surely, he himself did not take seriously, was that just
in order to know himself man must "take the compass well in
hand" [5] and investigate the laws of the globe on which he makes
his home.

The advance of Ptolemaic studies in the early part of the
century must have had much to do with this scientific direction taken by an essentially amateurish movement. The German humanists who searched the maps and text of Ptolemy for
information about ancient Germany could not have remained
unmoved by the Alexandrian's insistence that the primary task
of geography must be the critical collection of all materials
necessary for the correct representation of the earth's surface on a series of maps.[6] In other words, the geographer was
called upon to fix positions by latitude and longitude, determined astronomically. Ptolemy's distrust of descriptive geography[7] did not, of course, persuade his sixteenth-century
readers to abandon their beloved story telling. But it did lead
them to a recognition of the importance of the exact basis of
geography. The humanist scholar who did not want to face
charges of dilettantism had to take Ptolemy's directions seriously. He usually agreed with another ancient writer of even
greater influence on geographers, Strabo, that "the person who
attempts to write an account of the countries of the earth must
take many of the physical and mathematical principles as hy-
potheses and elaborate his whole treatise with reference to
their intent and authority."[8] The study of the earth and its features was not a subject for idle browsing. "The geographer,"
Strabo continues,

> does not write. . . . for the man of affairs of the kind who
> has paid no attention to the mathematical sciences proper-
> ly so called; nor, to be sure, does he write for the harvest
> hand or the ditch digger, but for the man who can be per-
> suaded that the earth as a whole is such as the mathema-
> ticians represent it to be.[9]

Nothing Strabo outlines here would seem forbidding to the
professional geographer. But what of the interested layman,
the person to whom the humanists addressed themselves? Was
it reasonable to expect that he would "first master those principles and then consider the subsequent problems?"[10] Was it
really necessary for him to burden his brain with recondite
data of mathematics and physics when he wanted only to know
the visible aspects of his country and his world? A glance at
the volumes that constitute the topographical-historical literature will indicate that the answer to this tacit question was
"yes." A great many carry their own introductions to scientific
geography, from Johann Cochlaeus' diminutive "Principia
Geographiae," which accompanies his textbook edition of Pomponius Mela,[11] to Rauw's comprehensive 140-page-long introduction to astronomy, astrology, mathematical and physical

geography, and projection, which precedes his great Cosmography.[12] Enea Silvio had also prefaced his Cosmographia with
just such an introductory treatise, seven chapters "de mundo
in universo," and German writers would surely have followed
his lead if Ptolemy and Strabo had not persuaded them.

One feels, to be sure, that this coupling of mathematical
geography and description is often perfunctory. Even Sebastian
Münster's introduction to his Cosmography of 1544,[13] though
it carried the authority of one who had recently published a
new edition of Ptolemy, scarcely bridged the gap between scientific and descriptive geography. His substantial contributions
to cartography and astronomy notwithstanding, Münster, too,
was pre-eminently and enthusiastically a narrator. He and his
colleagues took the dictum of Strabo literally: the exact principles first, description thereafter. One suspects that most
humanist writers would have been glad to leave the geometry
and astronomy to the experts and get on with their stories. But
the genre as it established itself, and the word of Ptolemy and
Strabo who were its patron authorities, required that the structure rest on a scientific foundation. If this was demanding to
the authors it was more so to their readers. But in the attempt
to make the principles of scientific geography palatable to the
public, the German humanists could draw on their singular a-
bility to popularize knowledge. A reader of Vadian's little introduction to general geography,[14] for example, will still appreciate the skill and understanding with which this universal
humanist brought sound professional knowledge to the layman.

Two modest volumes, above all others, advanced the geographical information of the general reader and served the
topographical writers as convenient sources of reference: Peter
Apianus' Cosmographicus Liber and Gemma Frisius' De Principiis Astronomiae et Cosmographiae. Apianus' fame spread
so rapidly after the publication of his brief work in 1524 and
its many subsequent editions and translations that he was made
instructor in astronomy to Charles V. Rainer Gemma, the Fri-
sian, slightly younger than Apianus, was his faithful follower
and offered as his first published work a continuation of his
master's Cosmography (1529). Apianus' constant endeavor was
to bring the enjoyment of astronomy and geography closer to
those who shied from computations and calculations,[15] and to
that end he attempted to reduce the mathematical part of these
sciences to a minimum by incorporating into his works a great
number of tables, statistics, and graphic representations.
Gemma employed what leisure he had in his position as professor of mathematics and medicine at Louvain improving
astronomical and geographical instruments and procedures.

Both writers included in their short volumes narrative accounts of the various countries of the world, and these indicated how the precise mathematical method of fixing positions—Ptolemy's method—might be put to use to turn out more accurate and therefore more useful descriptive geography.

Apianus' Cosmographia[16] begins with the Ptolemaic distinctions between Cosmography, Geography, and Chorography, then goes on to explain the motion of the spheres, the five zones, latitudes and longitudes, and climates. The reader learns further how to measure distance on maps and on the ground, how to determine his position, and how to tell the winds each from the other. Section two of the sixty-one-leaf booklet comprises a very concise description of the four continents, followed by a Tabula regionum which gives positions, in latitude and longitude, of regions, cities, and landmarks in Europe, Asia, and Africa.

Gemma's On the Principles of Astronomy and Cosmography[17] is a more substantial work. It follows, but elaborates on, Apianus, and a third part, "De orbis divisione," is a treatise on the four continents in the Germania illustrata style; that is, a correlation of the data of Strabo and Ptolemy with contemporary facts. The order of demonstration is exactly that of Ptolemy; only when he penetrates to regions unknown to the Alexandrian does Gemma depart from the traditional method. His account of America, by which he means Brazil,[18] is genuinely descriptive, even colorful. He introduces the inhabitants, all of them "cannibals, the worst kind of man-eaters"; we marvel at the continent's fabulous wealth, at its fairy-tale scenery, its improbable animals, the religion of the natives, and their buildings which are "comparable to the structures of Daedalus." His information is hearsay, of course, derived "from Spanish sailors and others,"[19] and the obvious exaggerations illustrate Ptolemy's warning that descriptive geography is a hazardous undertaking because it depends on tales of travelers and sailors, and these are unreliable, especially when coming from far-off countries.[20] But its lack of rigidity is refreshing, and one anticipates the conversion of such material into exciting accounts by later writers. Gemma's description of Germany,[21] however, is entirely in the conventional style and, like most of his passages, it conveys little about the land. But cosmography, Gemma said himself,[22] should not try to detail everything. "It ought rather to bring order to the confusion of the world's divisions in the manner of those pictures which suggest an image through its principal lines."

Apianus and Gemma were consulted, quoted, and imitated. An uncomplicated style, compact format, and helpful illustrations made their books ideal for reference. Gemma's little treatise on triangulation[23] and his new way of determining longitudes[24] proved invaluable to compilers of municipal and regional descriptions. The helping hand which they extended to the writers of the topographical-historical works was often and firmly grasped.[25]

As a foundation of the topographical-historical genre, the scientific base was most often taken as an assumption. The typical descriptive work did its duty to the exact disciplines either by commencing with a more or less comprehensive scientific review or by sending the reader to Apianus or Gemma, or to another colleague, for this information. It was not in scientific precision but in the combination of descriptive geography with narrative history that the genre attained its character. The Ptolemaic studies endowed the geography with that authority which critical investigation of sources and trained observation of people and events lent to the historiography of the partnership. Just as in geography only the results—reliably established and verified results—of mapping and measuring were revealed, so in historiography only the fruits of research and analysis found their way into the best of these works. Their historical content is thus often impressionistic rather than annalistic. A sketch rendered with a few characteristic strokes establishes the nature and the identity of a place, a person, an event. In descriptive history as in descriptive geography the writer communicates "in the manner of those pictures which suggest an image through its principal lines."[26]

It was Strabo who had shown the way in which the two arts might join forces. Strabo was to the sixteenth century quite as much an historian as a geographer,[27] and he was much cited and appealed to in the topographical-historical literature.[28] Though he accepted the primacy of mathematics and astronomy, it was political, historical, descriptive geography to which he devoted himself and which he perfected as a type. Far from being a specialized science, geography was in his handling a proper pursuit only for the polyhistor:

> The science of Geography, which I now propose to investigate, is, I think, quite as much as any other science, a concern of the philosopher;... In the first place, those who in earliest times ventured to treat the subject were, in their way, philosophers—Homer, Anaximander of Miletus, and Anaximander's fellow citizen Hecataeus.... In the second place, wide learning, which alone makes it possible to undertake a work on geography, is possessed solely by the man who has investigated things both human and divine—knowledge of which, they say, constitutes philosophy. And so, too, the

utility of geography—and its utility is manifold, not only as
regards the activities of statesmen and commanders but also as regards knowledge both of the heavens and of things
on land and sea, animals, plants, fruits, and everything else
to be seen in various regions—the utility of geography, I
say, presupposes in the geographer the same philosopher,
the man who busies himself with the investigation of the
art of life, that is, of happiness.[29]

It is easy to see how such a doctrine impelled the encyclo-
pedic proclivities of the German humanists. Aventinus, approaching from the historical side of the topographical-historical combination, felt that it is the task of history to know
"the most important things," and as he describes these, they
sound much like the "wide learning" of Strabo.[30] History must
be the mirror in which the multifarious facets of a country's
life are caught, just as geography gathers all the impressions
of a land's physical nature. In combination the view they render
is total and true, though trimmed and simplified because it
represents an ordering of the innumerable impressions which
meet eye and mind. Compared to such an ambitious design, the
old idea of a Germania illustrata seemed cramped and pedantic indeed.

Though the best of the topographical-historical works departed from their sources sufficiently to achieve a free narrative style, their authors never relaxed their conviction that
critical source study is the basis of sound historiography. The
impressive history of publication of classical and medieval
texts in the early sixteenth century has already been mentioned;[31] these sources served to create a more complete picture of the German past. Many a humanist found it worth a
parenthetical remark that his material came from "genuine
old sources, not only printed ones but manuscripts, also from
old letters and charters."[32] When documentary evidence is so
profitably utilized, one of the dangers inherent in the humanist
movement, that of remaining antiquarian out of preoccupation
with antiquity, is minimized. The topographical-historical writers distinguished themselves clearly from their more philo-
logically oriented colleagues by their positive attitudes toward
observation and experience. Vadian, for example, stated de-
cisively that in geographical instruction travel and the study
of maps must precede, not follow, interpretation of the authors.[33] With one voice his colleagues seemed to declare that
seeing is better than reading, that "the great store of knowledge obtained from the reports of those who have diligently
explored certain regions"[34] would lend firmer authority to
works already based on the word of established writers. Celtis

sometimes credited his geographical knowledge to his years
of roaming about,[35] and Braun and Hogenberg thought that in
their time no one would deny that "wandering or traveling, as
long as not business and gain but learning is the motive, will
increase wisdom and experience in all things."[36]

That journeying was still far from a routine occupation for
the average man may be perceived in the travel diaries of
such men as Dürer, Aventinus, and Stumpf. Distances covered,
towns and villages passed each day, amounts of money spent
at inns and lodging places, the weather during the voyage—these
were painstakingly, ingenuously recorded.[37] But accuracy demanded autopsy. Stumpf informs us that his description of the
lais is based on his own observation "as I myself have walked
from one end to the other of this splendid land and have, to the
limits of my ability, measured it and recorded the sights and
locations of all noteworthy villages, streams, and valleys."[38]
Another writer crawled through a long subterranean passage
about which the local people told weird tales and measured its
dimensions in order to determine its purpose.[39] And of Vadian
it was related that

> he was such a lover of the art of geography that he never
> shirked to undertake long and difficult journeys to Upper
> and Lower Hungary, Poland, and various parts of Germany.
> But far from letting it go at this, he also traveled to Ven-
> ice in Italy, crossed the Adriatic there, and climbed, nay
> crept, up the highest peaks of the Helvetian Alps not with-
> out danger and toil to his person, solely in order to see
> and experience for himself whether there was truth in the
> things which others said and wrote about these places.[40]

These men not only traveled about; they were eager to observe, to compare, to make acquaintances. "In foreign countries," a contemporary German proverb has it, "one gains
both knowledge and friends."[41] Francis Bacon might have written his familiar little essay Of Travel[42] as a description of the
German humanist en route, and the journeys of many German
travelers would illustrate that they were in agreement with
Bacon's advise on what to see and how to make the most of
their travels. Let anyone who does not know how suggestive
German travel literature in the age of the Renaissance can be
take up the narrative of the Augsburg physician and botanist
Leonhart Rauwolf, Description of My Journey to the East,[43] or
Siegmund von Herberstain's Russian Notes,[44] compiled during
the author's diplomatic service for the Austrian Crown. Or
let him browse through the many guidebooks like that of Hans
Georg Ernstinger,[45] or through Felix Fabri's Evagatorium,[46]

where that widely traveled Dominican Friar from Ulm set down
such a wealth of tales, impressions and solid information about
his two pilgrimages to the Holy Land that the whole Orient
seems to spring to life as we turn the pages. When such volumes as theirs, conceived with an almost Herodotean receptive-
ness for cultural diversity and written with enormous verve,
circulated in Germany, one can surely no longer speak of an
age or a country of parochial views. Nor can one possibly adhere to the notion that German humanists had little awareness
of what went on around them. Interest in the world at large, in
the manifold signs and expressions through which nature and
destiny spoke to man, was active and constant.

Because of the scope of their undertaking most topographical-
historical writers relied not only on their own systematic industry, but on the accumulations of facts and figures that humanist diligence was turning out in the form of special studies,
anthologies, and reference works. Many of these studies arrived
too late to be of help to the earlier and most original topographical authors, but later writers made good use of them. There
were many other fields besides the study of ancient Germany
in which specialized scholarship yielded useful results, and no
humanist felt any compunctions about appropriating the work
and, if desirable, the very words of others, with or without ci-
tation of source. Originality was never a humanist aim. The un-
abashed way in which some writers of the century declared
that much of the content of their works was appropriated from
others seems quaint to us today. Life is too short, says Münster,
to undertake a personal investigation of everything that a cosmographical author needs to know,[47] and Sebastian Franck freely admitted that his _Weltbuch_ was a "beehive of history, that
is, like a bee I have taken from each flower a little bit with
which to build my hive."[48] The German humanists, after all,
considered themselves joint members of an intellectual community; therefore such borrowing was really no more than an
exchange of information leading to the attainment of a common
aim. No one could have felt anything but gratification when
coming across a sentence, a passage, a whole chapter of his
own composition in the learned work of another.

Many volumes that were turned out during the century were
natural reference works and often were so intended, Konrad
Peutinger's _Emperor Book_ for example,[49] which listed all the
Roman emperors down to Maximilian, or Johann Herold's collection of Germanic law codes published in 1557.[50] A new kind
of historical manual also made its appearance, the _Calendarium
historicum_. The first of these seems to have been published by
Paul Eber, a disciple of Melanchthon, in 1550, and his method

was simply to list events of historical importance under the
years—and if possible the months and days—of their occurrence.[51] For biographical reference there was the useful and
unique dictionary of noted Germans by the Basel physician
and polyhistor Heinrich Pantaleon,[52] a work that surveyed
German history from earliest times through biographies of
its illustrious men. Since interest in biography extended to
the past, genealogy became another respected adjunct to the
topographical-historical literature. Münster's Cosmographia
has lengthy chapters full of names strung together: the Kings
of France from "Francus" to Francis I,[53] followed by all the
Dukes of Lorraine and of Flanders; the entire Habsburg dy-
nasty back to Charlemagne.[54] This last genealogy comes,
Münster tells us, "from the books of the experts,"[55] by whom
he means such genealogical specialists as Ladislaus Suntheim
court chaplain and historiographer to Maximilian I, and his
colleagues Johann Stabius and Jacob Manlius. These three
were commissioned by Maximilian to complete a history of
the House of Habsburg, and by other princely houses to under
take similar works.[56] Not all writers, incidentally, accepted
the intrusion of the genealogist into historiography. Johann
Stumpf, for example, despised them as flatterers and lick-
spittles,[57] and about one of them who had pasted together a
long and apocryphal list of Habsburg ancestors, he wrote: "It
is a wonder that he does not also include Alexander the Great
Philip of Macedon, Arthur of England, Godfrey of Bouillon,
and others....I am surprised that the dear man dares submit
such rubbish to the judgment of the learned!"[58]

　　The various writings mentioned here were in no sense preliminary studies for the topographical-historical literature.
Like the more comprehensive cosmographical volumes, they
were to be components in a collection of writings which, in
the aggregate, would tell the full story of Germany. Naturally
there was overlapping and duplication, and the effort must not
be thought of as being directed or systematic. But it was, I
believe, a conscious one. The agreement of motives and prac
tices which speaks to us from the prefaces of so many of thes
works was not achieved by mere imitation but by a consonanc
of individual aims.
　　However that may be, the topographical-historical genre w
formed out of many interests and many approaches—out of a
great expansion of Celtis' plan for a Germania illustrata and
the perfection of descriptive geography, out of critical sourc
studies, conventional chronicling, and new historical percep-
tions, out of travel reports, expressions of civic pride in pro

and poetry, out of the simple joy of telling a story. The combination came about easily and without artifice. Nor did it have
to await the perfection of any one of its components. The genre
had really always been there, ready to be perceived. Strabo
had known it, and Enea Silvio had written some of his best
pieces by its rules. The ancient and contemporary models
needed only to be tapped for their forms and methods.

It is now time to approach the topographical-historical works
themselves in order to determine the essence and character
of the genre as it appeared to their authors. Here the prefaces
and introductions come to our aid. They not only express an
author's motivating aims, but are often vehicles for methodological discussions which attempt to give some articulation
and coherence to the form of the work. As a rule these discussions are variations on the first chapter of the first book
of Ptolemy's Geography in which the Alexandrian determines
the limits of the science on whose study he has embarked.
"Geography," says Ptolemy,[59] "is a representation in picture
of the whole known world together with the phenomena which
are contained therein." It finds its true task in the fixing of
positions, in the determination of "the extent of the earth as
well as its shape and its position under the heavens, in order
that one may rightly state what are the peculiarities and pro-
portions of the part with which one is dealing, and under what
parallel of the celestial sphere it is located, for so one will
be able to discuss the length of its days and nights, the stars
which are fixed overhead,...in short, all things having regard to our earthly habitation."

Geography, Ptolemy continues, is distinguished from chorography in that the latter selects certain places for special attention to all particulars, "even dealing with the smallest conceivable localities, such as harbors, farms, villages, river
courses, and such like." Chorography is most concerned with
"what kind of places those are which it describes," not with
size and position relative to other places, which is the business
of geography. Chorography must render "a true likeness," and
to achieve this aim "chorography needs an artist, and no one
presents it rightly unless he is an artist." Geography, in turn,
requires the services of a man skilled in mathematics and
geometry.

As we trace these sentences through the humanist writings
of the sixteenth century we become aware of changes in tone
and emphasis. Obviously, what the topographical-historical
writers regard as their province is Ptolemy's chorography,
the detailed description of a particular region, not geography.
Both had been cartographical pursuits to Ptolemy, but his

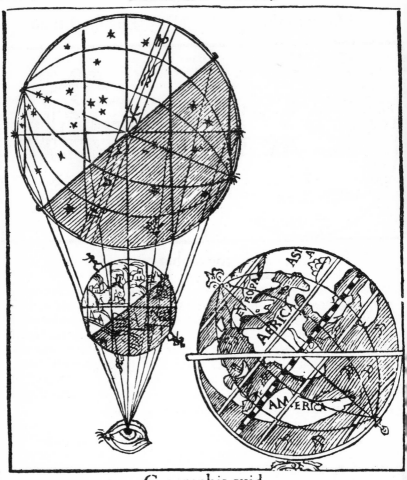

Geographia quid.

Geographia (vt Vernerus in paraphrasi ait) est telluris ipsius præ-
cipuarum ac cognitarum partium, quatenus ex eis totus cogni-
tusque terrarum orbis constituitur, & insigniorum quorumlibet,
quæ huiusmodi telluris partibus cohærent, formula quædam ac picturæ imitatio. Et a Cosmographia differt, quia terram distinguit per montes, fluuios, & maria, aliaꝗ insigniora, nulla adhibita circulorum ratione. Iisꝗ maxime prodest, qui admussum rerum gestarum & fabularu
peritiam habere desuderant. Pictura enim seu picturæ imitatio, ordinẽ
situmque locorum ad memoriam facillime ducit. Consummatio itaꝗ
& finis Geohraphiæ, totius orbis terrarum constat intuitu, illorum imita-
tione, qui integram capitis similitudinem idoneis picturis effingunt.

"Geography" (above) and "Chorography" (right)

Geographia.   Eius similitudo

Chorographia quid.

Horographia autem (Vernero dicente) quæ & Topogra phia dicitur, partialia quædam loca seorsum & absolute cō siderat, absᵩ eorum adseinuicem, & ad vniuersum tellu ris ambitum comparatione. Omnia siquidem, ac fere mini ma in eis contenta tradit & prosequitur. Velut portus, vil las, populos, riuulorum quoque decursus, & quęcunᵩ alia illis finitima, vt sunt ædificia, domus, turres, mœnia &c. Finis vero eiusdem in effigi enda partilius loci similitudine consummabitur: veluti si pictor aliquis aurem tantum aut oculum designaret depingeretque.

Chorographia   Eius similitudo

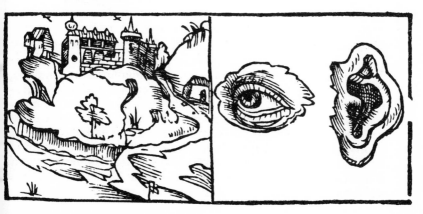

from Peter Apianus' <u>Cosmographia</u> (Antwerp, 1540).

definition was elastic, and it was understood as embracing
description. As the decades go by and the object of the topographical-historical writers is more clearly articulated in
their own minds, we find that their interpretations of chorography become more inclusive, more directly responsive to
their interests. Lines of division are less sharply drawn and
the names become interchangeable, so that when some writers
speak of chorography they may be referring to what others
call geography or even cosmography, a much more inclusive
term. At the same time the more professionally oriented
geographers show a tendency to stand aloof. A division becomes discernible between the "artists" and the geometricians
who hold their ground on the pristine Ptolemaic definition of
their discipline. To Apianus, for example, the distinctions
were as clear-cut as Ptolemy's had been: cosmography is the
consideration of the universe in its four elements, Earth, Water, Air, Fire. Cosmography sees the earth in relation to the
other celestial bodies while geography is "a faithful pictorial,
that is, cartographic representation of the land and its features."[60] Both are clearly mathematical pursuits, as they
seem to have remained to all but the group of humanists with
which we are concerned. On the subject of chorography, one
of lesser interest to him, Apianus repeats Ptolemy's observations.

Gemma's definitions are the same as Apianus'. Joachim
Rheticus, the Wittenberg astronomer, also held to the strictly
mathematical interpretation of geography and chorography.[61]
In the discussions of other writers, however, the distinctions
began to blur. Vadian, in the methodological preface to his
Pomponius Mela commentary of 1518, sounds a significant note
of departure from Ptolemy. Geography, cosmography, topography, topothesy, and chorography, he says, are words which,
though they all deal with the study and description of the earth
have often been confused by writers. "Now geography, if we
trace the etymology of the word, is the science which describes
the position of the continents relative to the ocean and the Mediterranean Sea, as well as places situated anywhere on these
continents." Cosmography, on the other hand, deals with the
heavens as well as with our world; its special concern is the
relationship between the planet earth and the entire cosmic
system.

> The geographer, in addition to listing places, concerns him-
> self generally with their histories and with inquiries about
> the origins of cities, races, nations, and peoples, and fur-
> thermore with the significance of names and with noteworthy

events not only in nature but also in the affairs of men, of which a great many can be observed on earth. The cosmographer mentions regions, cities, streams, oceans, and mountains merely to fix the boundaries and limits of lands or to indicate their situation relative to the constellations. ... The geographer's work is more akin to that of the poets and the historians ... for which reason, as we can see if we investigate carefully, Strabo, Pliny, and others were of much help to poets and historians in their descriptions of localities.

The cosmographer inclines more toward geometry and astronomy; but each is dependent on the other. Cosmography is a more precise science because, in its search for absolute axioms, it must base itself on exact laws (<u>certis</u> <u>axiomatis</u> <u>nitatur</u>). Geography, however, relying as it does on the evidence of literary tradition, "can be neither certain nor without internal contradictions, for time leaves no mortal thing unchanged." Chorography restricts itself to individual regions and describes them in the manner of a painting (<u>picturae</u> <u>similitudine</u> <u>observata</u> <u>prosequitur</u>). Chorography is limited to the local, the particular, which it depicts in all its precise details, while geography aims at a synoptic view of lands in their entirety.[62]

Though he retains the form of Ptolemy's definition, Vadian considerably enlarges the scope of geography to take in those historical, ethnic, and social investigations so important to him and his colleagues. Geography and chorography no longer differ in kind, only in compass. The exact sciences are now associated with cosmography where they are, in Vadian's definition, beyond the range of most of the topographical-historical writers. Literary sources are considered proper geographical evidence.

As the <u>Catechesis</u> was one of Vadian's most widely read works—it has with good reason been called "the manifesto of the political geographers"[63]—and as his subsequent publications elaborated and exemplified the method outlined in it, Vadian's words can be taken as the inception of an effort to evolve the rules of a distinct geographical form. Precise men might deplore the loose way in which "cosmography" and "geography" were bandied about by amateurs,[64] but the definitions had to be stretched to suit the purpose.

In the "cosmographical" works of the middle and late periods of the century the topographical-historical type was worked out in accordance with these definitions. Vadian's fusion of chorography and geography was extended to include cosmography. To Münster cosmography meant simply "description of

the world" and geography "description of the earth."[65] No dif-
ferentiation is made, but he is sure what his task is to be. His
Cosmographia, a huge work of some 650 folio pages in the
original, and nearly 1,200 in the enlarged edition, describes
the whole world, country by country and region by region,[66] in
other words, chorographically, and is packed with information
considered appropriate to geography by Vadian. "For this art,
Münster writes, speaking of "the Gentle Art of Geography,"
deals "not only with the countries, states, and customs of sun-
dry peoples, but concerns itself also with many other things
on earth and in the oceans, such as strange animals, trees,
metals, and similar useful and harmful things found in the soil
and in water." All these his Cosmography will put before our
eyes. "I shall lead you from land to land," Münster promises,
"and we shall even venture out to sea so that I may point out
to you cities, mountains, rivers, deserts, and many other
things profitable and diverting to know about, such as the customs, characteristics, and practices of foreign peoples, also
the plants that grow in the countries they inhabit and the treas
ures found in their soil."[67]

Johann Stumpf, like Münster, wishes to guide his reader
along a path of geographical and historical discovery, but his
description of Switzerland is referred to as a chorography.[68]
To Rauw, cosmography and geography are one and the same,
both "indicating the situations of cities and places,"[69] the former with substantial preliminary notices on the heavenly bodies. Braun and Hogenberg, the printers of majestic volumes
of city descriptions, regard geography as a summary representation of the physical features of the whole earth while the
chorographer (or topographer, as they write) "describes each
section of the world individually with its cities, villages, is-
lands, rivers, lakes, mountains, springs, and so on, and tells
its history, making everything so clear to the reader that he
seems to be seeing the actual town or place before his eyes."[7]

Whatever the endeavor was to be called, then, its character
was fixed. The topographical-historical work was to contain a
minute and comprehensive description of as much or as little
of the world as its author set out to survey, "leaving out not a
mountain, farmyard, creek, house, tower, wall, or wood,"[71]
and telling everything necessary to a consummate understanding of its nature, that is, explaining "Locus, Tempus, and His
toria."[72] Descriptions and generalizations were to be based
on accurate investigation, and the reader was, if possible, an
especially in the larger cosmographies, to be made aware of
the majesty and design of the realm of nature and its laws.
In form it was to be a refurbishing of the ancient periegesis[73]

in which we are transported from place to place on the winged words of the writer. In spirit, finally, it was meant to bring the world at large, and especially his own native land, closer to the reader. Germany was to be illustrated not just by demonstrating the survival of her ancient habitations, but through the description of a living, changing country.

In the estimation of the German humanists the topographical-historical genre had a rightful place among the humanistic studies. What other literary form created so many opportunities to examine man in the manifold guises of his earthly habitat? What other study called for observations on such a variety of matters? In fact, was geographical investigation not the beginning of all knowledge? Vadian, the most reflective member of his group, makes this highest claim for his discipline when he associates it with the cognitive act itself:

> For as long as the human mind lives in the body it obeys that law of knowledge which decrees that the intellect can only grasp that which is conducted to it by the senses, and that all our thinking and imagining is analogy. This law of knowledge requires first and foremost the study of geography so that we may begin our quest for knowledge by understanding the earth, the scene of human habitation.[74]

Most humanists took a less exalted view. But they were no less certain than Vadian that chorography, geography, and cosmography were fitting pursuits for learned men.

4

The Regional Chorographies   I: Germany

HE VOCIFEROUS nationalism of the German humanists notwithstanding, their closest affinity was to the regions which held their roots. The topographical-historical literature is, as a consequence, essentially a territorial one. There is no reason to doubt the sincerity of expressed national senti-ments, but the associations raised by patriotic thoughts were local. When Felix Fabri, returning from a long voyage to the Holy Land, wrote in his diary, "O how my heart was glad to behold my Germany! Once she was poor in wisdom, power and wealth; but now she puts to shame all other nations,"[1] the im-age before his mind's eye was Swabia and his native Ulm. When Aventinus discussed Germany he meant Bavaria. When Wimpheling invoked his country his voice was attuned to the ears of Alsace. "Germany" was still an amorphous designation, and only such men as Hutten who were active in the high poli-tical contests of their age could rise to a truly national con-sciousness. The territories, on the other hand, were concrete in their ethnic and geographical characteristics, and for this reason the chorographic literature offers us many regional descriptions, the products of <u>Stamm</u> fidelity and familiarity with native traditions. Only the cosmographies of Franck, of Münster, and of Rauw took the whole empire for their province, and even these volumes were, as we have seen, essentially patchworks of regional descriptions furnished by widely scat-tered contributors.

Not every region, of course, produced descriptions of sig-nificance. Indeed, some were not described at all during the century. A glance at the distribution of the chorographic lit-erature shows that the German south is generously represented the north but little. The close personal and institutional con-nections which bind the southern territories to Italy in the age of humanism cannot fully account for the disparity, though they

explain much in German history. Nor can the theory, already
mentioned in an earlier chapter, that national consciousness,
and therefore incentives to topographical description, were
first generated along the lightly drawn borders of the empire.
The Rhine delta was an area of conflicting loyalties and the
seat of a lively and cosmopolitan culture. Antwerp, as one who
visited the city describes it to us, was "always full of Frenchmen, Germans, Spaniards, Englishmen, and Italians," and the
whole town was magnificent with the opulent quarters of its
bourgeoisie and the lofty spires of its many churches. But
Adrianus Barlandus, the author of this description, attached
it, along with some glimpses of other Dutch and Flemish cities,
to a historical treatise on the Dukes of Brabant which was not
likely to attract widespread attention.[2] For the rest, our knowledge of the lower Rhine area must depend on a sparse general
survey of the delta by one Cornelius Aurelius,[3] a little pamph-
let on Netherlandish town names written by Gerardus Noviomagus in the style of Willibald Pirckheimer,[4] and an account
of Dutch antiquities by Petrus Schrijver.[5] The Low Countries
had to await the following century for a school of geographers
worthy of their material and intellectual civilization.

In the northeast the cultural situation seemed to hold little
promise of humanistic chorography. The three principalities
of the northern plain, Mecklenburg, Pomerania, and Brandenburg, oriented eastward, and with few and recently established
universities,[6] were tardy in their assimilation of the themes
and forms of the humanist age. But the persistent efforts of
their rulers to attract men of learning to these remote lands[7]
bore fruit. From one of them, Pomerania, came a gem of a
description, and the need for geographical investigations
seemed to have been felt elsewhere too. Joachim Rheticus,
one of the humanists in residence at the court of Albrecht of
Prussia, the Grand Master of the Teutonic Knights who had
secularized the Order, tried to stir up some local interest in
chorography. In 1541, Rheticus, who is better known for his
early publication of the Copernican theories, sent to Albrecht
a provisional map of his duchy, hand drawn and done from his
own reckonings. In the dedication he explained:

> Since in these times our Christian rulers are burdened
> with high and weighty matters concerning religion, the
> preservation of peace and the prevention of civil wars,
> and the stand against the Turk, it is left to the learned in
> all our lands to devise Chorographicas Tabulas, that is,
> maps, in order that a capable mathematician may go to
> work on them, and, in the manner of Ptolemy, renew the
> art of geography for us.[8]

Sebastian Münster had argued similarly in his circular letter
of 1528. But Rheticus was interested in cartography, not description, and the thirty-two leaves of his <u>Chorographia</u>, which
remained in manuscript, merely suggest a number of methods
of representing Prussia on a detailed map. Description was
not part of his program, and none was attempted.[9]

However, beginnings had been made elsewhere, tentative
ones, to be sure. The Hamburg churchman and chronicler
Albert Krantz, for example, wrote a number of brief descriptions of such cities as Rostock, Stralsund, Greifswald, and
Lüneburg for his historical volumes on the northern peoples.[10]
They bear the marks of personal inspection, but they were not
sufficiently elaborated to be revealing to the distant reader.
Had Krantz lived a quarter century later he would surely have
been more responsive to the demands for informative descriptions. The continuations of his works by the Protestant theologian David Chytraeus, a professor at the University of
Rostock, contain a number of deft descriptive passages which
illustrate much that remains lifeless in Krantz.[11]

The writings of another Low German author beat with a
quicker pulse. Thomas Kantzow, author of four versions of a
description of Pomerania, secretary in the Chancery of the
Ducal Court of Stettin, and a chronicler with a high opinion of
the power of historiography to instruct men, tells us in his
many pages not merely what he has heard "from the oldest
citizens of this land and what I have been able to observe and
experience for myself," but conveys a lively image of his country and people. Kantzow was a most conscientious writer. Not
only did he so industriously revise and augment his chronicle
that it never quite got ready for the press, but the subsequent
versions gradually extended themselves backward, so that a
chronicle meant at first to be a record of the immediate past
became at length a full history of Pomerania.

The first attempt was in the Low German vernacular of his
region,[12] but the later versions, written in the 1530's, were set
in the High German style of the Pomeranian Chancery.[13] Though
his narrative, like that of Krantz, is unrelievedly chronological,
it is interspersed with items that revive our interest: fires,
earthquakes, heavy snowfalls, price increases, and depressions
When he describes the rebuilding in stone of Stralsund after
the wooden city had been gutted in a war with Lübeck, or when
he offers his diagnosis of a mysterious four-day paralysis, he
displays a noteworthy response to significant detail. Here and
there in the long chronicle there are fine descriptions—the account of the Duke's pilgrimage to the Holy Land, for example,
quite amusing in its tales of adventure and mishaps with Italians

and Turks, and the description of his visit to the site of an ancient Saxon city where he traced the submerged foundations
with a long pole while being rowed back and forth over the area.

Most interesting to us is Kantzow's meticulous topography
of Pomerania, an effort in the best manner of the genre. "Now
that we have outlined the history of Pomerania," he begins,
"it may not be without merit to say something about her present appearance, her customs and characteristics, so that her
history might be better understood. Since everything in human
affairs changes and reverses itself, posterity will thus have a
record of the country as it was in my time." First he describes
the land:

> The country, as much of it as is subject to the Dukes of
> Pomerania and to the German Empire, is fifty great Pom-
> eranian miles in length and is shaped like an angle, nar-
> row at the ends and wide in the middle. Around Stettin,
> located in the very center, the land is broadest, but just
> this side of the Vistula, near Danzig, it narrows down to
> seven miles, and on the other side, at Rostock, it is like-
> wise very narrow.... It is a level, plain land without any
> hills ... full of rivers which flow in the direction of the
> ocean and are all navigable. The soil holds no ore deposits
> ... nor are there vineyards, except around Stettin. Grapes
> could be grown there, but the inhabitants are so shiftless
> that they refuse to go to the trouble of cultivating them.
> Beer seems to be all they want.
>
> Other than that, the land grows a great plenty of grain and
> fruits, and there are forests and pastures where cattle are
> raised. Thus the people lack nothing.... For this reason
> the country is well populated and has thriving cities.[14]

Kantzow describes the Baltic Sea and the rivers that enter
it. He traces the course of the Oder from the Moravian mountains to the ocean. The Frische Haff, the great lagoon at the
mouth of the Oder, merits a special chapter, as does the fishing industry thereabouts:

> In the summer more than 500 Zesekhan [net boats] are
> made ready. These are small trawlers which can sail
> against the wind as well as with it. The fishermen let out
> a net, called by them Zese, and with this spread out be-
> hind them they sail up and down the Haff. The larger fish
> are at once salted or else brought fresh to market in the
> cities along the Haff. But the small ones are dumped over-
> board, and it is a pity to see so many of them go to waste.

> In the wintertime, when a thick sheet of ice covers the Haff, the fishermen come out with huge nets, so heavy that it takes twenty or thirty strong men to pull one. They cut large holes in the ice and push the net under water with poles, drawing it back and forth. Often a single such catch brings in fish worth a hundred to three hundred Gulden. [15]

As for the inhabitants, they are simple, decent folk, honest but stolid. Few care for learning and the liberal arts, and all lean to immoderate pleasures, especially gluttony, the national vice:

> When a child is born, the women must have their feast, and baptism is another occasion for public celebration. When the mother returns to Church after her confinement, there will be still another eating bout. A wedding calls for a carousal of three, four, five, even six days with invitations to friends and strangers alike.... When someone has died, the bereaved family is obliged to entertain all mourners.... There is not a holiday in the year which is not stretched into a week-long orgy of guzzling and gorging. [16]

The local cuisine, incidentally, is unimaginative and coarse, and so are the fashions. But all in all, the Pomeranians are not a bad sort, he concludes; they are upright, faithful, and, since 1534, pious Lutherans.

An epitome of the history of government in Pomerania follows, and when the account has been brought up to date Kantzow turns to the land in his own time. He explains the duties and privileges of the three estates and the confusion of legal codes in force; then he begins to enumerate the products of the region "twenty times what is needed to sustain life." A long section deals with Pomeranian animals, and we are instructed in the lassoing and breaking of untamed horses, herds of which may be seen running wild on the plains. There are also bears, wild pigs, deer, wildcats, wolves, foxes, and beavers. Hunting and fishing, needless to say, are superb. A mere catalogue of varieties of fish and wild fowl takes up seven pages.

So much for the country in general. The remainder of Kantzow's topography of Pomerania is devoted to descriptions of some two dozen of the larger cities. [17] These are brief sketches, and the pattern of exposition remains constant. Only the details vary. Still, each is a little vignette of sixteenth-century life, for we hear about the architecture of town halls and churches, about costumes and dialects, crafts and industries, about the domestic habits of citizens and their intellectual pursuits, if any. Kantzow was a shrewd observer. Not much escaped his notice, though he kept his narrative sparse.

In the east as in the west of Germany, the rivers dominate
the geography of the land. Kantzow followed his river courses
diligently, enumerating tributaries and the towns on their
shores. In the west it was the Rhine which held the attention
of every chorographer who worked in the area. The bustling
life of the Rhine cities is preserved in the jingles of traveling
poets who thus recorded their gratitude to the hospitality of
officials and townspeople. A stroll around Cologne in 1531 with
one such rhymster, Johann Haselberg, reveals all the tourist
sights: walls, Town Hall, arsenal, and granary. But he also
takes us to the docks to watch the ships tie up:

> Five cranes we see down by the shore,
> They load and unload a great store
> Of goods, some of enormous weight,
> And never drop a single crate.

He guides us to the market place:

> When through the Lindgasse you've been led
> You'll see the market place ahead,
> Where wool is sold, and textiles rare,
> Velvet and silk, and camel's hair.
> Dealers in herbs and apothecaries
> Here have their shops; and pears and cherries
> And cheese and cabbage are for sale,
> And pubs dispense fine wine and ale.[18]

We cannot be sure that descriptive accuracy was not occasionally sacrificed to the need for making a rhyme, but these
little poems are wonderfully evocative. We shall meet others.
Less concerned, unfortunately, with the local color of the
Rhineland towns, but informative and eminently useful, is a
careful chorography of the whole Rhine valley by Sebastian
Brant. That the busy Brant found time for such an undertaking
is evidence enough of the widespread interest in describing
the German scene. Brant was, as a native Strassburger, familiar with the western regions of the land. His title, Description of Various Localities in Germany, Such as Rivers,
Mountains, Cities and Borders, with an Indication of Miles
and Roads from Town to Town,[19] sounds impressive, but it
is deceptive. Brant's main concern is with Alsace and lands
to the north, and Strassburg is his specific point of orientation.
Unlike other Alsatian writers, however, he has his local patriotism well under control. The familiar national motive is
struck in the closing lines—he has written his book "for foreign states to reflect that not they alone are great and

NVREMBERGA

The city of Nuremberg, drawn in 1493 by Michael
Wolgemut for Hartmann Schedel's <u>Liber</u> <u>cronicarum</u>.
View from the southeast. Left, the Spittler Gate; next
to it St. James's; then the Carthusian monastery and

the tower of the New Gate. The two churches of St.
Lawrence and St. Sebald are topped by the castle
with its four ancient towers. In the foreground, the
Pegnitz.

mighty"[20] —but there is no ambiguity of motive in the text. The purpose of his description is to describe.

Brant permits himself only the most rudimentary general survey. A few pages on the Danube valley and some other eastern German sites are mere preliminaries to his concentration on the Rhine region. And his description of the great stream, when he comes to it, is worthy of his zeal. We first, of course, learn something of the opinions of the ancients on the river's sources and length, but before long Brant begins to draw on his own notes to render an exact, if unvaried, account of its course and its many tributaries, its cities and carefully cultivated hillsides. As he moves north out of the mountains and into the valley proper, his information becomes abundant, and he shares it all with us: "From Rheineck...the Rhine enters Lake Constance. Around this lake lie the following cities: Lindau, Buchhorn, Mörsberg.... West of Constance the Rhine leaves the lake at Stein. There a bridge spans the river." Brant lists every bridge, toll station, and ferry crossing as he follows the Rhine towards the sea. At Basel, for example, "the Rhine separates the Big and Little Cities. It is spanned there by a bridge with wooden and masonry arches; altogether eighteen arches are needed to cross the river. The Birss here enters the Rhine from above and the left, the Wiese from the right and below. At Neuenburg, no bridge but a toll station. At Breisach, a bridge and a toll station." Bridges, their construction and their conditions, fascinate him: "Strassburg has a long bridge, but because of a series of floods and some settling of the ground this bridge is badly in need of repairs. It is not merely useful but indispensable to local citizens and to travelers." All this is information not only interesting but most useful to the voyager in an age in which maps were not abundant and transportation unreliable. Brant also takes some notice of cultural matters, especially of the changes which had been wrought since the days of Caesar. These he points out, but briefly and in passing. We have the sensation of moving along while we listen to him. The finest Rhine wine, he tells us as Bacharach comes into sight, is produced there. The place is named after Bacchus, "that is, <u>Bachi ara</u>, because Bacchus, who was held to be a god of wine in pagan times, once had a sanctuary there and sacrifices were made to him." The larger cities, too, are dealt with in a mere paragraph, though in each case a building, an institution, or a little scene is brought to life:

> Cologne, as I have said, lies on the left side of the Rhine, like Strassburg and all other important Rhine cities, for

they were originally fortresses built by Romans against
the Germans on the other side. Here we have a Cathedral
with a mighty spire, but only half of it has been completed
so far.... Its nave is somewhat larger than that of the
Strassburg Cathedral, but it has not yet been roofed over.
...

When the Bishop of Cologne goes to Mass he is preceded
by the "Sendgraf," that is, the Criminal Judge, who bears
a heavy white cudgel, thick as a man's arm and a yard and
a half long. A retainer beside him carries a golden sword
in a scabbard. Behind the Bishop two servants carry a
green flail and a white flail, each on a velvet cushion, to
indicate that Cologne is an architect and a builder of the
realm, and its Bishop one of the Empire's heads.[21]

"From Cologne it is three miles to Suntz...," and on we go.
We stop only when we come to one of the tributaries, where
Brant turns left or right, picks up the river at its own source,
and pursues it with its bridges, ferries, towns, and castles
until he arrives again at the point where he arrested his journey. We continue until we reach the North Sea, and following
a brief look at England and Scandinavia Brant switches the
scene and transfers to the Danube. But here the treatment is
curt indeed. The entire course of the Danube with all its sub-
sidiary rivers and its cities occupies a mere six pages; then
Brant is back in the west with a series of mileage tables of
which it would be tedious to give more than a suggestion here:
"From Strassburg to Ettlingen 8 miles, From there 7 miles
to Esslingen, Then to Gisslingen 5 miles,..."
    Strassburg is the center of the road map he now draws:
Strassburg to Trent and points south, Strassburg to Prussia,
Strassburg to Silesia, to Nuremberg, to Trier, to various
places in Switzerland, to Paris, and so on. Not only the mileage itself, but also the best travel route is indicated, again a
useful service to his readers. But a loftier theme must be
struck before concluding, and therefore Brant ends his little
work with a "Summary of the Might of the German Nation,"[22]
a roster of the Electors and other secular and spiritual Lords
of the realm which sounds the customary patriotic note.
    Brant gives us the facts, but not much more. His book is
useful to have but we miss detail and personality. But, as it
happens, an earlier traveler on the Rhine noted many of the
sights that Brant must have seen but failed to register or record and we may turn to him, Felix Fabri, for a description,
and a vivid one, of the scenery of the southern Rhine.

Fabri is not, to be sure, a geographer in the humanist sense.
Vadian would not have accepted him into the guild.[23] His designation of the boundaries of Europe according to Orosius and
Isidore of Seville, his confounding of the names of Alamannia,
Germania, Teutonia, and Francia in obliviousness of, or indifference to, the fact that contemporary maps gave a far more
trustworthy picture of these territories, must have touched
the professional nerve of later writers. Fabri here accepts
wholeheartedly St. Jerome's dictum that in the composition
of chronicles, a man's independent judgment is his very worst
authority.[24] But where he operates without sources, when he
is forced, because he can find no guide, to recreate what has
impressed itself on his own senses, he is very much a chorographer. In fact, he is a very good one.

The chapter on the course of the Rhine in his Descriptio
Sueviae[25] is an example. Before we reach it, to be sure, we
are regaled with much lore of an etymological and pseudo-
archaeological nature, and the description of the Rhine, too,
begins with speculations which have little resemblance to geographical fact. But once these are out of his system, Fabri
switches to a pleasant descriptive style and we float with him
down the Rhine from its sources to Cologne while he points
out noteworthy features:

> Emerging from the lake [Lake Constance] which it has
> thus replenished with its waters, the Rhine now turns west,
> running in a deeper bed and a more peaceful course. But
> wherever it meets obstacles which hinder its path it turns
> so violently on the rocks in its way that those who see the
> force of the waves as they break on the cliffs and hear the
> thunderous noise are overcome with terror. Between the
> town of Schaffhausen and the city of Basel there are a num-
> ber of such obstructions. These are mountain passes where
> the cliffsides form tight gorges and the Rhine, angry at the
> narrow opening, begins to roar so fearfully that a spectator
> can barely remain on his two feet so does the earth shake.
> You observe this especially at Schaffhausen where the
> Rhine falls in a headlong descent and with such force that
> no one can think of proceeding by boat. Below the town of
> Laufenburg a tightening of the rocky bed compels the river
> to squeeze through with impatient rage so that you see no
> water at all, only white foam.
>
> In this region boats are emptied of passengers and cargo
> and are guided over the cataracts by means of ropes. A
> few skilled boatmen, however, manage to lead their craft

down without the use of ropes. But the people thereabouts
say that the Church denies the Holy Eucharist to these pi-
lots because they expose their lives to danger for the sake
of money. I have often myself seen both methods of navi-
gating the rapids employed.[26]

Fabri follows nearly the whole course of the Rhine, though
only his descriptions of the southern portions have the clear
ring of his own observation. Germany's south was familiar to
him, and he felt able to depict it accurately. The rest of his
Swabian Description is of little interest to us. Enea Silvio's
Europa is his guidebook here.[27] Soon the geographical unity
of the earlier sections is lost; instead we get a dynastic account of the fortunes of the House of Habsburg, and it is very
dull.

Just west of Fabri's Swabia there was a community of writers
whose purpose admitted chorographic description to a mere an-
cillary place. Alsace, forever a contested region, was the point
of contact between two ethnic groups, two languages, two cultural traditions which contended with one another. In such regions patriotic feelings are apt to be high-pitched, and in Alsace
they expressed themselves in what a modern historian has
called a "typical border nationalism."[28] The debate with the
French and with German supporters of French claims concerned the right of Germans to the Imperial crown and the
ethnic character of Alsace and its inhabitants.[29] Both were
questions with acute political implications in the first quarter
of the sixteenth century, when the throne itself was at stake.
Much more heat than light was generated by this controversy,
but in its process the land and the people of Alsace did come
in for some critical inspection, though never without ultimate
references to the political argument.

The first and most violent of the Alsatian publicists was
Jakob Wimpheling, who appeared in Strassburg in 1500 after
half a century of studying and teaching in Schlettstadt, Freiburg,
Erfurt, and Heidelberg. Wimpheling's fervent and tiresome
patriotism is well known. Jean Bodin must have had him in
mind when he remarked of some German historiographers
that "they did not, in order to exalt their nation, have to vilify
all others."[30]

In Strassburg Wimpheling published his Germania, a tract
addressed to the magistrates of the city, in which he demon-
strated the German character of Alsace and tried to promote
the foundation of an institution of higher learning in the city.[31]
He also wrote an Epitome of German History, published in
1505, and intended as a text for a reformed course of studies

at this institution.[32] Given the political purpose of his writings,
Wimpheling could have no real interest in description for its
own sake. The last of the seventy-two short chapters of the
Epitome does, however, summarize the "Fertility of Alsace,"
whose good soil, temperate climate, shady forests, and abundance of water have earned it the name of "Germany's Pro-
vider." Moreover, he asserts, the mild air produces clear
heads, hence the region possesses more than its share of
learned and distinguished men, who are named in due course.
When there is detail in this book on German history it is always Alsatian, but even so only the most rudimentary description of the cultural scene fits into the narrow frame. German
architecture, he claims at one point, is the most sublime artistic creation of man. Take the Cathedral of Strassburg:[33]

> I would say that there is nothing more magnificent on the
> face of the earth than this edifice. Who can admire this
> tower sufficiently? Who can adequately praise it? With its
> stone tracery, its sculptured columns, its carved statues
> which describe so many things, it exceeds all buildings of
> Europe in beauty. Its height is over 690 feet![34] It is almost
> incredible that such a massive structure could have been
> raised so high! If Skopas, Pheidias, Ctesiphon, and
> Archimedes lived today they would have to admit publicly
> that our people exceed them in the art of architecture and
> that they prefer this building to the Temple of Diana at
> Ephesus, to the Egyptian pyramids, and to all the other
> works counted among the seven wonders of the world.

No deep appreciation of High Gothic should be read into these
phrases, only civic patriotism. And nothing else appears in
any of Wimpheling's writings. The didactic purpose, the political ambition, spawned them all.

Wimpheling set the tone for Alsatian writing. Its political
direction remained unchanged. In 1521, Wimpheling's friend
and associate Hieronymus Gebwiler, a former rector of the
school of Schlettstadt, produced a laudatory poem to celebrate
the arrival of Charles V in Germany, the Panegyris Carolina,
whose copious glosses by the author's own hand hold some interest for us.[35] Gebwiler uses the occasion to call attention to
his native Alsace. He mentions two theories to account for its
name, and delineates the boundaries. The customary statement
on fertility and smiling skies follows, and here too we have a
procession of distinguished Alsatians whose fame has carried
far the renown of their homeland.

Some short time after this Gebwiler found time for a little
chronicle of Schlettstadt, the town to whose fame he had him-

self contributed. Here he had no political axe to grind and no
apple to polish, and the pleasant description of the town ranks
with the best of the chorographic literature. We travel to
Schlettstadt over roads whose every turn Gebwiler knows,
and we are made to notice their state of repair at the time of
writing. We trace with him the foundations of the various walls
that encircled the town in its periods of growth, then we hear
about the government. "Three things are indispensable to a
sound municipal government," he writes, "a conscientious
priest, a wise and cautious mayor, and a good schoolmaster."
These Schlettstadt has, but we learn other things as well about
life there. One may buy a fine meal for four or five pence.
Wine is seven or eight pence a measure. These good things
being so inexpensive, the Schlettstädter spend much time con-
suming them in their inns. "They have such cosy and cheerful
parties that even Princes and Lords and Prelates do not disdain their company." Gebwiler places much stress on the demo-
cratic ways of the Alsatians; they recognize no inequality of
civic status, they take each man for what he is, not for what
his forbear was.

But back to the town: the public bathhouse has splendid equip-
ment, for the Schlettstädter, as indeed all Alsatians, like to
keep themselves scrupulously neat. Even in their habits of
cleanliness they are gregarious. Baths are not taken in privacy
but in association with others, though "each has his own tub
which is filled with hot water by employees of the establishment." The markets and periodic fairs are social occasions
too; in fact, all activities are carried on in the friendliest manner. The Ill River provides pretty scenery and fish, and the
landscape is picturesque for miles around. A paragraph on
the famous school which he headed until 1509 follows, and
Gebwiler does not neglect to mention that the town profits not
only from the renown the school brings, but materially from
money spent by the students. We sense a recollection of town-
gown troubles in the remark. Once more a catalogue of famous
men, Wimpheling prominent among them, concludes the account.

Gebwiler and Wimpheling told their stories well. Münster,
whose knowledge of the region came largely from them, thought
that "in all of Germany no land is to be compared with
Alsace."[36] And though the strident dispute over the Rhine
caused the loudest reverberations in Germany,[37] those who
responded were not likely to remain ignorant of the nature of
the land. Beatus Rhenanus' Alsatian pages[38] were more accurate and more widely informative, but the enthusiastic zeal
of Wimpheling and Gebwiler was more likely to impress the

Alsatian landscape on the minds of those to whom it had been
a mere name before 1500.

Current political and social interest was always a major
stimulus to chorographers and an incentive to publishers. Often it resulted in something of more lasting value than Alsatian
chorography. Not everywhere was the promise offered by situation and conditions fulfilled. The accomplishment of a proper
regional description required a subtle relationship between
the challenge, the presence of a learned and talented person
to take it up, and the active interest of a community of readers
Silesia, for example, though there the problem of contested
borders and divided allegiance prompted native sons to turn a
sharper eye on country and people,[39] did not produce any notable descriptions. Lorenz Corvinus, a Silesian humanist close
ly associated with and influenced by Konrad Celtis, did, in his
<u>Geographia</u> of 1496,sketch a little portrait of his native region,
but it is a meager account, and the impression he conveys is
blurred.[40] The book was, to be sure, a text, written expressly
for his pupils at St. Elisabeth's School in Breslau, but even
in this narrow compass the author felt compelled to include a
description of his homeland. "The geographical writers have
not treated this country sufficiently," he declares, "and I deem
it wrong to report here on well-known countries while saying
nothing about... Silesia, my native land."[41] What he does say,
however, is little enough and of doubtful chorographic value.
Following the trail of his mentor, Celtis, Corvinus "describes"
Silesia in two odes, one of them on his native city, Neumarkt.
And there is no other Silesian writer to make precise what
Corvinus left vague.[42]

But elsewhere in Eastern Germany new conditions and the
excitement aroused by them called for a more vigorous ap-
praisal. This is the ore country of the Bohemian and Saxon
mountains where the glittering treasures which were then being unearthed caused a lively interest in the land. Following
a general decline of European prosperity during the fourteenth
century that had affected mining as it affected everything else,
a new epoch for the pits of Central Europe began in the 1450's
and 1460's. New seams of ore were discovered; cinnabar, the
ore of mercury, and calamine, which yields brass when combined with copper, found their uses, and it was realized that
silver could be separated from argentiferous copper ore by
means of lead. This latter discovery, especially, stimulated
production in the Central European copper mines. Responding
to the demand, the mining experts—most of them active in the

Tirol, Saxony, Bohemia, and Hungary—designed more powerful drainage engines and devised new methods for ventilating
shafts, most of which may still be seen in Georg Agricola's
fascinating De re Metallica. Tens of thousands of people were
drawn into the new operations, and the resulting boom was reflected in a vastly expanded rate of production of silver and
copper in these regions.

Peter Albinus, the writer of a description of that part of
Saxony which then bore the name of Meissen, thought these
mining operations of such interest that he appended a wholly
new volume on Meissen's pits and shafts to the second edition
of his main work, the New Chronicle of Meissen.[43] Albinus
was born in one of the centers of the Saxon industry, Schneeberg
in the Ore Mountains. Though he went on to higher studies and
attained a chair of poetry at Wittenberg, he never seems to have
lost the contact with his native region, which makes his description a revealing one. Published near the end of the century, the
Chronica is at once a history of the Margraviate of Meissen
and its three bishoprics, and a description of its geography. It
was Albinus' contention that a country's topography must be
known before its history may be understood; therefore he enumerates Meissen's physical features, the cities and towns, the
castles and monasteries, rivers, and lakes, as well as "The
Endowments and Attractions or Beauties of the Land." What
these "Attractions" are, we are soon told in detail: profession
of the liberal arts, true (that is, Protestant) religion, universities and learned men who study and instruct there, public
schools also, with able masters, good government, fair laws
and impartial courts, clean and prosperous cities, and, best of
all, citizens of sturdiness and courage.

Not to be counted as the least among these blessings is the
"fertility of the land,"[44] by which Albinus means all that is tak-
en from the soil, is raised or built on it, or which lends beauty
to it. He treats us to a detailed account of the cultivation of
grain and grape, of cattle, lumber, and mining activities, the
stupendous beer production and consumption. Then rivers,
cities, and the inhabitants are discussed in particular. The two
great streams of the region, the Elbe and the Saale, receive
meticulous antiquarian attention; following this they are described scenically—the vegetation on the banks of the streams,
the river rafts and their hardbitten crews, fishermen trapping
the many kinds of fish, the latter so delectable that Albinus
cannot refrain from naming each succulent variety and advis-
ing on its gastronomic properties.

In the cities of Meissen it is the neatness of streets and
houses which makes the most lasting impression. The townsmen,

no less than their domiciles, gleam with cleanliness (their
godliness has already been praised), and the popular saying,
"Meissner Gleisner," hardly needs Albinus' labored explanation: "There can be no doubt that the old epithet given to our
citizens, 'Meissner Gleisner,' originated in their habits of
neatness and the care with which they kept their bodies and
clothing, food and living quarters free from dirt and shining
with cleanliness." The bustling life of the towns shows the
Meissner to be industrious as well, and the region could live
comfortably on its textile manufacture alone, even if the mines
did not exist. The Naumburg and Merseburg fairs bring in outside products and market domestic ones. His picture of Meissen is one of solid, honest prosperity with middle class virtues
and rewards, though the arts are by no means neglected. The
learned men of Meissen have been renowned since the thirteent
century, and Albinus recounts their accomplishments in severa
long paragraphs.

Nine years after the <u>Chronica</u> first went to press a second
edition appeared, enlarged and handsomely illustrated.[45] Appended to it is a special section on the mines of the Ore Mountains[46] which is surely a response to general interest in mineral and metallurgical matters. Though the introduction ascribe
its genesis solely to the author's conviction that God reveals Hi
wonder-working powers most dazzlingly in the precious metals
which, long hidden underground, were now coming to light,
Albinus must have been aware of the great popular curiosity
about this subject. More than a generation before, Sebastian
Münster, with his sure sense of popular taste, had added an illustrated chapter on mining to the greatly expanded 1550 edition of his <u>Cosmographia</u>.[47] Albinus now wrote the definitive
work on the mines themselves. He had first, however, to con-
vince the reader that there is no impiety in man's eagerness
to tear open the soil and extract from it metals for his gain
and adornment. Arguments from reason and from Scripture
are marshalled against what appears to have been a persistent
sense of guilt.[48] Credit for establishing the dignity of the mining profession is given enthusiastically to Georg Agricola,
whose writings are so informative that they are read by others
besides professionals in the industry. What technical and linguistic difficulties had to be overcome before the subject of
mining could be adequately described, Albinus only implies.
He, it is acknowledged, has drawn freely from the publications
of Agricola, Lazarus Ercker, and others.

Albinus embarks now upon a methodical discussion of the
Saxon mines. Each location is taken individually: time and circumstances of its discovery, the method of its exploitation,

productivity in weight and value, ownership and disposition of
profit, finally the names of engineers and Bergmeister in the
various mines. A number of brief chapters survey the pits of
other European countries, then Albinus is back in Meissen
with an account of the metals taken from its hills. There are
gold and silver, of course, and also copper, mercury, tin, bis-
muth, lead, and iron. A description of steel-making by means
of the blast-furnace method, discovered not too long before,
is of special interest. But Albinus does not stop his recital of
Meissen's underground treasures there. Eager to establish
his land as deficient in nothing, he lists minor products too:
zinc, gravel, cobalt, precious stones, marble, alabaster, all
sorts of building stones, exquisite clay, pigments, salt and
saltpeter, alum, coal, and, finally, thermal springs.

Albinus thought of his Chronicle as "a complete chorography
of the land of Meissen."[49] It may not be all that, but his book
does leave us with some vivid ideas about one German region
at the close of the sixteenth century. Of the inner territories
of the Empire we have no descriptions as revealing. The political divisions of their day, Maximilian's administrative
Circles of 1512 for example, never meant much to humanist
writers who began their treatises with Tacitus and preferred
to base their descriptions on the old tribal territories. Those
deep and mysterious woods of interior Germany, whose ancient
collective name of Hercynian Forest they never abandoned, attracted their attention as nothing else in German geography.
Most authors liked to contrast the vastness and dramatic power of their country's landscape with the gentleness of the Italian scene, and in the great German forest, especially the Black
Forest with its towering firs, they found a subject worthy of
their adjectives.[50] Many of them never went beyond a summary
description of the range. To the scenery of Swabia, of Franconia,
Thuringia, and the Palatinate, therefore, the comprehensive
cosmographies of Münster and Rauw are our best guides. The
regional descriptions of these territories are uneven. Some,
like Philip Apianus' elaborate catalogue of Bavarian topography,
are painstakingly detailed, though hardly descriptive. Others
convey only fleeting impressions.

There is Felix Fabri's Description of Swabia, already mentioned for its views of the upper Rhine. Fabri, a Dominican
friar and world traveler, had returned in the late 1480's from
his adventuresome journey to the Holy Land. The account of
this pilgrimage is preserved in his Evagatorium,[51] the sum of
his diary entries and recollections, an extraordinary book written with magnificent gusto. In continuation of this tale he composed a description of Swabia and of the city of Ulm, the native

region for which, he says, he had longed while among strangers.[52] It was first designed as the culmination of his book of
experiences, but as the account of his journey grew to unsuspected lengths, it had to be revised as a separate work. The
Descriptio Sueviae[53] is, geographically at least, of interest,
but since Fabri had not traveled extensively through the entire
territory, he did not trust himself to depart very far from his
written authorities. It is his little work on Ulm, the Tractatus
de Civitate Ulmensi,[54] based entirely on his own observation
and his own knowledge, that conveys to us something of the
character of the region.

Ulm was Fabri's home. It was, he writes, "the destination
from which my journey was undertaken and to which it returned at long last." His sense of perception sharpened by a
year's absence from the familiar scene, he drew a brilliantly
vivid picture of the town's aspects and life, a close-knit chorography, more purposefully constructed than the loose-jointed
Evagatorium, and wonderfully descriptive. A good deal of antiquarian lore must, of course, be set down too. Fabri feels
obliged to establish the origin of the city, the key to which mys-
tery, he thinks, is concealed in her name. He therefore examines with a great show of learning in Biblical lore and classical
chronology more possibilities than we would care to hear about
if some of them were not so amusing, such as the theory, set
forth in all earnestness, that Ulm is MLV spelled backward
and therefore signifies the city's foundation date, though whether it is 1055 before or after Christ Fabri cannot say.[55] But he
soon leaves this world of fancy for more substantial matters.
He describes the growth of the medieval town as it may still
be traced in the archaeological remains. He dwells at some
length on the great building projects. In a chapter touched with
the bright tones of a miniature he describes the laying of the
cornerstone to the great Cathedral:

> Now in the year of our Lord 1377 the citizens of Ulm dis-
> solved their old parish, the Church of All Saints, and car-
> ried its treasures to the spot where the new cathedral was
> to be built. When everything had been carted to this place
> the workmen dug the foundation until they touched ground
> water, then sunk piles of hardy timber into the soil for the
> building stones to rest on. This gaping mudhole was a grue
> some sight indeed, for it measured no less than 464 paces
> in circumference.

> When the foundation was ready for the masons the crew
> masters notified the members of the Council, for it was

A detail of Philip Apianus' map of Bavaria, Bairische Landtafeln XXIIII (Munich, 1568). Original size is 32 x 42 cm.

to be the privilege of these dignitaries to lay the first stone.
... According to the decision of these grave men the venerable Herr Ludwig Krafft, at that time Lord Mayor of the
city, descended into the pit, accompanied by other notables,
in order to put in place the huge block of stone which hung
suspended in the claws of a great clamp. At precisely three
o'clock ... the block was lowered, not by workmen, but by
the august members of the Council, some of them turning
the great wheel, others guiding the ropes, ... and all this
was done most seriously while the people prayed, the monks
chanted, and the town band played. ... And when the first
stone had been laid the Lord Mayor opened his purse, took
out a number of coins and adorned the hewn surface with
100 glittering gold pieces. When he had done so the other
patricians stepped down, each in his turn, and covered the
stone with gold and silver, and the men of the people did
the same. And so, on this day, was collected a great fund
for the building of the new church.

Fabri takes us on a tour of the industrial outskirts, and exhibits the points of interest of the spacious town within the
walls. He makes an excellent guide, genial and informative,
never obtrusive with his explanations. He can arouse our interest in the municipal pumping station with its system of lead
pipes and twenty-three public fountains, and he can make us
identify ourselves, as he does himself, with the proud families
of the upper middle class, the Kraffts, Ehingers and others,
whose hands firmly hold the government of the town. Fabri did
not quite complete his treatise; a concluding epitome of the history of Ulm remained unwritten.[56] Even so, the little book is
a model for municipal descriptions.

We cannot close the _Tractatus_ without regret that Fabri's
travels had not taken him to other German lands and cities.
Only Nuremberg was as attractively portrayed, in Celtis' colorful description of its scenery and its public life which he submitted to the Nuremberg Town Council in 1495.[57] Here, too, the
geographical setting is made tangible, the official buildings
stand out in prominent relief, and the activities of citizens become part of our world. For further details of Nuremberg town
life we may turn once again to the popular poets. Hans Rosenplüt,
like all the others of his tribe, says encouraging things about the
thickness of battlements and the depth of the moat, but from him
we also learn that on every Sunday of the year the authorities
donate 312 loaves of bread and 624 pounds of good meat to 156
needy households, that the Pegnitz drives the wheels of 67 mills,
that Nurembergers can claim as their own one of Germany's
great organists, Konrad Paumann, and that the skill of Nurem-

berg metal-workers (of whom he was one, by training) sur-
passes belief:

> No masters like them you'll find anywhere:
> Name the creature that flies through the air,
> Crawls on the ground, or swims in the sea,
> Let it a worm or a fish or an angel be,
> A beast or a man of whatever class,
> And you'll see they can cast it in iron or brass.[58]

There are many other interesting bits of information, but a
graver contemporary thought Rosenplüt frivolous:

> He does not in one line relate
> The things which make our city great:
> The arts which bring her fame and weal
> Through many a commercial deal,

wrote Kunz Hass, a mastersinger and clothmaker who informs
us fully on the business affairs of his city.[59] More learned,
and therefore more elevated humanist poets, eschewing heavy-
footed German rhymes, rhapsodized no less warmly about
Nuremberg's and other cities' attractions.[60] But somehow
they tell us less, and their arch hexameters do not often bring
the place before our eyes. Still, a diligent reader of all these
encomiastic poems would be well informed, though the reading
would weary him more than the grand tour itself. For there
are a great many poems and they are all very much alike.[61]

Of Swabia there is another description, this one by a proper
humanist. The learned Tübingen professor Martin Crusius,
whose compilations of ancient and modern Greek erudition had
much fame in his day,[62] completed his <u>magnum opus</u>, a <u>Swabian
Chronicle</u>, in 1593.[63] It is a vast and shapeless work, little
more than a storehouse of materials he had spent his life collecting. His biographer tells us that Crusius wrote the work
"with one single pen and without ever sitting down,"[64] and we
have no difficulty imagining the man at work, arranging his
notes, sifting, copying. His method is rigorously chronological,
and topography does not fit into the scheme.

But Crusius was conscious of his public's interests. He had
already shown his sympathy with the popular taste for description by writing or obtaining brief topographical accounts of
eastern European areas then under Turkish domination.[65] If
the form of his chronicle did not permit the inclusion of such
material for Swabia, Crusius knew how to add it in the
<u>Paralipomena</u> which served as a catchall for stray bits not
utilized in the main narrative or acquired too late for use there
In these appendices the localities of Swabia are quite adequately

surveyed, though the reader must make his own transitions
from place to place. He must also make his way through much
undigested extraneous matter. Before any vital information
about Stuttgart, for instance, is conveyed,[66] Crusius must tell
us about several clocks in the town, about an inn where a
thousand guests may dine at three hundred tables, a giant
bird cage, swans and cranes in the castle pond, a troupe of
dancing bears who learned to walk upright when their forelegs
were bound to their backs, and a few other such trifles. But
sounder facts follow, and other places are more incisively
portrayed. Usually we get at least a sketch of the surrounding
countryside, a description of the town's architecture, and some
comments on its government and schools. But there is little
life in Crusius' phrases. Swabia does not receive her due
from him.

Bavaria fared much better at the hands of her chorographers,
though it seems strange that the natural beauties which she offers so conspicuously to the eye went unnoticed, or at least unrecorded. Bavarian topographical writing in the sixteenth century was businesslike and competent. The land was explored,
its features and resources registered, its history told. But the
great Bavarian chorography which these activities seemed to
herald was not written.

Bavaria's most distinguished author, Aventinus, was a historiographer by preference and by training. Though in spirit
one of the topographical-historical writers,[67] he never turned
his declarations of principle into a finished piece of writing.
We have already seen how little Aventinus' _Germania illustrata_
of 1531 partook of the ideas of the genre. The description of
Bavaria in his major work, the _Bavarian Chronicle_,[68] is more
genuinely descriptive, but though Aventinus refers to it as a
"chorographia"[69] it is essentially an antiquarian inspection of
the ancient tribal territory in its three divisions, the _Nordgau_,
the _Sundergau_, and _Noreinland_, now Austria. Only the _Sunder-
gau_ merits a somewhat detailed survey, and that because "this
is the land where I was born," as Aventinus writes with cavalier disregard of geographical significance.[70] "I shall describe
it more carefully and with greater attention to its attractions,"
he announces. The Lech is traced from its source in the Swabian
Alps across the historic Lechfeld that divides Bavaria from
Swabia and past Füssen, Augsburg, and Rain. The courses of
the Inn and Isar follow. He presents Alpine Bavaria to us:
sparsely populated, thickly wooded, almost impenetrable with
its many lakes, rapid streams, its wild boars and bears, and
its deer which run in herds of a hundred or more. Lower Bavaria, which lies between Alps and Danube, is, on the other

hand, densely settled and carefully cultivated. Again Aventinus enumerates cities and towns, rivers and streams.

Aventinus was an indifferent chorographer. He loved Bavaria he was gifted with a keen sense of observation, and his pen was sharp, but his abilities took him in another direction. If he had been interested, we would have today a vivid description of six teenth-century Bavaria. But since we do not possess this prize we may at least turn appreciatively to an extensive inventory of Bavarian topography, one of the most ambitious topographical surveys ever undertaken in Germany. This is the work of Philip Apianus, the son of the famous cosmographer Peter Apianus. Himself a versatile man, mathematician and doctor of medicine, Philip was called to fill his father's chair at the University of Ingolstadt upon the latter's death in 1552. Two years later he received a ducal commission to draw up a detailed map of Bavaria, and he responded willingly.[71] With an assistant or two he traveled through the country,[72] measuring distances, computing the positions of towns and villages, and studying the topography. Completed in 1563, the finished product was a complicated piece of work in more than forty separate sheets which, when pasted together after printing, would form a map nearly five-feet square. This map was to be entitled

> A New Description of the Principality of Upper and Lower Bavaria and Neighboring Regions, Complete with Cities, Towns, Monasteries, Villages, also Valleys, Heaths, Moun tain Ranges, Forests, Rivers, Lakes, Ponds, and many other such Items, all painstakingly observed and now described by Philip Apianus,

and each of the enumerated features was there on paper, show in drawings and symbols. But the cost of printing such an intri cate work of cartography precluded publication at that time, and Apianus was ordered to prepare a reduced version. This he did, in the XXIV Bavarian Maps, printed in 1568 in Munich. At the same time he set to work on an explanatory text to go with the large map if and when it could be published, and this explanation proved to be Apianus' major undertaking, so elabo rate an endeavor that when he died in 1598 it remained unfinished.

The text is called Exposition of the Map or Description of Bavaria, and it is a most precise enumeration of Bavarian natural features and habitations. Like the map, it was a product of Apianus' systematic travels through the hills and valleys of Bavaria in the 1550's. Following some general remark on the hydrography of the land, Apianus describes the country first in its four administrative sections, Munich, Landshut, Burghausen, and Straubing, each called a "tetrarchia," then according to its "prefectures" or centers of local government. We hear of the natural divisions of each and are given a list of towns and hamlets, distances from one to another, and proximity to mountains, streams, and roads. Here is an example, on the tiny prefecture of Leonsberg:[73]

> The castle which forms the center of the prefecture of Leonsberg is the stateliest in all of Lower Bavaria. It is situated on the slope of a hill in the plain of the Isar, about a mile northwest of the town of Landau.

> Formerly the castle was called Leonberg or Lewenberg and was the ancestral seat of the Counts of that name. It is supposed to have been built by Diethmar, the son of Babo of Abensberg, Count of Leonsberg, who also founded the monastery of Elsenbach, near Neumarkt. The Counts, however, lie buried in the monastery of Viebach on the Isar. During the wars of 1504 the stronghold was burned to the ground, but it has been rebuilt in our day by Duke Ludwig of Landshut, the father of our present Duke Albrecht, with stones taken from the ruined fortress of Wolfstein which is located about a mile below Landshut on the Isar....

> Now to the localities of this prefecture: Kölnbach, a large village with a church and a castle, on the brook of the same name.—Tunting, a village with a church.—Oberdaching, a village with a church.—Petzenhausen, an estate on the edge of the Hübholz wood.—Etzenhausen, a village.—Grafflkoven, a village with a church.—Heiling, a village with a church, located on a brook.—Hankoven, a village with a church on the same brook.

This is the pattern of the entire work, dull, but highly informative. Read with patience and with the aid of a map, Apianus' catalogue portrays the active community life of a highly cultivated land. There is little attempt at lightening the reader's burden; only occasionally are bits of historical material included. Ample illustrations brighten the manuscript, however: more than seventy drawings of cities, some Roman antiquities, and hundreds of escutcheons belonging to the families and municipalities of Bavaria.

Descriptive literature in Austria was the direct result of the encouragement and support of the emperor. We are used to the complaint of German humanists that territorial rulers were

crude in their tastes and unsympathetic to the ambitions of the
learned. But Maximilian not only endowed but also actively
participated in scholarly activities, bestowing special favor
on historical studies. Maximilian was said to have known the
topography of his lands so well that he could jot down an im-
promptu map of any region.[74] But even if true, this was no
more than a game to the imperial humanist. He cared less for
the history of Germany than for the destiny of his family, and
it was his House and his crown lands which dominated his attention. He sponsored a collection of materials to be used as
sources for a dynastic history, and soon his historiographers,
genealogists, and other officials were searching through German archives for chronicles, charters, and documents.[75] The
project does not appear to have progressed far, but nearly all
the persons engaged in it published the results of their studies

One such researcher was Ladislaus Suntheim, whose genea
logical compilations have been referred to in another chapter
Suntheim became the emperor's court chaplain in 1496, but it
was not long before he embarked on a series of investigations
that took him to the far regions of the empire. Though Suntheim
interests, reflecting Maximilian's own, were genealogical, he
must have had a quick eye for the characteristics of places he
visited. When Vadian calls him "a most diligent geographer"[76]
we may assume that his genealogies and histories contained
more than tables of descent. The Vallis Danubio, for example
written around 1500 following one of his journeys, lists and
occasionally characterizes the cities, towns, villages and ham
lets along the Danube from Donaueschingen to Buda and Pest:

> Stockerau, an important market town; many fisherman liv
> there and a great many turnips are grown; hence the prov
> erb "What do you know about the price of turnips in Stock
> erau?" Here St. Colman was hanged and martyred. His
> memory is sacred to the Austrians, and he was a Scot, of
> royal Scottish blood.—Greiffenstain, a castle of the Bisho
> of Passau, there is a prison for priests in the castle.—
> Groritschenstain, a mountain castle near a wood; it belong
> to the King of the Romans.—Kritzendorf, a village where
> fine wine is grown, called Kritzendorfer.—Höfflein, a vil-
> lage and ford which also raises fine grapes.—Kornneunbu
> where there is an Augustinian monastery, a largish town
> in a narrow plain; it engages in agriculture.[77]

Sometimes a unique or a queer custom impressed him and wa
duly noted:

> Cannstadt, a little town and castle on the Neckar. . . . It lie

on the highway to Frankfurt. Every year they have a feast
there called The Day of the Homely. Whoever is judged
the ugliest man wins a new suit and accessories, and the
ungainliest of the women wins a girdle, a pair of gloves,
and other things.[78]

Suntheim's writings, one gathers, were replete with glimpses
of this kind.[79] They hardly, however, constitute a systematic
treatise on the land and past of Austria. That task was achieved
by another of Maximilian's official scholars, Johann Cuspinian.
This versatile humanist, who had lectured at the University of
Vienna at age eighteen, was honored with innumerable titles
and offices by an emperor who appreciated his talents. "The
imperial councillor," we hear of Cuspinian,[80]

> personal physician and historiographer to the Emperor,
> prefect of the city of Vienna, Professor of rhetoric and
> medicine, divided his time among affairs of state which
> often kept him and the Emperor up half the night, visits
> to patients, historical research, university lectures, pub-
> lic addresses, editions of scholarly works, and philosophi-
> cal discourse with his humanist friends.

His friends included the foremost men of letters of his time.
Celtis had probably impressed him most deeply, but his colleagues at Maximilian's court, the mathematicians Johann
Stabius and Georg Collimitius, were his most immediate collaborators in the collection of historical sources and the study
of Austrian geography.

The _Austriae Regionis Descriptio_,[81] Cuspinian's most ambitious work, directly responds to Maximilian's grand design
and is its most successful single expression. The volume re-
views Austrian history from the Margraves of Babenberg to
the reign of Charles V, and describes the land as it was known
to one intimately familiar with its features. The conventional
motives led Cuspinian to undertake the work: earlier writers,
he says, have, "partly from malice, partly out of jealousy,"
depreciated Austria in order to increase the glory of their own
countries. Now the fame of the empire as well as the attractiveness of Austria demand such a volume as he has just completed. Austria's history and scenery, her beauty and her glory,
must be broadcast. His geographical portions were meant to
be the commentary to a companion piece, the Austrian map of
Stabius.[82] But the map is now lost, and this is a double mis-
fortune, for it would have been interesting in its own right, and
without it Cuspinian's _Austria_ is only half a chorography.

Cuspinian begins in the usual fashion, with the etymology of

the country's name, and this leads him, because of its original
designation as "Ostmark," to an outline of the migrations of
East and West Goths, Huns, and Suevi whose passing across
south-central Europe was of importance to the country now
called Austria. The relationship between "Austria" and the
territories known in the old days as Upper Pannonia and Noricum is then discussed, and his assertion that Austria is essentially equivalent to ancient Noricum is proven not only from
authority but with the report of a recent archaeological discovery of his own: two Roman sarcophagi, each with the in-
scription of a Roman legion stationed in Noricum.[83] Following
a brief digression on his own place of birth, Cuspinian launches
the customary Laus Austriae in which the natural blessings
with which Austria is wonderfully gifted are counted:

> mighty streams, cities, towns, castles, temples, and
> churches; broad forests and high mountains. Nothing that
> is useful, pleasant, or beautiful is lacking, ... and there
> is such abundance in the production of food stuffs (from
> which neighboring countries as well as ours live) that the
> ancient proverb "Austria has no equal among the nations"
> seems today as true as ever.

What few things need to be imported—spices from Venice and
some gold and silver—are easily and economically purchased.
    Now to the definition of Austria's boundaries: Here Cuspinian
falls into professional stride as he turns to the thorny job of
determining the limits of the country. They have varied much,
he points out; wars and competing claims of sovereignty have
shifted border lines again and again. But the natural boundaries
may be found by means of diligent geographical and historical
research. Cuspinian follows the rivers: in the east the Raab
and Rabnitz set Austria off from Hungary, while the Great
Schütt Island, formed by two arms of the Danube south of Pres-
burg, divides it from the Balkan lands. In the west Austria is
defined by the Inn which joins the Danube at Passau. Next he
turns to the history of Austria's territorial divisions in order
to discover what information these may provide regarding her
present limits. Lower and upper Austria are discussed first,
then the present administrative divisions, the seven Gaue. As
he traces river courses and mountain ranges, as he examines
town names and tests the archaeological evidence, there emerge
the shape of a country, set off from its neighbors and internally
coherent.
    That problem out of the way, Cuspinian proceeds to the cen-
tral portion of his book, dealing with the course of the Danube,
which he now pursues from source to mouth with a great deal

of pleasure in its majestic journey. Through Bavaria, Austria, and the other Danubian states we go, crossing all sixty-three tributaries from the Iller to the Pruth and passing through most of the towns located at them. Though it is in the main a mere list, Cuspinian manages to convey a sense of the grandeur of the river and of its dominating position over the political and economic geography of Europe.

This description proves most informative to the student who uses it with a map, as was intended. It is followed by a discussion of some Austrian cities and geographical features whose names are of etymological and historical interest. Ehrenburg was built in the time of Honorius, we learn. Pressburg was Posonium but should be Pisonium after L. Calpurnius Piso. But this is rather thin fare; and we hurry on to an interesting account of Austrian political and ecclesiastical institutions and an elaborate list of Austrian prelates and some of the more colorful lay personalities. We are impressed, and that is Cuspinian's aim, for there are many dignitaries, and the ancient traditions to which they have fallen heir, the powers which they wield, are resplendent evidence of Austria's greatness. A fine description of the capital city forms a final section. A glance at a contemporary plan and profile of Vienna, drawn in 1547 by the Nuremberg artist Augustin Hirschfogel,[84] reveals the close correspondence between description and object. Cuspinian ends on a note of brilliance, with a view of the Cathedral of St. Stephen in Vienna, its splendid architecture and opulent appointments, and its lavish liturgy.

Cuspinian's work lacks the detail and the local color to rank with the best of topographical-historical volumes. But a tone of high seriousness and severe craftsmanship speaks from its pages. Like the more evocative examples of the genre, the _Austria_ aims at a total picture of a geographic region. It does not excite us, but it tells us a good deal about the land.

5

The Regional Chorographies II: Switzerland

WHEN WE CROSS the uppermost Rhine we are approaching
the center of German chorographic activity. Nowhere wa
the technique handled with such mastery, nowhere was civic pa
triotism as vigorous, as in Switzerland. Nowhere was there as
much to write about. Switzerland was by far the most intensive
ly surveyed region in the sixteenth century. Not only do the
works produced by its citizens bulk large in number, but they
are in style the most attractive, in spirit the most forceful, in
content the most informative part of German chorographic literature.

At the beginning of the century, we are told, men of letters
as well as men of affairs looked to the Alpine cantons with interest. In the Burgundian wars of the 1470's the Swiss had show
the stuff of which they were made. The peasants of the Confederation who had won the day at Grandson as they advanced toward the enemy, solid squares of men with halberds raised an
pikes sticking out in all directions while the battle trumpets
made barbarous music,[1] had become renowned throughout
Europe as the best foot soldiers to be found anywhere, and the
most determined fighters for national independence. "Who can
nowadays be ignorant," writes the earliest humanist historian
of Switzerland, Albrecht von Bonstetten, to the Doge of Venice,
"of the valor and of the hard-fought wars of the Confederation
which have won fame not only in Europe, but even in Asia and
Africa? What country is not today full of the news of our toil
and struggle? Who is not eager to know the land and its people,
its ways and its history?" This was a year after the conclusion
of the wars with Charles of Burgundy, and the Doge Giovanni
Mocenigo was not the only ruler who watched Switzerland's
territory and affairs from afar. Louis XI of France showed
keen interest.[3] Not long afterwards the virtual secession of
the Swiss Confederation from the Empire increased its noto-

riety. Though heretofore loyal subjects, and always eager to
affirm their cultural kinship with the other German lands, the
Swiss would not abide by the decisions of the Diet of Worms of
1495 which would have deprived them of the freedom from imperial taxation and judicial authority which they had tradition-
ally enjoyed. Refusal led to hostilities, but it was the last war
which the Swiss had to fight for their independence. In the
peace treaty which ended the conflict, Maximilian was forced
to extend to the Swiss de facto recognition of their sovereignty.
    That the Swiss were independent was generally recognized
in 1499. That they thought of themselves as forming a distinct
region and people within the German language and culture domain is also clear. That their writings should reflect civic
pride and their descriptive works in particular should have
"come to life out of the love we bear our fatherland" is natural. We can still hear the wonder in the words of Heinrich
Bullinger, the Zurich reformer and successor to Zwingli, as
he marveled how "our Confederation, which was once poor and
without any special distinction, has been so raised by God that
now its borders come to within one mile of Milan and include
Basel, Lake Constance, the Rhine, and Geneva."[4] But mere
military success would not have justified Swiss pride. Foreigners may have judged the Swiss by their mercenaries who
were said to be even a cut below the German Landsknechte in
humanity, but the citizens of the Confederation took greater
pleasure in their constitutional achievements. Nor did they
pursue the civic arts alone. Swiss historiography was lively,
popular, and instructive. The cities boasted scholars, artists,
and men of letters of wide reputation. Of Basel, especially, it
was impossible to forget that Erasmus had found there men
who understood Latin and Greek, even Hebrew, and scholars
in history, theology, mathematics, and jurisprudence.[5] The
enterprises of the Swiss printers were cosmopolitan in their
far-flung contacts and interests. But it is not urbanity which
makes Swiss writings of the period attractive to us. It is, rather, the direct, uncomplicated approach to life, and the pithiness
of expression and utter frankness of self-revelation which establish spontaneous rapport between author and reader.
    Even the earliest descriptions of Switzerland show a verve
which is lacking elsewhere. The widely traveled and respected
Albrecht von Bonstetten, descendant of one of the few remaining aristocratic houses and Dean of the monastery of Einsiedeln,
was the first to attempt a general depiction of his land. His
work formed the pattern for many subsequent efforts. Though
Bonstetten's interests were in the main historical, his description[6] is evidently based on such observation and experience

as he had gained in his busy diplomatic and scholarly career.
His inspiration was Enea Silvio, whom he had briefly known in
Italy, and whose writings he had studied assiduously,[7] and if
the Swiss does not possess the genius of the Italian he is at
least a good disciple. He indicates the central position of Switz
erland in Europe before giving a general idea of Swiss topography, and continues with a survey of each of the old cantons:
Zurich, Bern, Lucerne, Uri, Schwyz, Unterwalden, Zug, and
Glarus. We learn not only the location of each, but hear about
its climate and products, its political history, the characteristics of its inhabitants, its commerce, its flags and escutcheons, and—a matter of special interest at the time—its military
resources and skills. "Are these not marvellous things to relate?" he calls out, interrupting his recital of the great battles
of the recent wars, "are these not struggles to be compared
with the Punic Wars?"[8]

Military concerns were uppermost in Switzerland during the
last decades of the fifteenth century, and the usefulness of topo
graphical descriptions from a strategic point of view was not
lost on the Swiss. "I have been asked," writes the learned municipal physician of Zurich, Conrad Türst, "to describe the
regions of our Confederation and their environs so that you ma
realize... how useful such a description is to all those princes
who are about to take the field with their armies."[9] Written in
the early 1490's and addressed to the magistrates of the city
of Bern, Türst's Description makes a strategically valuable
complement to Bonstetten's more historical survey. Eighteen
entirely topographical chapters describe the political divisions
of the Confederation and plot the location of its cities:

> And now I shall name the situation of each town: Zurich is
> situated from Chur on the Rhine 66,000 paces, from Con-
> stance 34,000 paces, from the Gotthart 70,000 paces, from
> Basel 50,000 paces.—Bern: from Lake Geneva at the point
> where it drains into the Rhone 70,000 paces, from Con-
> stance 90,000 paces, from the nearest Alps 70,000 paces.[10]

In addition, each township is made the subject of a chorographi
study which describes the terrain and its villages, monasteries
castles, and other features. A map of Switzerland with a work-
able grid accompanied the manuscript, though no reference to
it is made in the text.

But Türst's little work would not be a true chorography if it
did not also convey a visual image of the land. A series of por-
traits of notable cities accomplishes this. Freiburg, for example,

> is a town of great magnificence, well-built with strong

walls and gates, a credit to its architects and a boon to the
security of the citizens, for her defenses are altogether
impregnable. The fortifications on the rocky heights are
further protected by the Saane, which circles the town. A
Dominican convent is within the walls, as is a House of
the Knights of Jerusalem, a Franciscan monastery, and an
Augustinian one.... The lands of the Count of Griers, whose
castle and subjects belong to Freiburg, touch Lake Geneva.
Freiburg also enjoys authority over the city of Murten,
7,000 paces away.[11]

These are direct, unassuming sentences, and the entire book
is as free from artifice. The most successful of Swiss chorographers were, in fact, simple men. Their modesty kept ped-
antry and pomp from their works while their closeness to
people and soil brought to them a unique freshness and vigor.

The man of deeper learning, however, stood behind these
works. His name does not appear on the title pages, but his
researches and his encouragement often made the difference
between wishful thought and accomplishment. This is above all
true of the most universal figure in Swiss humanism, Joachim
Vadian. The significance of this cosmopolitan and versatile
man in the development of the entire topographical-historical
literature has already been noted; Vadian stands particularly
close to the Swiss achievements in the genre. He was born into a prosperous commercial family, distinguished for a long
record of public service in its ancestral home, St. Gall.[12] From
the Latin school in his native city he went to study, then to
teach, at the University of Vienna. There he lectured on Strabo,
on Aristotle's physical works, on Pomponius Mela, on Pliny's
Natural History, occasionally filling in for Cuspinian, who held
Celtis' former chair of rhetoric and poetry but was often away
on diplomatic business. In 1516, Vadian succeeded to the post
in his own right, and shortly thereafter he became rector of
the university. But all this time Vadian had been preparing
himself for a new career in medicine, and when he received
his doctorate in that science in 1517 he returned to his native
town to practice and to teach.

Teaching was Vadian's vocation, and his importance was primarily pedagogical. In his geographical studies he was not original, but he was uniquely able to express his conviction that
there was an intrinsic purpose to geography aside from its value as a key to the classics. At Vienna he had been tutored in
mathematics by Collimitius, whose lectures on the second book
of Pliny's Natural History, that is, on astronomy, meteorology,
and general geography, he attended, and of whose Sodalitas
Collimitiana he was a member. At Vienna, also, he had fallen

under the sway of Celtis[13] and had been influenced by the older man's advancement of geography and historiography for the
purpose of national descriptions. In his notes on Pomponius
Mela he had given a clear exposition of what such a description
should be and how it must be assembled. But the very fame of
his erudition, his scholarly achievements, and his familiarity
with the notables of the world of learning prevented him from
making full use of his own maxims. When he returned to his
city he became so deeply involved in political events that there
was little time for the geographer's toil and the historian's labors. His voluminous correspondence, a running commentary
on the important events of his time, reveals how often projected
studies had to be abandoned and how rarely Vadian enjoyed the
inner calm so essential to scholarly pursuits. "I often wish,"
he once wrote to his friend Heinrich Bullinger, "that I could
hide in a forest for a month or two!"[14] His letters also show
how closely Vadian was connected with every matter of concern to the humanist and Protestant causes. If he had larger
creative schemes—and we know that the political and religious
changes of his time moved him to plans for a major historical
work[15]—he was not able to complete them. His plans, however
were mostly incorporated in the works he caused to be undertaken and helped produce.

Among these, his contributions to Johann Stumpf's great des
cription of Switzerland are of cardinal interest. Vadian was re
sponsible for the description of St. Gall and the Turgau, that is
the northeastern regions of Switzerland. It is to be found in
Book Five of Stumpf's work and, in its original and more extensive form, in Vadian's corpus.[16] The description of the
Turgau opens with a brief topographical survey of the "general situation" of the land, followed by a long history of monasticism which Stumpf abbreviates considerably, though not
sufficiently to avoid later confessional criticism. Then came
the history of the monastery, biographies of its abbots to the
year 1530, and, finally a view of the city of St. Gall and of Lake
Constance. There is much geographical description in all this,
but the underlying purpose was "to instruct the general reader
in what our customs have been since ancient times and what
innovations have taken place."[17] The sketch of the city of St.
Gall[18] is very lively. It begins with notes on climate, fertility
of the soil, St. Gall's distance from landmarks such as the
Rhine and Lake Constance, and surrounding geographical features. Vadian carefully explains the historical and political
ties which exist between town and monastery, these relations
having been complicated by recent events. The mention of flax
weaving, the traditional craft of the city, leads him next to

consider the guilds and their role in the government of the
community through the Little and Large Councils. Then he
turns to agriculture, to the markets and fairs—the time of
their occurrence and the products exchanged there. He describes the churches and lists the learned men of the town,
among whom, since his manuscript was to be published under
another's name, he numbers himself.

Nearly as famous as Vadian in his day was the Swiss humanist Heinrich Loriti of Glarus, whose slim contribution to
the topographical-historical literature entitles him to a place
here. He had studied at the University of Cologne and gained
such renown as poet and musical theorist that in 1512, by which
time he was called Glareanus after his birthplace, he received
the poet's laurel from the hands of the Emperor Maximilian.[19]
In 1514 he went to Basel to teach. At his gymnasium there, we
are told, geography was one of the subjects taught.[20] He was
interested in maps and in the mathematical basis for an exact
geographical representation of the earth, and these occupations
resulted in the composition of one of those introductory manu-
als to scientific geography which were so popular in his time.
A slight book of thirty-five leaves, the Geography[21] paraphrases
some chapters of the first two books of Ptolemy's Astronomy,
then goes on to deal with zones, latitude and longitude, climate
and winds, projections, and so on.

This treatise was too slight to make more than mention of
Switzerland; however, Glareanus had at an earlier time published a description of Helvetia[22] in elegiac verse, as the art
for which he had been crowned required. Its description of the
Swiss scene is exceedingly bookish, but the preface strikes
the political note which so often provides the muted counterpoint in the chorographic literature. Everywhere in Europe,
Glareanus writes, Switzerland has her detractors who be-
grudge and deny her just fame. Envious of her strength and
angry at her refusal to bow before a tyrant, these enemies continue to spread their vicious falsehoods. He, however, will not
reply in kind. A description of the Swiss and their country will
be sufficient answer to these slanderers.[23]

Probably because of this tenor, the verses achieved fame,
or at least currency, so that five years after their publication
Glareanus' friend, the Basel reformer Oswald Myconius,
thought it necessary to reissue the poem accompanied by a
massive and very tedious commentary which was intended to
clarify the innumerable mythological allusions and elaborate
upon the description of the country.[24] Myconius prepared himself conscientiously for the job; he asked Vadian to examine
his geographical notes for accuracy,[25] and added many an

interesting gloss to Glareanus' laconic references, but his
worthwhile contributions were engulfed by a torrent of learned
trivia. Both poem and commentary are mediocre humanist pro
ducts, of which Switzerland, as all other countries, had its
share.

Just as the topographical-historical literature was regional,
so the regional writings were often local in scope, as the definitions of chorography demanded. In Switzerland such local
descriptions tended to illuminate those sections of the country
which were involved in the diplomatic struggles of the period.
In the early sixteenth century the political alignment of the independent members of the Swiss Confederation was not regarded as permanent; shifts were expected and occurred. Attention was on those regions which politically and territorially
were   still in a state of flux. Such a region was Raetia, or
Graubunden, the easternmost salient of Switzerland, whose
topography and institutions must have been matters of general
concern during the century, as they were often and well described.

Ancient Raetia had comprised parts of the Tirol, Switzerland
and Lombardy, but as the Swiss humanists use the designation
it refers chiefly to the territory of the Three Common Leagues
During the fifteenth century, and especially as a result of the
joint struggle against the Habsburgs in 1499, these Leagues,
the Gotteshausbund, the Graue Bund or Grisons, and the Zehn-
gerichtenbund, formed a permanent union among themselves
and then joined other Swiss lands as members of the Confederation.[26] It was from Raetia that the Swiss invaded northern
Italy in 1512 to begin a series of conquests which reached their
climax when Maximilian Sforza received the keys to his city
of Milan from a Swiss deputation. Though the success of the
war was terminated by the French victory at Marignano, the
domain of the Confederation had been extended to Lugano and
the Valtellina. With Austria not only maintaining its territorial
rights in Raetia, but actually threatening to extend them, the
region had, in the sixteenth century, an unusually current interest for the Swiss. Under the circumstances, questions of
terrain and of ancient boundary lines might have great significance.

The best known of the Swiss chroniclers, Aegidius Tschudi
of Glarus, wrote a little explanatory work on Raetia in 1528,
the only one of his writings to be published during his lifetime.[27] Tschudi enjoyed some fame as a cartographer in addition to his renown as a historian, and we learn that his
treatise was illustrated by a fine map of Raetia.[28] The task

Tschudi set for himself, however, was to determine the extent and character of Raetia in the time of Strabo and Ptolemy. There was no time, therefore, for a chorographic description, though Tschudi compares at least in summary the contemporary appearance of Raetia with the facts reported by the ancients. Points of special interest like the Breitgau Valley, the Schalberg, and the Adula Alps are depicted somewhat more graphically, but his main object was the precise delimitation of the region and the demonstration of its essentially Germanic character.

Other Swiss writers followed Tschudi in describing Raetia, but we need not read all of these works because they are admirably reviewed in the introduction to the best of them, Guler von Weineck's magnificent Raetia, written nearly a century after· Tschudi's effort.[29] We learn from Guler that Franciscus Niger has written a pleasant little description, in verse, of Raetia; that Johann Stumpf has well covered its history, especially the wars; that Münster really should have done better by the region; that Josias Simler composed a treatise on her government; that Kaspar Brusch described her bishoprics and monasteries; and that Franz Guillimann and Marcus Welser portrayed her inhabitants. Many others, Guler tells us, have given us a little of this and that on Raetia in their books on various subjects. Only one really comprehensive work exists, says Guler, and that is the Topography of Ulrich Campell. But this author "has been so industrious with minutiae, most of which, in my opinion, should have been left unrecorded," that it is often hard to discover the forest among the trees of facts.

Ulrich Campell's Raetia is indeed a pedantic work.[30] But the dry tone and the overabundance of detail which disturbed Guler were parts of a careful scheme which the author laid in advance for his ambitious work. Campell's description was planned on a large scale, and was to be a definitive survey of Raetia.[31] He canvassed his humanist colleagues for the kind of help which had been given to Johann Stumpf when that writer was at work on his Description of the Confederation,[32] and such aid did, in fact, come to him too, chiefly from Josias Simler, who was at the time himself busy with a number of historical and descriptive works. So much did Simler's suggestions become part of the volume in progress that Campell could speak, at least to him, of a joint authorship.[33]

The manuscript was divided into two distinct parts, a topographical survey, written first,[34] and a comprehensive historical narrative for which Johann Stumpf was the evident source. This cleavage meant ease of organization, but it also took much life from the chorographic form and made monotony in-

RAETIA ist das land/
da sich Rætus/vnd ander
Italisch volck/ in dem
Alpgebirg zů den alten
einwohneren deßelbigen/
haußhäblich hat niderge-
lassen/ vnd was durch jre
nachkommen darzů ero-
bert worden/sambt allem
dem/ das nachwerts die
Römer/als Oberherren/
vnter disen namen ge-
schoben haben : als da ist
das gantze *Vindelicia,*
vnd ein großer theil Hel-
vetierlands/sambt einem
strich in groß Deütsch-
land/dardurch Rætia zů
einer vornemmen Pro-
vintz gerahten : welche
mit der zeit in zwo vnterschiedliche Vogteyen ist
vnterscheiden worden:
namlich in ———

I.
Rætiam die erste:
welche begreifft

Die alte vrsprüngliche Ræ-
tiam/ so in dem Alpgebirg
gelegen.

Etlich
hinzů ge-
setzte vñ
von an-
deren lan
den hin-
weg ge-
nomme
theil: als

Erstlich das Gastal
oder Rheingöuw.

Demnach ein theil deß
Thurgöuws/ oben herab
biß gen Pfin.

Endlich das gantze Thur-
göuw/ sambt dem Zürich-
göuw.

II.
Rætiam die andere/
so sich erstreckt vber

Gantz *Vindeliciam,* so von dem Bodense
Donauw dannen/ zwischen gesagter
mittägigen gebirg/ biß an den Yhn gela
theilt durch den fluß Låch in das ———

Einen theil jhenseit der Donauw gege
ben vrsprung deß Näckers vnd Nördli
hertzschung die Römer vnd Alemanni
biß endlich/nach vilfeltigem abwechsle
gleichwol ein theil deßelbigen lands de
Rieß genennt wirt : welches sambt de
Hertzogthumb Schwaben vnd Alem

Dise
schun
demn
komm
bigen
schun
jeder
dem
auch
Alem
beßäff

A schematic outline of the historical and geographical divisions

Entweder mit ewigen Bündten zu samen geträtten.

Dise werden in drey vnterschiedliche theil abgetheilt/ die man die drey Bündt nennet: regieren sich in democratischem stand/ vnter allgemeinen satzungen vñ ordnungen: neben welchen auch ein jeder Bundt für sich selbst/ vnd dannethin schier ein jedes Gericht im selbigen Bundt sein sonderliche vnterschiedliche Policey führt vnter etlichen eigenen satzungen vnnd alt härgebrachten breuchen. Dise drey Bünde seind/ Der OberBundt: Das Gottshauß: vnnd die x. Gericht.

Ihenseit gebirgs gegen mittag: namlich dise

- Ein theil der Fürstlichen Grafschafft Tyrol.
- Abt zu S. Marienberg.
- Tarasp.
- Vältlein.
- Grafschafft Cläven.
- Die drey Pleven.
- Grafschafft Bellentz.
- Vbrige Lepontier.

r herr=
x/ vnd
cken
ensel=
r=
ein
vnter
lang
n zu
aben

Oder aber ausser dem Bundt verblieben/ zum theil

Gallischer seiten Rheins/ als

- Vrsern.
- Haldenstein.
- Pfävers.
- Sarngans.
- Gastal { Windeck. / Schänis.
- S. Johan Durthal.
- Werdenberg.
- Gams.
- Herrschafft Sax.
- Rheintal.

Disseit gebirgs gegen Mitternacht/ auf

Germanischer seiten Rheins/ als

- Gütenberg.
- Valdutz.
- Schällenberg.
- Fäldkirch.
- Sonnenberg.
- Pludentz vnd Walgöuw.
- Blümeneck.
- Montfort.
- Nünburg.
- Embs.
- Brägentz.

nd durch die Ale=
e entzogen worden/
ckischer herrschung/
öm. Reych vnd die
tien kommen/ vnd
n worden.

Was disseits deß Lächs gegen dem Bodensee gelegen: das haben die Schwaben eingenommen vnnd biß auf ons besässen.

Was jhenseit deß Lächs gegen dem Yhn gegen: das ist durch die Bayrn erobert/ vnd biß an jetzo ingehalten worden.

ßen Deütschland/
cher gelegenheit in der
s ander gemachet/
fäld behaubtet: da
nen behalten/ vnd im
t der Donauw an das

of Raetia. From Guler von Weineck's Raetia (Zurich, 1616).

escapable. The topography, although at least partially based
on personal observation, offers very little detail, and Campell
moves so swiftly that he conveys only a bird's-eye view of the
land. It could not have been the geographical information here
presented which Guler found excessive. Only occasionally does
the description become concrete: when Campell sketches the
location of towns and villages, for example, with surrounding
scenery, churches, and municipal buildings. Maps were to be
included to illustrate these sections and also the major regions
of Raetia. These, too, were carefully outlined by Campell in
advance, and a set of detailed instructions to the engraver was
drawn up.[35] But the text is too often involved with elaborate attempts to trace town names to Tuscan origins and to associate
saints and martyrs with Raetian localities. This is where the
description bogs down; Campell had himself suspected this.[36]
In 1575 he ran into difficulties with the historical portion of
his work,[37] and though he later managed to complete the text,
it found no favor among his colleagues and remained unprinted.
The careful preparations, however, were not altogether in vain,
because in 1586 Guler von Weineck happened upon the manuscript and adopted it for his own use.

    Johann Guler von Weineck was born in Davos, near the center
of Raetia, in 1562, and was active most of his life in the diplomatic service of the Three Leagues.[38] When, in his twenty-
fourth year, he found Campell's <u>Raetia</u>, he realized that here
was the germ of something valuable. He extracted excerpts
from the manuscript, and what he was able to do with Campell's
material is the measure of his skill. Denying himself the easy
separation of geography from history, Guler intertwined the
two strands of Campell's treatise and, in so doing, breathed
life into the other man's work. The historical material follows
Campell closely, although also incorporating data from Tschudi
and Simler, but it is quick-paced, not a bit stuffy, and even today rings with the tone of authority. At the outset, the territorial divisions of Raetia down to villages and hamlets are
indicated on a chart meant for orientation. Then, in ten books,
the general history of Raetia is unfolded. The story moves all
over Western Europe, and we are made acquainted with Roman,
medieval, and modern affairs, but never is the focal point,
Raetia, out of sight. The narrative moves around and towards
Raetia, never away from it.

    Guler possessed a unique genius for description, and took
full advantage of it. Many a picturesque scene becomes, in his
handling, a real presence:

    The next place is Morbenn, called <u>Morbonium</u> in Latin, the

chief town of the region, which derives its name from the
word morbus, that is, disease. It seems that a long time
ago, when the Bitherbach still ran in its old bed, the whole
plain of Morbenn was covered with swamps and marshes
produced by the seepage of moisture from the hills. There
was not a sufficient amount of this to form a brook and the
water remained stagnant. In the summertime, when the
heat of the sun beat upon the land, all kinds of vermin and
evil stenches used to arise there so that the local people
suffered a great many afflictions from the corrupt air.
The old town, furthermore, was situated a good deal below its present site, in fact, where the church of St. Martin
now stands, which is known to be one of the oldest buildings thereabouts....

One spring, however, during a mighty flood, the old bed of
the Bitherbach was dammed up with timber and debris so
that the stream's course was shifted from the pass con-
necting Regoledo and Cosio to a side valley which runs between Castle Morbenn and the Old Tower, the two structures
that frame the present town of Morbenn, the former on the
right, the latter on the left side of the stream. Gradually
working its way into the ground, the Bitherbach carved out
a new bed for itself and deposited the material taken from
the soil in the plain beyond the valley, filling up nearly all
the puddles there and draining the swamp. Soon the whole
place was dry, the insects gone, and a gentle and healthful
air hovered over the place. You cannot find cleaner breezes
anywhere than now at Morbenn. Not long after this the
Bitherbach again left its bed and returned to its former
course. The inhabitants thereupon took advantage of the
deepened and broadened valley where delightfully cool
breezes blew from the mountain slopes,and began to build
just below the castle, first a house or two, gradually a
whole town complete with encircling walls and suburbs beyond them.

This town, when it was complete, stood on the right bank
of the stream. On the southern side it touched a suburb
called Burgus Salvus, itself protected by a moat and walls.
Another suburb, New Mirandola, was erected on the left
shore of the Bitherbach and was joined to Morbenn by
means of a bridge at exactly the same spot where the magnificent new single span now stands. From there a winding
road led to Castle Morbenn, and another descended to Ber-
lenda where the bailiff used to have his official residence

before he moved to the house of the physician Zoyen and
later still to the Menapasius mansion which stands opposite
the bridge just mentioned, and where he has remained to
this day.

The walls which surrounded Morbenn have long ago col-
lapsed to the ground, and their rubble has been used to
fill up the moat. Nevertheless, the place,as it is now,
may be spoken of as a little city, for it not only has state-
ly edifices and prosperous citizens but keeps its regular-
ly scheduled weekly and annual fairs which attract visitors
from afar and bring fame and wealth to the whole neighbor-
hood. Morbenn's houses are well constructed, in the medieval manner. They are noted, among other things, for
their wine cellars which are cut into the rock on which the
city is built, often one on top of another and both beneath
the ground, so that you may have to descend forty steps
to reach bottom. In the winter these caves are pleasantly
warm and in the summer delightfully cool and fresh, so
that even during the most extreme heat you can have your
wine clear and cool.

The slopes around Morbenn produce not only excellent
wine but also grain in abundance, beef and dairy products,
fish and crabs from the stream, most especially the delectable species of trout called <u>Trutte</u> by the inhabitants.
All the wood they can use is brought to them by the Bitherbach itself.[39]

Guler's geographical narrative is not only precise, it is logically constructed, with every paragraph organically related
to the whole work. When Guler pauses to describe the architecture of a building, we do not forget where we are, nor do
we fail to remember that after some words of information, we
shall be moving on. The description follows the courses of rivers, descends mountain slopes, and proceeds along the natural
lines of drift. Without effort, unjarred by stops and spurts, the
reader accompanies his guide on a leisurely but carefully
planned walking trip through some of the most grandiose scenery in Europe. On the way he hears about the history of the
landscape, who inhabited it first, where the original towns were
built, what sort of people lived in them, how they governed them
selves, and what their relations were with each other and with
the outside world. He learns of noteworthy events, of men of
renown who were born there, of the pursuits of the present popu
lation, of their crops and their handicrafts. He may even meet
a local citizen who stops for a moment's chat. There is not a

page in the long book to bore the reader, scarcely a paragraph
which will not delight as well as teach him.

Any one of Guler's chapters would illustrate his method and
style, but one of the finest is his description of the Valtellina,
or Veltlin,[40] that very beautiful and strategic valley of the Adda
which today belongs to Italy, but in Guler's time was Swiss, having been seized by the soldiers of the Three Leagues in 1512. It
was a much contested pass, vital especially to the Habsburgs
as the only link between their possessions in Italy and Austria.
Spectacular scenery and political significance lent the valley un-
usual interest, and Guler seeks to capture both in his description.

He commences with a historical sketch of the valley under the
Milanese dukes, the Visconti and the Sforza, and follows the
customary etymological inquiry into the region's name:

> The name "Veltlin" is, in Latin as well as in Italian, writ-
> ten and pronounced in several different ways. Some hold
> that the earliest inhabitants of the valley were the Ven-
> nonetians, which name was corrupted during the Middle
> Ages into Ventos nini and finally into Veltolini; hence in Ital-
> ian the valley is referred to as Veltolina. Others call it
> Vallis Tellina, Italian Val Tellina, in German Theller Thal.
> ...Still others prefer the name Vallis Tyrrhena...because,
> they say, the first inhabitants were descendants of the
> Tyrrhenians, otherwise called Etruscans or Tuscans. There
> are also those who claim that the valley ought to be called
> Valturrena, that is, Valley of the Towers, because of the
> many fortifications which it held at one time.

Guler himself found the theory that the valley takes its name
from the Etruscans most plausible, and he points out that they
named their capital in the region Volturena, which, in German,
is rendered Veltlein or Veltlin.[41]

The necessary preliminaries out of the way, we proceed to
the description itself:

> The magnificent valley of the Veltlin lies alongside the
> southern end of the Raetian Alps which forms the water-
> shed for the northern Italian rivers. It touches, in the East,
> the valley of Münster and the Duchy of Tirol, in the South
> the Val Camonica and a segment of the Venetian domain;
> in the West it borders, at its lowest point, on Lake Como,
> in the North on Bregell and Engadin. From all these re-
> gions (except at the point where it adjoins the lake) the
> valley is set off by wonderfully tall and mighty mountains.
>
> From the source of the Adda, which coils its way through
> the land, to the spot where the river enters Lake Como,

the Veltlin measures 60 Italian miles, which come to 10
German miles, taking six Italian for one German mile. It
takes two hours to journey from the source of the Adda to
Worms [Bormio]; from there to Tirano it is six hours,
from Tirano to Sonders [Sondrio] four hours, from Sonders
to Morbenn another four hours, from Morbenn to Dalebio
two hours, and from Dalebio to the lake two more hours.
Altogether that makes twenty hours which amounts to ten
German miles, as I said.[42]

The width of this valley varies a good deal, for at some
places it opens up, elsewhere its sides huddle close together, and this happens several times. Near Worms it is
wide, but narrows down considerably until it becomes a
tight gorge near St. Britio. Below that point it expands
again. . . .

The entire valley is, by its situation, exposed to the sun
which does not (as elsewhere) traverse it crosswise with
slanted rays. But rather it rises high up in the mountains
and travels the length of the entire valley in its daily
course. The fiery heat of the sun brings high temperatures
to the area, but these are made comfortable by cooling
mountain breezes and by lovely and refreshing springs and
waterfalls, so that the entire region is not only scenically
beautiful, but so productive as to furnish the inhabitants
with everything they need to sustain life, the only excep-
tion being salt. . . .

Guler now permits himself a lengthy and very informative discussion of the characteristics of the local wines and methods
of producing them. Virgil, he says, sang the praises of the
Raetian wine, and no other grape was valued as highly by the
great Augustus.[43] The red wine, Guler informs us, loses its
color as it ages; a barrel of red wine stored by his father in
the year 1540 and recently (1616) opened, came out "white, pure
and as clear as a veritable crystal, and strong as brandy." The
local wine is exported, he goes on, to all of Switzerland, to Ital
Tirol, Swabia, Bavaria, Austria, and many other lands. To sug
gest the volume of trade, he quotes some figures which he procured, he says, during his term of office as Landeshauptmann
for the Three Leagues of Graubünden.

   Reluctantly, we feel, Guler leaves the pleasant subject of the
Veltlin grape and turns to a consideration of other products of
the soil. He catalogues them, stating their characteristics,
their growing periods, and the problems connected with raising them:

It is common there for one plot to produce four annual
crops, one after the other. Between the grape harvests,
which fall in the early autumn, wheat, rye, maize or such
grains are sown; when these are brought in, millet is
planted, and then beets. When fruit trees are also tended,
as is the case in many places, the return from the soil is
that much greater. The sunniest acres permit harvesting
to begin in May, and the gathering in continues until the
products of the highest fields are brought by. A yoke of
oxen, in many places a single animal, can pull the plow.
In fact I have seen some peasants do it with just one old
cow, so willingly does the soil lend itself to husbandry....

Guler next gives us an idea of the variety of fruits that are
grown. There are all the ordinary sorts, but also more exotic
ones like almonds, figs, pomegranates, olives, and lemons.
Above all, the Valtellina has an abundance of edible chestnuts
which are the staple of the humble people. The valley's trees
yield many other edible and useful products, and they have
aroused the interest even of the haughty Venetians who are
looking at the tall trunks as a possible source of timber for
their fleet. As for pasture land, there can be few places in the
world to compare with the Veltlin's rich meadows:

The valley supports on its pastures, especially in the high
altitudes, not only horses, mules, and donkeys but also
great numbers of cattle, as well as sheep and goats. In the
winter the inhabitants feed them on hay, in the spring and
autumn they let them graze on pasture land near the crest
of the mountains. There the animals graze on rich, shady
alps, whose nourishing grass and clear air make them
strong and stout.... For this reason these regions possess
a great plenty of milk, cheese, whey, fat, and butter, also
of meat, leather, and tallow....

There follows a catalogue of indigenous game and fish to tanta-
lize any sportsman. Trout, he says, weigh an average of thirty
pounds ("taking the pound at ten ounces"), and anyone may
catch them to his heart's content in the Adda. His knowledge
of the habits of the Adda trout, incidentally, reveals many leisure hours spent at the rod.[44]

But there is a dark side to the hydrography of the valley.
Guler interrupts his recital of the valley's peace and plenty
with a scene of nature at her most inhuman. The lovely streams
and falls occasionally change their character and turn on the
men who dwell beside them:

For since the mountains attain such great height and have

steep and precipitous slopes, rain water rushes headlong
into the valley toward the streams. When the rains have
been heavy or the snow has melted on the heights, these
streams swell enormously and carry tree trunks, rocks,
and lumber with them. When this floating cargo reaches
the Adda where it is broadest a great deal of damage en-
sues. And this is aggravated by landslides, which are fre-
quent there because of the rotten, soggy, and clayey soil
of the upper mountains. Cloudbursts and thundershowers
are also injurious and terrible. Often the Adda increases
so in height that its raging waters flood fields and pastures
carry away good top soil, wrench out trees and bridges,
fill in ditches, set huge rocks adrift,and tear away houses
and barns....

But the waters do not ordinarily destroy. They make the soil
fertile and provide hot springs and baths of healthful properties. The air of the valley is pure and wholesome, except in
the lowest section where a warm air current known as Breva
infects the atmosphere during the summer months. But at that
time all who can do so move up to the plateaus. And now to the
people of the valley:

> Most of the inhabitants have quick, agile, thoughtful minds;
> they think highly of books and of schools and they also at-
> tach importance to military exercise,... hence there are
> among them doctores in all disciplines as well as brave
> and valiant fighting men.... Their aristocracy possesses
> true nobility of character and is well endowed with the
> knightly virtues....

As an example of the local qualities of head and heart Guler
narrates at some length the story of a simple peasant girl of
the valley, Bonna Lombardin, who innocently arouses the passion of a passing knight and is abducted by him. Bonna's loyalty and courage make her subsequent career reminiscent of
the life of patient Griselda. Her knight disdained to marry her,
though he dragged her from adventure to adventure, until she
ingeniously secured his release from captivity by Alfonso of
Naples. Thenceforth she shared his mercenary profession,
distinguishing herself as a doughty heroine until her death in
1468.
    Following a brief glance at the language, which is the Lom-
bard dialect of the Italian tongue, Guler outlines the government of the region. At first the valley was under the aegis of
the Bishop of Como. Later, under the Dukes of Milan, governors were stationed there, the chief of them in the capital of

Teglio. He was assisted in his duties by a podestà at Tirano
and another at Morbenn:

> Each of these officials had his own vicar who was a <u>doctor</u>
> or at least a man experienced in imperial law. These of-
> ficials governed the entire country and sat in judgment
> over all civil and criminal cases, though appeals could be
> made to Milan. Their term of office lasted one year. If
> complaints were raised against them they had to justify
> their actions publicly at a specified time each month. . . .

There are some words on the harsh taxation practices of the
Milanese. Then Guler concludes: "So much for this valley as
a whole. Now let us look at its sections in particular and take
up one by one each place, town, village, and hamlet as we make
our way through them."

He then begins a minute examination of the region of which
he has just rendered a general picture. In the various sections
of this next part of his description, Guler subjects every corner of the valley to patient consideration, and the result is the
most precise and detailed study in chorography ever attempted.
The first section to be described is the most spectacular one,
because it is the highest, the Wormser Domain:

> At the summit of the Veltlin lies the Domain of Worms.
> [Wormser Gebiet, Bormio.] It is surrounded by snowtopped
> mountains just as a city is enclosed by walls. But there is
> one gap through which the Adda hurls itself downward to-
> wards the valley, and at this spot the cliffs of the moun-
> tainsides crowd so close together that the stream, running
> in a canyon far down below, has only a narrow egress on
> whose left-hand side the mountain road just barely clings
> to a ledge in the rock. In this narrow ravine, now called
> St. Britio, there stood a long time ago an ancient fortress.
> A thick wall extended from one cliff to the other and a tow-
> er rose above the road which could be blocked off by shut-
> ting a gate. . . .

The description here is so extraordinarily vivid that one is
tempted to quote the whole of it. Guler describes the individual
sections of the valley much as he did the whole region. First
a general scenic description, then a discussion of fertility and
products, climate and notable features of the landscape such
as mountain peaks, streams, waterfalls, hot springs, and so
on. Next the government is discussed, both the internal admin-
istration and the political contacts with Switzerland and Italy.
Then follow descriptions of churches and monasteries, then
towns and villages , with distances one from the other. A word

on notable individuals usually concludes the discussion of each
section of the valley.

No Swiss or German writer can match Guler's descriptive
genius. We turn from him to other surveys of Swiss regions
and find ourselves once more in the midst of ordinary humanist productions. One wishes, for example, that the Berner
Oberland might have been viewed by as responsive a person
as Guler, but the chorographer of Bern was far from the mark

> The Jungfrau is a towering mountain, covered with perpet-
> ual snow and ice so as to make it inaccessible. For this
> reason the local inhabitants supposed that the name Vir-
> gin—that is, untouched—was given it.... Although the Jung-
> frau is only one mountain its top is bifurcated into two
> peaks which are so distant from one another as to appear
> to be two distinct summits. For this reason I hold that we
> have here not one, but two mountains which, however, go
> by the same name, that is, the Anterior and Posterior
> peaks.[45]

Still not in Guler's vein, but with a good deal more life than
the pedestrian sentences just cited, are two Alpine treatises
of the theologian and historiographer Josias Simler. Though
in their present form mere fragments, they had been intended
as sections of a comprehensive descriptive work. The plan
aroused the enthusiastic interest of the French jurist Pierre
Pithou, who offered his knowledge of Swiss antiquities and remained in touch with Simler while work was in progress.[46] But
time passed, and completion seemed far away; therefore in
1574, two years before his death, Simler published two excerpt
the Description of the Valais and the Commentary on the Alps,
"to afford a foretaste of the enterprise...hoping that my studies and labors may encourage learned and erudite men—of
whom, thanks be to God, Switzerland possesses today many—
to undertake similar studies."[48]
Simler's aims were modest. "My goal," he writes, "is not
to discern the causes and reasons of the things which nature
keeps hidden from us, but simply to describe systematically,
like a historian, the phenomena themselves."[49] In a modest
way he succeeded. The extent of the Upper and Lower Valais
is defined, the source of the great Rhone is located, the
"Vallesiae fertilitas," of course, is lauded, and the inhabitants
customs and activities, characters and costumes are apprais€
It would be difficult for anyone writing on the Upper Valais to
ignore the grandeur of the mountains, and Simler expresses hi
admiration, though in moderate tones:

In this region one finds marvels of nature, above all the
mountains which encircle the Valais. Our compatriots are
no longer very impressed by them because they see them
each day. But strangers are struck with awe after one
look at the Alps.... Surely we must marvel at the power
of nature which has built these mountains to a prodigious
height, which has covered their summits with eternal snow
and ice, which has caused mighty torrents to gush from
them, which—under the very snows of the Alps—raises me-
dicinal plants unknown elsewhere, and spreads excellent
pastures and magnificent trees.[50]

The second of the two treatises contains "in one commentary all the facts about the Alps that I have either read in the
books of worthy authors, have heard from reliable informants,
or have witnessed myself."[51] Much of this is, indeed, compiled
out of the ancients. But the reader does suspect that the dignity
of the Alpine landscape did not leave Simler unmoved. "It is a
most beautiful sight to watch, from the height of a summit, the
sun rise slowly above the eastern horizon," he writes,[52] and
though the passage stands alone, one feels that the sentiment
is not unique.

The western sections of Switzerland also found their chorographer, the Basel mathematician, theologian, and chronicler
Christian Wurstisen, whose <u>Bassler</u> <u>Chronik</u> offers a substantial survey of the geography and history of northwestern Switzerland. Its lengthy title promises to "treat not only of the city
and the bishopric of Basel, but also of the rest of the Confederation, as well as of Burgundy, Alsace, and Breisgau with
their adjacent regions." Seven of its eight books are primarily historical, but throughout, Wurstisen's copious topographical knowledge is nicely combined with the material from the
chronicles. He writes with restraint, but not without color, and
the book is amply supplied with illustrations which anyone familiar with the stock of the Basel publishing firm of Petri will
recognize as old friends. A general description of the environs
of Basel, "a mountainous land, but well populated and well cultivated, with ten cities and about 150 parishes,"[53] is elaborated
on in a great number of sketches of particular localities:

A mile away from this place lies the little town of Laufen,
situated in a fair and lovely plain. Its name comes from
the cataracts or rapids of the Birs which, though not violent, cause trouble for the river rafts. For if they are not
skillfully guided they are apt to come to grief on the rocks
of the falls.... In our time Laufen belongs to the Bishopric
of Zwingen.... The fairs are held on May Day and St.
Bartholomew's Day.[54]

Glimpses such as this, many longer and more informative, occur on every page. Wurstisen gently guides us along the roads:
"Now we enter Basel as we cross the Rhine bridge...," and
not infrequently he pauses on the way to point out the most dra
matic features of the landscape.

It is, of course, this spectacular nature of Swiss geography
which forces even the most chronicle-bound of writers to look
up. Moreover, no Swiss locality or group of localities can be
known at all except in their relation to these physical surround
ings. In Switzerland, therefore, more than in other German
regions, the fusion of geography and historiography took place
in descriptive literature, and this in close correspondence
with the rules evolved by the theorists of the chorographic
genre. Only the most successful authors, of course, were able
to construct a genuine literary form out of this fusion, and only one writer accomplished it in a work whose compass is
more than local. This was Johann Stumpf, "the finest writer
on Swiss affairs,"[55] whose plain talk has been much quoted in
these pages, and to whose description of all Switzerland[56] we
now turn.

Stumpf has been called "the first author of a Swiss history
whose work was influenced by the Italian humanists,"[57] but
there is little in the modest incidents of Stumpf's life to lead
one to suspect such a relationship. He was born in 1500 in
Bruchsal in Baden, studied theology without much enthusiasm,
joined the Johannite order, and won the priorship of one of the
order's houses. But he fell in with the Zurich reformers and
became a Protestant, settling in Switzerland and laboring for
the remainder of his life in a number of ministries. He died
in Zurich in 1578. Though the catalogue of his library shows
him to have had an acquaintance with a substantial body of literature[59] he does not appear to have been a learned person;
the Description of the Swiss Confederation reveals a genuine,
warm-blooded, fervent personality, but not a distinguished
intellect. What influence the Italian humanists exercised on
him came through his conscious imitation of their forms, for
it is more than likely that Stumpf had Biondo's Italia illustrata
in mind when he set out to compose his major work.

The Description was not Stumpf's earliest undertaking. When
he was in his thirties he first took up the historian's task by
continuing the manuscript chronicle of Heinrich Brennwald,
adding to it two books on the Reformation in Switzerland.[60] To
Brennwald, his father-in-law, Stumpf gave credit for having
awakened in him a taste for historical research and description,[61] but the younger man left the older far behind.

Stumpf's temperament clearly shows through his chronicling

of events and his description of places, and his strong views
account for his more than ordinary troubles with censorship.
Even the universally admired Description was excluded from
circulation within the Empire because of its enthusiastic republicanism and outspoken Protestantism,[62] and the cautious
religious politics of the Swiss authorities, particularly of the
city of Zurich, kept many of his other works out of print. These
other works comprised an account of the Luther-Zwingli controversy, a treatise on the Council of Constance, a sympathetic
history of the tragic life of Henry IV of Germany, and a theological study of the Last Judgment and the second coming of
Christ. But if we had only these we would not today remember their author. It was the Description of the Confederation
that won for Stumpf the respect and gratitude of his countrymen, and the notice of the scholarly world. In Jean Bodin's
catalogue of historians, Stumpf's name stands as the only representative of Swiss historiography,[63] and a modern student
has found that "until the beginning of the eighteenth century
Stumpf's description remained our major source for information about Switzerland and her history."[64]

If this is so, it is not only because the Description is the
most exact and complete of the chorographic works on Switzerland, but also because it is the sum of much of the finest
scholarship of which Switzerland was capable. Stumpf had the
unstinted support of the foremost men of letters among his
compatriots. Vadian, Heinrich Bullinger, Aegidius Tschudi,
Nicolaus Brieffer, and many others were constant in their encouragement and helpful with their contributions. Bullinger
and Vadian especially were Stumpf's mentors, as a study of
Stumpf's correspondence reveals.[65] In 1544, Bullinger was
able to enlist Vadian's interest in Stumpf's project. "You owe
this to our country," he wrote to him,[66] but the patriotic appeal was not needed. Vadian proved an invaluable counselor
whenever a problem called for more than Stumpf's own skill
or experience. Books and documents were suggested and procured by him, and it was Vadian who acted as intermediary
between Stumpf and the printer, Christoph Froschauer.[67] When
a dispute with Tschudi, himself an early contributor to the
Description but also a vigorous spokesman for the Swiss Catholics, threatened to scuttle the whole enterprise, it was Vadian
who drafted a long response to Tschudi's charges.[68] Bullinger,
too, remained concerned throughout the years of planning and
writing. The title and introduction were from his pen,[69] and
after publication he saw to the sale of the volume and did his
best to appease the many minor theological and political
tempests which it aroused.

But Stumpf was by no means a mere writing tool. It was he who managed to give the _Description_ a soul and a voice. Out of raw material sent in by dozens of major and lesser collaborators[70] he fashioned an organic structure. His supporters recognized his talent before preparations had gone very far. "Stumpf seems to be born for this work," wrote Vadian to Bullinger in the summer of 1545.[71] Not only did Stumpf stamp the manuscripts submitted to him with his personal style, but he gave them direction and infused the whole with a point of view. His general purposes were to illuminate nature, the magnificent handiwork of God, and to indicate the progress of history through time. But his affection for his country had no small part in prompting him to embark on a writing and editorial job of such magnitude. Switzerland, he, too, points out, has been neglected by ancient and modern authors.[72] "People in other countries," he notes,[73] "assume that the Alpine lands are nothing more than rocky wastes. . . . If they will but read this book they shall see that even the highest Alps have their fertile valleys and in them smiling pastures." The world should be made aware of the land and the deeds of the Helvetians, but it is just as important to remind the Swiss themselves of their ancient glory so that the sterling characters and sturdy habits of their forefathers may be the inspiration of the present.[74] History, he knows, is a stage on which "good and bad men, praise- and blameworthy deeds, . . . noble virtues and bad vices"[75] display themselves so that we may draw our object lessons.

But never does this moral intent, nor the bitter streak of disillusionment and resignation which runs as its counterpoint through the entire work, obscure the task Stumpf set himself: the depiction of his country. Nor is there the extra cargo of learning which makes lumbering vehicles of so many humanist works. Stumpf applied an energetic blue pencil to much of the material submitted to him. The book on the Turgau, for example, which had been first outlined by Stumpf and then submitted to Vadian for elaboration,[76] contains in the version included in the _Description_ very little of the etymological and antiquarian information with which Vadian's draft was weighted. A note refers the reader to Vadian for further details,[77] and Stumpf moves on to other matters.

His mission, as he saw it, was to describe. Much of Switzerland he knew himself, and much in the book is based on his personal observation. A diary which he kept during a research journey in the summer of 1544, the year in which he began systematic work on the _Description_,[78] enables us to observe his exact method of investigating and recording.[79] He examines

documentary material: "As soon as we arrived we called on
the abbot and inquired about the monastery's charter. The abbot then brought out a magnificently illuminated volume in
which the foundation charter had been recorded. . . ." He includes copies and German translations of records bearing on
municipal histories. He makes mention of details of architecture and decoration: "<u>Nota bene</u>: the fine floor mosaic behind
the altar." Above all, he notes topographical detail: "Lake
Roth, a half hour's walk from Lucerne, extends northeast to
within a half hour's walk from the village Ebikon. . . ." And:

> Distance in miles[80] from Zurich to Grimsel: from Zurich
> to Zug 2 miles, from Zug to Lucerne 2 miles . . . from Engel-
> berg to Grund on the Aare 2 miles, from Grund to Guttan-
> nen 1 mile, from Guttannen to Spittal a little more than 1
> mile, from Spittal to Grimsel 1 mile. Total 12 or more
> nearly 13 miles.

Such precision is reflected in the fine maps which enhance
the usefulness of Stumpf's volume. To know where we are,
says Stumpf, we must see "how each country touches its neighbors."[81] The maps lead us from canton to country to continent
and, finally, to the frame of the whole world, each map designed to show the relationship of the smaller geographical
area to the larger. Stumpf took the maps of the world, of Europe,
and of Germany and Gaul from Sebastian Münster's Ptolemy
edition of 1540, but those of Switzerland and of the Swiss cantons are his own, though based on the manuscript maps contained in Tschudi's Swiss chronicle.[82] They impress us far
more than do their models; eleven different styles of lettering
assure clarity, and there is a serious attempt to indicate visu-
ally the comparative height of the mountains. Small inset maps
in the text are a further help; these and two thousand or more
topical illustrations[83] make Stumpf's work not only instructive
but most delightful reading.

Stumpf's <u>Description</u> is divided into thirteen books, of which
the first is a survey of Europe and its countries and peoples
(including the Turks), and the second and third are descriptions of
Germany and France. Each book is prefaced by a short geographical section, restricted to general terms; then the settlement and history of the countries are traced from Trojan and
Old Testament times to the present. Book Thirteen, the final
section, is "a summary view of the history of all of Switzerland," a straight chronicle which lists events since 1314 of concern to the entire Confederation.[84] Stumpf, like Guler and many
other topographical-historical writers, made an emphatic distinction between general and local history. The former is

initially set forth, but the latter belongs with the chorographic
descriptions of individual localities and regions.

Books four to twelve make up this chorography of Switzerland, the substance of the work. But this main body is preceded, again, by a general survey of early Swiss affairs which
brings the narrative to a point of current interest. This section has an impressive visual opening: five pages of the coats
of arms of noble houses formerly resident in the country.
Stumpf's republicanism, we see, could not spoil his pleasure
in the pageantry of aristocracy. A few remarks on Swiss geography in antiquity introduce us to the ancient Helvetians, whose
character and courage we admire in a recital of their traits
and in an account of their campaigns against the Romans. Medieval history follows: the conquest of Switzerland by the Aleman,
incorporation into the Frankish realm, the country's fortunes
der the Holy Roman Empire, and finally the salient events of
the early Swiss struggle for independence, culminating in the
league of the Three Forest Cantons and the defeat of Austria
at Morgarten.

Now we are in a position to examine each of the Swiss sections individually. The cantons have come into being and their
institutions formed. It is now time to describe the land in detail, chorographically (subsequent history is narrated later).
Beginning with the divisions of Switzerland known to Caesar
and proceeding thence to the sections joined to ancient Helveti
by more recent events, Stumpf renders a full chorography of
each important canton. The pattern remains constant: references to the region by ancient authors, description of the general geographical nature of the region, discussion of the cities
and towns, each with its particular thumbnail chronicle. In the
case of St. Gall, for example, Vadian's general history of monasticism precedes an account of the foundation and growth of
the monastery. The mention of Zurich calls for an outline of
Zwingli's reformation. Stumpf goes on to describe lakes and
rivers and the localities situated on them; then come places
of topographical interest, such as waterfalls, passes, glaciers,
steep ledges, and peaks. Finally, there is at least a mention
of lesser features of the landscape—villages, minor rivers,
etc. He does not let us forget that these places are inhabited.
While only the renowned citizens are mentioned by name, the
men and women of the countryside are always before our eyes
through their customs and costumes, their dialects, and in an-
ecdotes of their folkways.

This is the form, but there is variation in it because the
chorographic method tries to glimpse each place in its singu-
larity. Important cities such as Zurich, Basel, and Solothurn

receive meticulous topographical and historical consideration
and are displayed in large woodcuts for which Schedel's Nuremberg Chronicle was the model. Important events are related,
year by year as they happened, down to Stumpf's own time.
Extraordinary occurrences—famines, plagues, conflagrations,
the birth of a monster—are faithfully recorded and, if possible,
illustrated. Inscriptions are reproduced. When antiquities are
in evidence, these are shown. Often a legend connected with
some ancient ruin is worth retelling: the Treasure of Augst,
for example,[85] that famous collection of coins supposedly
buried under the remains of a Roman building. We are told
how a poor devil, made desperate by privation, crawled into
a long subterranean passage and advanced toward a chamber
where he believed the hoard to be hid, coming instead upon a
heap of human bones. We hear a lot about animals too, notably
the stranger Alpine species, and most of them are illustrated
for us, some fancier than nature made them.[86] There is also
a liberal sprinkling of dragons and monsters, for no less an
authority than Pliny affirms that such creatures once existed
in Switzerland.[87] The arrival of a band of gypsies merits a
paragraph,[88] and there is room for a pseudo-medical digression on the therapeutic properties of hot and cold springs,
which are said to cure everything from blindness to sterility.[89]

   Work on the Description proceeded slowly, but in the winter
of 1547 it was complete. At least five of the thirteen books had
been examined by Vadian, first in manuscript and then in
proof,[90] and he and Bullinger pronounced the work sound. Public reaction was gratifying, in the Catholic as well as in the
Protestant cantons. Stumpf's adolescent son, Johann Rudolf,
was well received wherever he presented one of the thirteen
dedication copies.[91] In November and December of 1547, immediately after publication, he traveled in the Five Forest
Cantons.

> On the 27th of November, 1547 [he reported], I was on my
> way to Zug, which is located 2 miles from Zurich.... At
> Zug, I called on the Chief Magistrate, the brother of Peter
> Collinus. On the 28th I handed him a copy of the Chronicle
> and the covering letter. On the 29th I journeyed to Lucerne
> and spent the night at the Crown Inn near the Reuss bridge.
> ... On the 30th I presented Chronicle and letter to the
> Council and received, on the 1st of December, 10 crowns
> from the hands of the bailiff. On the following day I con-
> tinued my journey to Winkel, a village one mile from Lu-
> cerne, where I boarded a vessel which took me on a stormy
> trip to Altnach, where I spent the night. On the 3rd, bright

and early, I traveled to Sarnen, the chief town of Unterwalden, and that very afternoon presented Chronicle and
letter to the Council there. Both were received with expressions of high gratitude....[92]

The city of Zurich made both father and son honorary citizens.
From the canton of Schwiz came ten crowns, from Uri twelve,
and more was expected.[93] In some quarters, however, there
was anger at Stumpf's and Vadian's blunt comments. The Abbot of St. Gall is said to have been outraged at the history of
monasticism in Book Five, and, Stumpf wrote Vadian, "stated
that he is waiting only to meet me one of these days to call me
a liar to my face."[94] Tschudi objected to what he considered
irrelevant and gratuitous observations on the habits of monks,
on the efficacy of good works, and on images. Such matters,
he thought, are for theologians, not historians, to consider.[95]
The German aristocracy was irked at Stumpf's egalitarian
sentiments.[96] As late as 1554 the Council of the City of Zurich
was obliged to draw up a list of complaints being voiced against
the book, and called on Stumpf to furnish answers.[97]

After that the controversy seems to have run down. Catholic
resentment over the views of the Zurich authors was, after
all, a very minor incident in the course of Swiss religious
struggles, and Stumpf's Description of the Confederation was
a major accomplishment. It was soon recognized as such. The
work's merits had been obvious to Tschudi even while he objected to its obiter dicta.[98] Popular response was lasting,[99]
as the editions of 1586 and 1606 show, and modern critics have
sustained Stumpf's reputation as one of the most effective of
the sixteenth-century chorographers. He was informative,
plain-spoken, a source of enlightenment and entertainment to
his readers, and a mine of facts for subsequent writers. The
grand ambition of the German humanists to portray their country and capture its spirit produced few better works.

The Great Cosmographies

T HE REGIONAL compass of most of the topographical-historical works invited a local point of reference that was apt to distort the natural relationship of German territories to each other and of Germany to the world. The chorographer looked at his map through a magnifying glass, and, holding it over a single spot, he often lost his sense of proportion. In view of the zeal of German humanists and the fullness of facts from which many of their works were constructed, it is quite remarkable that so little exaggeration does appear; a Stumpf, an Albinus, a Brant made it clear that his favored region was part of a larger geographical and political body. But local writers were chiefly intent on the attractions of their own spheres of interest, and their attention was not usually on all of Germany.

The writer of a cosmography whose purview includes the whole inhabited world is more likely to approach his task with detachment from the local scene. The three comprehensive cosmographical works of the sixteenth century, Sebastian Franck's Book of the World, Sebastian Münster's Cosmographia, and Johann Rauw's Cosmographia, remained in possession of the perspective which their colleagues often lost. This perspective, of course, was extended only to the borders of Germany. None of the three writers saw his country as just one among many. The territories of Germany were their absorbing interest, and their aim was to create a balanced portrayal of the whole land of Germany rather than of the entire world. Franck's second book is on "Europe, principally Germany," and Rauw, who takes about one thousand pages to describe the whole earth, devotes nearly half of them to Germany. Münster's book, too, gives almost half its volume to a description of Germany, a fact which made Jean Bodin refer to it as "Münster's Cosmographia, or rather Germanographia."[1] Its title promises

111

the reader that he will be shown "the whole world and especially Germany," and a prefatory note elaborates:

> Further, dear reader, you must know that my first intent
> has been the description of the German nation with its re-
> gions and cities, and to tell you how their history began,
> with what useful things nature has endowed them and what
> human art has invented, also what has occurred and hap-
> pened.[2]

Cosmographical writers no less than regional authors were
responsive to the calls for national description. But though
they gave principal attention to the German lands, they brough
to their writing a far more cosmopolitan outlook than the regional authors. God, says Münster, scattered his gifts without
favoritism, and we who can become familiar with the peoples
of the globe by flicking the pages of a book ought to learn that
"no man can live without his fellow men and no land without
its neighbors."[3] Rauw agrees: "When one compares the countries of the world one generally finds that each and every land
has its gifts and also its shortcomings. The old saying is true:
no country is worth three pennies more than any other."[4] Frar
as a true Christian (though both Catholics and Protestants re-
jected him), held all races in equal esteem and disliked the
sort of historian who gloats over the renown of his own nation.
"Others we defame, ourselves we praise to the skies";[5] and
among the men he judges guilty of this presumption there are
many names from the title pages of our chorographic volumes
Franck did not bring to his cosmographical studies a schola
objectivity, nor was he much impressed by the demands for
national historiography which his colleagues heeded. It is true
that one can find in his work a number of references to the
historiographical neglect of Germany and the malicious dis-
tortion of German history by foreigners. But such statements
are lifted bodily from the writings of more patriotic humanists.[6] He himself feels that too much brooding and wrangling
about these "useless and subtle matters" is dangerous. These
disputes lead to veritable wars over the nomenclature of cities and mountains, and in all the shouting we forget the essential truth of existence, that God is in all and above all and that
all life reveals the word and deed of its Creator.[7] Historiography and cosmography are for Franck the display of God's
wonders; only such facts as reveal "a special secret, a purpose, or a wondrous work of God"[8] are pertinent. That is why
the motto of his Book of the World is taken from the psalmist,
"Come, behold the works of the Lord," and why Franck's cosmography is an organic part of his religious writings and

amounts to a passionate confession of faith.

Franck's pitiful nomadic existence, compelled by the intol-
erance of his fellow men against one who strove to remain
religiously unattached in an age of violent confessional com-
mitment, was bound to be reflected in his opinions. His early
adult years were spent in Nuremberg, where the air was quick
with the historical and ethnographic interests which then occupied him. In 1529 he moved on to Strassburg to publish his
first major work, the Chronicle and Bible of History.[9] Out of
the history of the world as he here relates it, Franck attempts
to formulate a neutral point of view, different from that of
Catholics, Lutherans, Zwinglians, and Anabaptists—a non-
partisan, simply Christian view. Turks, Pagans, Christians
he holds to be all the same.[10] The powers over our spiritual
and secular lives, he charges, foster hatred of all that is
strange to us as a means of securing their own authority. The
masses are too dense to understand, and follow their leaders
blindly. Enlightened men have always been and always will be
called heretics. The book made Franck an outcast. Expelled
from Strassburg in December of the year of its publication, he
settled first in Esslingen, later in Ulm as a soapmaker, then
as a printer. In 1534 he was able to publish the concluding section of his Chronicle, now printed separately as the Book of
the World,[11] but the agitation against him by his Protestant
enemies, to whom he was worse than an Anabaptist, forced the
municipal authorities of Ulm to drive him from the city in 1539.
He went to Basel or perhaps to Holland, and died in 1542 or
1543.

Written from the fund of such experiences, the Weltbuch
could have few points of contact with the relatively unruffled
world of the chorographers. Its title and form are, to be sure,
those of the professional cosmographical works, but Franck
cared little for professional canons. He was hardly conscious
of the techniques of exact geographical description. Nor did
he keep this unconcern from his readers. "You must not," he
tells us at the outset,

> expect to find in this Book of the World (which is scarcely
> worthy of being called a "geography") a detailed likeness
> of the whole earth, for such a task was never my intention
> and would not have been within my powers, and I leave it
> to others more skilled than I. I myself want to spread out
> before your eyes the characteristics, beliefs, and laws of
> the earth and its land, pointing out how the desolate, wild,
> gloomy world is split and rent by innumerable sects so
> that there are nearly as many creeds and rites as there

> are people, countries, even cities and souls. In order to
> bewail this state of affairs and to demonstrate to the blind,
> foolish world its blind and stumbling ways ... I have under-
> taken to write this book.[12]

Geographical accuracy, historical perspective, logical organization hardly count, therefore. In fact, preoccupation with detail would have obscured the religious theme of the work; for
his purpose it was sufficient "to sketch and outline the world
as with a piece of charcoal, not to copy nor portray it exactly."[13] Such a cavalier attitude towards cosmographical precision did Franck no good with his colleagues, who were only
too ready to believe the worst of him. Melanchthon called the
Chronica a "book of libels rather than a history."[14] Franck's
zeal in the exposition of his views must have alienated many
readers who had purchased a copy out of their interest in
world geography.

     This is not to say that other cosmographers did not also
profess a religious motivation for their scholarship. Like
Franck, Münster believed that man meets God most intimately in the world He created,[15] and that man may learn from an
investigation of this world that human achievements are tran-
sitory and only God's work permanent.[16] Johann Rauw also
thought of his craft as "a _famula_ and guide to God's Creation."
His writing, too, is full of awe at the wonders of nature revealed by cosmographical study—the order and proportion of
the elements, the confinement of water to its place in the ocea
basins "as though held there by walls and ramparts," the sus-
pension of the earth in the center of the universe "without pillars or columns," and, most enigmatically, the revolution of
the spheres:

> Just observe the sky a little bit: how neatly God has de-
> vised its arrangement into heavenly Circles or Spheres,
> how steadily and with what amazing speed they revolve!
> For you must know that the outermost sphere moves all
> the other heavens in a complete revolution in just twenty-
> four hours. This is so great a speed that human reason
> cannot even imagine it.[18]

Therefore it is as a cosmographer, and not merely as a Chris
tian, that Rauw pledges to keep his gaze on God and heed the
call: "talk ye of all His wondrous works."[19]

     Such sentiments are prominent in the prefaces of Münster's
and Rauw's cosmographies, but they do not extend to the texts.
Franck's narrative is saturated with religious fervor; Münster
and Rauw's theology rarely reaches beyond the introductions—

it is the aegis under which their works flourish but not the
spirit by which they live. Johann Rauw, who was by profession
a minister in various places in Hessen, had published a theological treatise and a book of Protestant hymns in addition to
the Cosmographia, which appeared in 1597.[20] Nothing is known
of the circumstances surrounding the composition of this work,
nor can we guess why Rauw undertook to write a huge volume
of some one thousand folio pages on a subject alien to his training. His Cosmographia, like all such books, is not an independent effort, but rather a patchwork of oral and written reports
from men familiar with topics and localities described. It is
a dry book, and was not well received at the time, but it is at
least a very exhaustive job. We can imagine how Rauw's notes
and reports accumulated on his desk and how the fat volume
was compiled from them: "I had originally intended only a
Compendium Cosmographicum, but it grew under my hands
and is now larger than I myself meant it to be."[21]

To an overwhelming extent Rauw's work is based on Sebastian
Münster's Cosmographia, "the most respected of all cosmographical writings," as Rauw himself admitted,[22] published
for the first time fifty-three years before Rauw's volume.[23]
Münster, like Rauw, had once been a cleric. In 1505, in his sixteenth year, he had become a Franciscan friar, but Luther's
writings caused him to become a Protestant, and his studies
in classical and Hebrew philology, mathematics, and astronomy
provided him with a new and absorbing discipline to which to
dedicate his life. The Cosmographia is in no way the summing
up of his life's scholarship, whose flights were too diverse to
be brought between two covers. But the book holds the essence
of both his craft and his convictions, being the labor of eighteen
years, and, as we have seen, the product of painstaking and
highly skilled personal investigation[24] as well as tireless in-
quiries with residents of various German regions:

> For eighteen years [he writes], I have been making inquir-
> ies throughout the German lands and have sought help every-
> where, as the nature of a work of this kind requires, and
> wherever I found an informed person I called on him, ac-
> quainted him with my purpose, and often found him coop-
> erative and willing to aid me with reports, descriptions,
> and the loan of books.[25]

But the finished work was not a mere aggregate of facts. Like
the bee whose habits Francis Bacon recommended to the scholarly world, Münster gathered his matter from the flowers of
the field, digesting and preparing it by his native powers, building
his work of a substance he had not only mastered but clarified

and refined. He was not unaware of the uniqueness of his endeavor: "There were some among the ancients and now among
Christians," he writes, "who have made attempts to portray
the German nation, but as far as I know no one has as yet undertaken a true and right description of the cities and territories and peoples of the German land."[26] What Münster meant
by a "true and right description" we already know: a view of
the whole country, region by region and town by town; not the
obvious geographical features alone, but the singularities known
only to the native, the peculiar traits which identify the local
resident. And the result was to be not merely scientifically
accurate but also pleasant to read and serious enough to instruct.

The desire to instruct was strong in all German humanists.
Only Franck is here again outside the fold. Though he exhibits
"Germans to Germans in German,"[27] Franck despairs of the
capacity of human beings to learn. When a donkey once falls
on the ice, he comments sadly, it knows enough thereafter to
avoid slippery surfaces. But man never profits from his mis-
fortunes.[28] Franck's colleagues, however, not only believed
man capable of improvement but felt that they, as investigators
of the world, had a special mission to communicate their wisdom to him. Johann Rauw's entire volume is designed to
teach. It is schoolmasterly in tone, and in question and answer
form throughout. Every paragraph carries a marginal summary. Münster commands a richer style, but he too likes to
instruct. He often sends his reader to the atlas which accompanies his work, and he provides rudimentary instruction in
its use. "Don't forget it!" he cautions us when he has made
an important point. Above all, Münster recognized the place
of such books as his in the lives of his contemporaries. Men
are naturally inquisitive, and the world is large and full of
fascinating things. But who may, like Odysseus or Marco Polo
roam over the vastness of it and see it all? Few ever could,
and in these times the unstable political situation, the religious animosities, and the presence of the Turks in Europe
have thrown more obstacles than ever in the sight-seer's way.
But, says Münster to his readers,

> nowadays you no longer need to wander about the earth in
> search of knowledge of countries, cities, rivers, mountains
> and valleys, or the customs and manners, laws and con-
> stitutions of men, or the habits and habitations of animals,
> or the properties of plants and herbs. You now find such
> things written in books and may know from them more
> about this or that country than someone who has lived in
> it for a year or longer.[29]

The cosmography was to be a receptacle for everything
worth learning, an encyclopedia of knowledge—knowledge of
the world and of man, of the marvels of nature and the fruits
of human inventiveness, of the scene and plot and actors in
the great drama God allows us to play on His stage. No wonder that Jean Bodin's catalogue of historians refers to Münster
as a "universal geographistorian."[30] But all this information
is not merely poured into the cosmographical form. It is ordered and related by the descriptive geographical method
which is the catalyst of the genre and to which all else is sub-
ordinated. Fortunately, this descriptive narrative, which proceeds leisurely over the surface of the globe as the available
material demands and limitations of space permit, is the most
elastic of all forms of writing, and along the way there are innumerable opportunities for comment and interpretation. For
it was Münster's conviction that "the description of the whole
world, which is my aim in this book,... requires an open mind,
much reading, much observation, much experience. Yet even
these would not be enough if the author's critical judgment
were lacking."[31]

The cosmographical form, as Franck, Münster, and Rauw
employed it, developed out of the much shorter, more technical treatises of such men as Peter Apianus and Gemma
Frisius, which had borne the name but had little resemblance
to the format of their offspring. Through Münster, their most
articulate spokesman, the narrative cosmographers altered
the direction of cosmography, making it primarily descriptive
geography. Tradition and interest, however, continued to demand that the reader be given some instruction in the mechan-
ics of the universe and its nucleus, the earth. With Apianus
and Gemma this technical initiation had been primary; the
brief description of continents which they appended was merely an application of the principles they had expounded. But in
the greatly enlarged volumes of the younger men this technical
material served only as an introduction to the main work, although usually it was itself of substantial length and caliber.
Even Franck deals in his introduction[32] with the position of
the world and with its shape and size. The material is taken
from Apianus,[33] but is mingled with biblical cosmogony and
punctuated by moral injunctions and professions of human fal-
libility. Münster and Rauw keep Bible and Ptolemy segregated.
Creation is the beginning of the universe and God the master
of its laws, but these laws have an independent logic. Rauw's
introduction, the "Description of the Divine Work, the Universe;
both its Celestial and Terrestrial Regions," 140 pages long,

technically competent and pedagogically skillful, first relates
the six days of creation, then explains the spheres and their
motions, treats of meteors, thunder and lightning, winds, and
earthquakes, and finally surveys the globe's climatic and physical divisions and their geographic properties. Münster goes
directly to the source of his own knowledge and gives long excerpts from the first book of Ptolemy's Geography. Following
this, he provides an underpinning for the historical part of his
work by tracing the rise and fall of some of the great empires
of the past: Assyria, Macedonia, Carthage, and Rome.

These are the fundamentals, the rules which operate eternally under the myriad phenomena of existence. We must know
them in order to comprehend what follows. The cosmographers
are first of all teachers, but they never forget the character
of the cosmographical form so far as to be pedantic about it.
They are masters of ceremonies, raising the curtain on an
extravagant spectacle. Even Rauw, who often plods along without much spirit, communicates the animation of his own discoveries. Franck and Münster never cease to marvel at what
they are relating. The world is full of incredible things, and
there is excitement in the telling as well as in the listening.

Münster and Rauw commence their surveys of the inhabited
world with a description of Europe, but Franck lingers first
in Africa, where he enjoys himself with tales of men who live
in holes in the ground, eat snakes, have one-eyed or dog-headed
kings, are headless with eyes and mouth on the chest, and many
others possessing weird characteristics,[34] some of whom turn
up again, handsomely illustrated, in Münster's book on the dark
continent. Franck is, of course, fascinated by the astounding
variety of mores which fact and legend report concerning the
African tribes, all of them God's children. So absorbed is he
in the open-air lovemaking of Herodotus' Nasamonians, the
grasshopper diet of others, and the custom of still others to
shave the left side of their heads, that he quite forgets the geography of Africa. Münster and Rauw more soberly describe
the African terrain, Münster especially successfully by means
of a fine map which is included in his volume. But they, too,
must rely on hearsay, and therefore cannot altogether avoid
the pitfalls of which Ptolemy had warned the descriptive geographer.

It is with the descriptions of Europe that their founts of information take on both fullness and credibility and their words
authority.[35] But all our writers move rather rapidly over Western Europe; Britain, Spain, France, Italy is the order which
leads to Germany, the heart of the continent, or the area of the
vitals as Rauw declares in his elaborate comparison of the

shape of Europe to that of a reclining woman—Spain and Por-
tugal forming her head and crown of hair, the Pyrenees a neck-
lace, Italy her right arm thrust loosely away from her body.[36]
Much of the best writing occurs in the descriptions of Germany
which follow. Here those regional sources already available
could be utilized and impressions of contemporaries brought
together into a re-creation of the German lands. We need not,
of course, expect a description as detailed as that of the local
chorographies. The cosmographers aimed at something else.
Out of the wealth of local scenes, each of which they tried to
grasp in its individuality, they fashioned a composite picture
of the Germany of their time, stressing not only the uniqueness of each area but also the relationships between them, and
implying, though not stating, the national denominator under the
distinctively regional traits.

Again, this applies only in part to Sebastian Franck. His er-
ratic personality permitted no consistent exposition. He begins
not with the country itself, as does Rauw, nor with its earliest
inhabitants, like Münster, but instead with his contemporaries,
whom he scathingly upbraids for their gluttony, their vindic-
tiveness, and their addiction to gambling.[37] Only when this is
out of his system does he render a brief general impression
of German geography, consisting of a few remarks on the
courses of the Rhine and Danube. After the conventional avowal
of the land's fertility, he moves on to descriptions of particular
German regions. Many of these are mere sketches:

> Moving north we go from Moravia to Silesia, not an ignoble
> land, touching Poland in the east. The famous river called
> Oder flows through it toward the German Sea. The length
> of this region amounts to about eight horse journeys, its
> capital is Breslau, situated on the Oder. Its former Lord,
> called Bulco and resident at Glauco, believed neither in
> angels nor in the devil and held that body and soul die and
> dissolve at the same time. The language of the people
> thereabouts is mostly German, though Polish is spoken
> beyond the Oder. For this reason, some have thought, not
> without justification, that the Oder forms Germany's bound-
> ary in that particular area.[38]

Of Swabia we learn a little more circumstantially that it is
located between Bavaria, Alsace, Franconia, and the Alps,
that it is a "well-cultivated, well-irrigated, sufficiently fertile
land with many mountains, lakes, rivers, woods, and pastures,"
that it is "filled with renowned and formidable towns and castles," and that it is populated by clever and courageous inhabitants about whom the following is to be noted:

Their religion is fourfold, Papist, Lutheran, Zwinglian, and
Baptist. But read elsewhere about that. Their income derives not from agriculture, as in ancient times, but from
the formation of companies for the undertaking of commercial ventures, and also from various crafts. Now, a
company is a group whose members get hold of a sum of
money and buy up everything they can lay their hands on,
such things as pins, mirrors, grain, wine, cloth, and so
forth. These they sell abroad and, in turn, bring to this
country useless stuff like silk, velvet, musk, pepper, cin-
namon, and so on. And what the workman has sold to them
he cannot buy back at double the price....[39]

With such spot observations and much acid comment, Franck
moves through Bavaria, Lithuania, and Russia, then back to
Western Germany, ending with the Netherlands, Alsace, and
Switzerland. The other European countries come next, but the
climax of the European section is a long dissertation on the
Turks,[40] broadminded in conception and cosmopolitan in tone.
This is followed by an outline history of the Christian creeds,
including the eastern denominations. Parts three and four, on
Asia and America, close the Book of the World on the exotic
note which Franck had struck at the beginning.

From Franck we turn with renewed appreciation to Sebastian
Münster's purposeful and methodical exposition. No single-
minded preconception meets us here, no aimless rambling,
but there is no genius either, not even genuine originality.
Münster's working methods reveal many of the peculiarities
of his time: faith in authority, an irresistible urge to show off
his considerable philological and antiquarian learning, and a
tendency to cater to the taste of his age for the marvelous and
improbable. But the end product has the life which only its
author's many-sided career could give it. It also has an integrity which few other works could match.

The great Cosmography was a long time in taking shape. As
early as 1530 an explanatory treatise of Münster's appeared
as a companion piece to the renowned map of Germany by
Nicolas of Cusa.[41] It restates the case for a topographical and
historical description of the many delightful features which
Germany now possessed in contrast to the wild country which
the ancients had seen. It then addresses itself to some technical problems, and ends with a list of all town names found on
the Cusa map. A similar but more popular work followed six
years later, called Cosmographei or Mappa Europae,[42] and
certainly suggested by Franck's Book of the World. It contained an excerpt from Pirckheimer's nomenclature of German

geography, as well as a chapter "On Germany's Shape, Location,
her Peoples, Institutions, Laws and Customs, Taken from
S. Franck." There were also sketches of various German territories and a few brief glimpses of other European countries.

Not much could be done in the thirty-six quarto pages of
this essay, but the germ of the <u>Cosmographia</u> on which Münster
was then actively engaged was there. Eight years later, in 1544,
the first version of the major work came off Heinrich Petri's
press, already generous in size and makeup, but not yet in
harmony with the author's ambitions. The third edition, which
was issued in 1550, was much more lavish in representation,
and richer, more authoritative in text. We know that the appearance, in Zurich in 1548, of Johann Stumpf's splendid <u>Des</u>-
<u>cription</u> <u>of</u> <u>the</u> <u>Swiss</u> <u>Confederation</u> had much to do with this
new version. Compared to the superb first edition of Stumpf's
book, the 1544 <u>Cosmography</u> was a poor country cousin, "different from yours as black is different from white," Heinrich
Bullinger had written to Stumpf.[43] With some misgivings,
Münster had observed from Basel his rival's progress. "Are
these people imitating me," he asked a friend in the other
camp,[44] "are they excerpting me?" He was especially afraid
that Stumpf's original plan of a survey of Switzerland and surrounding regions might be enlarged into a global description
like his own. Heinrich Petri, he writes, cannot bring out a new
edition without great loss if a similar work is to be issued in
Zurich. He was soon reassured on that point; Stumpf's <u>Des</u>-
<u>cription</u> did not aspire to the compass of his own <u>Cosmography</u>.
But Stumpf's opulent format, with its maps, its ornate borders
and devices, and its nearly two thousand illustrations, including many large spreads of Swiss cities, set both author and
publisher to work on a resplendent volume of their own. However, Münster used the occasion to turn out more than an expansion of his original plan. The 1550 edition was practically
an entirely new work. The many municipal descriptions were
more detailed, and were magnificently illustrated with drawings procured from local sources and transferred to large
wood blocks in Petri's shop.[45] Many sections were greatly altered—that on the New World was expanded from six to fourteen pages; the description of Palestine was augmented with
a history of the crusading movement; the peoples of the world
were pictured in their ethnic garb; animals and plants were
illustrated; and all other accounts were brought up to date.
Münster's dedication to his task is evident in the mere bulk of
the volume, but its quality is not less impressive. The direct-
ness and personality of the original were not lost in its elaboration.

At the outset of his third book on Germany, the central section and by far the longest, Münster reiterates what he asserted in some of his earlier writings, that the new Germany
needs a comprehensive description. But here as everywhere
he is moderate; he does not think that Germany has been too
unfairly treated by older writers, nor does he accuse any of
them of malice. "Everyone did the best he could," he writes,
referring to the general uninformativeness of ancient
sources,[46] and though this prefatory note is enlarged
in the later edition, the issue is not belabored. The important
thing is to create in the reader an awareness of the antiquity
and tradition of his country, and to that end Münster includes
from his earlier works the comparisons of ancient and modern
Stamm names. He then occupies himself with the Germanic
tribes. He narrates the history of the long and bitter wars between Romans and Germans, calls upon Tacitus to show what
manner of men these Germans were, and casts a general
glance at the country through which they migrated, but of
whose fertility they made no use. Medieval history, as Münste
presents it, is marked by the enlargement of the German domain. Regions adjacent to the original home of the tribes,
Noricum, Vindelicia, Raetia, and Pannonia, were occupied,
while territories beyond the Danube, such as Holland, Lorrain
Alsace, and Austria, were conquered. Soon the victorious tribe
wrested the imperium itself from the eastern remnant of the
Roman state, and their imperial dignity as well as the true
Christian faith they now sincerely professed made Germany
the hub of the world in the centuries that followed.

Münster passes over these centuries quickly, not dwelling o
the procession of medieval kings and emperors, and only when
proaching his own time does he arrest his narrative to let us
look around in this German Empire which has now attained its
definitive form. We inspect its principalities and domains, are
acquainted with the hereditary titles of the great lords, the
laws and decrees by which the realm is governed, and the pom
of an Imperial election. We also penetrate into the homes of
more ordinary German citizens and learn to distinguish the
estates by their customs of dress and their mode of living.
One more point and we are done with this initial section: much
of the description which follows will have to do with the towns
and cities of Germany, so we must know something of their
names. Münster therefore demonstrates the shifting of sound
through which Latin designations became German and explains
the obvious reasons for the endings -heim, -tal, and -bach, by
which the newer German towns are identified.

With the past now fixed and established as heritage, Münste

may proceed to his proper task: the survey of Germany region
by region. Reminders of the ancient and imperial period will
recur, but the glances into the past of German territories will
be distinctly local, not national, history. We begin with a close
look at Switzerland, perhaps because this was Münster's home,
or perhaps because, as he says, "Germany extends west as
far as the Rhine or a few miles beyond, and the source of the
Rhine lies in Switzerland."[47] The Rhine is for him, as it was
for Sebastian Brant, a fixed line of orientation. He himself
had studied its path, and his own maps of the river departed
significantly from the more inexact indications of his colleagues.
From its source we move north through Western Germany,
then shift to the center, again moving up the map, then go eastward, and conclude with Bohemia and Silesia.

It is in this regional part of the Cosmographia that the difference between the two editions becomes clear, most of all
in its purely topographical portions. To get a clear picture of
Münster's method in enlarging his volume, we may examine
the chapter which takes us through Franconia in Central Germany, not one of his longest or best chapters, but a good survey of a land not especially favored by any of the local
writers.[48] "Where the Franks Originally Came From" is the
title which begins his survey:

> Franconia, located about the Main, got its name from its
> inhabitants, the Franks, who resided formerly near the
> Rhine in the Netherlands....Originally this people came
> from the land of Scythia where the Danube enters the
> Sea....

It was the Goths, pushing from behind, who were responsible
for the migration of the Franks westward. At that time they
were called Sicambri, but they soon adopted the proper name
of their wisest and most beloved King, Francus. This migration, Münster says, occurred in 24 B.C. They moved into Gaul,
later called France after them, but not all remained there. The
story goes that the Thuringians, then, as always, at war with
the Swabians, called on the Franks for aid, offering a portion
of their land as inducement. Genebaldus, brother of the Frankish king, responded with 32,680 men, their wives, animals,
and other possessions. He won the war for the Thuringians
and then settled his followers between them and the Swabians
to keep the rivals at peace. The region became known as
Franconia, and Genebaldus became its first Duke.

In the 1550 edition this account of earliest Franconian history is left unchanged, but it follows a general view of the country. In 1544 one paragraph of description had sufficed:

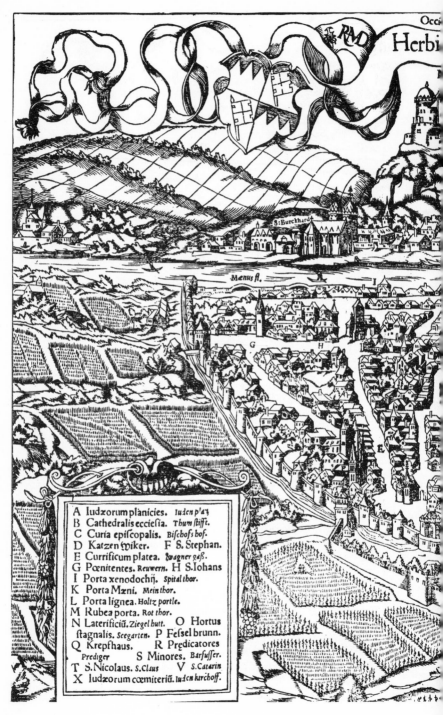

A Iudæorum plànicies. *Iuden pl'az*
B Cathedralis ecclesia. *Thum stifft.*
C Curia episcopalis. *Bischofs hof.*
D Katzen wiker. F S. Stephan.
E Currificum platea. *wagner gaß.*
G Pœnitentes. *Reuwern.* H S. Iohans
I Porta xenodochij. *spital thor.*
K Porta Mæni. *Mein thor.*
L Porta lignea. *Holtz portle.*
M Rubea porta. *Rot thor.*
N Laterificiũ. *Ziegel hutt.* O Hortus
stagnalis. *Seegarten.* P Fessel brunn.
Q Krepfhaus. R Prædicatores
Prediger S Minores. *Barfusser.*
T S. Nicolaus. *s. Claus* V S. Catarin
X Iudæorum cœmiteriũ. *Iuden kirchoff.*

The city of Würzburg.

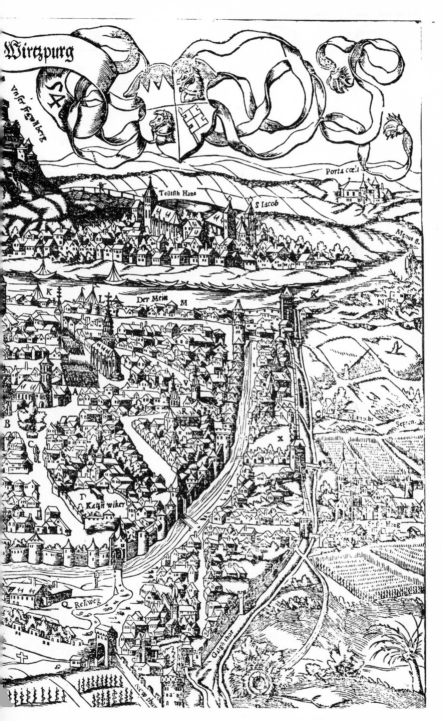

From Sebastian Münster's <u>Cosmographia</u> of 1550.

> Franconia lies in the center of Germany and is surrounded
> by dense forests and rugged mountains. The Main and the
> Tauber go through it and support vineyards on their banks.
> The soil is fertile, and of barley and wheat and sundry
> fruits there is a great plenty. No German land can boast
> larger onions and turnips than Franconia. Around Bamberg
> grows a honey-sweet root called licorice.... Franconia is
> densely populated and there are also many kinds of domes-
> ticated animals. The rivers and creeks are full of fish and
> the woods teem with game.... The Franconians are an in-
> dustrious lot; women as well as men may be seen at work
> in the vineyards. No one is allowed to be idle.

But the 1550 edition gives us a second description of Franconia
following upon the historical passage already quoted, and a set
of genealogies of Franconian dukes and counts appended to
it. Now the writing is more vivid, and is illustrated by inset
drawings:

> I have already indicated that Franconia lies in the center
> of Germany and is enclosed by thick forests and rugged
> mountains. It is crossed by the Main and the Tauber, whose
> shores furnish the inhabitants with an excellent wine....
> The Franconians are just like all other Germans in ap-
> pearance. They are most diligent workers.... In our time
> Franconia is under the rule of five princes: the Margrave
> of Nuremberg and the Count Palatinate are the two secu-
> lar rulers; the Bishops of Babenberg, Würzburg, and Mainz
> are the three ecclesiastical Lords. There used to be a
> Duchy of Voigtland between Babenberg and the Bohemian
> forest with its own prince, but it is now defunct and its
> authority has been divided among the March of Branden-
> burg, the Bishop of Würzburg and the Bishop of Babenberg.

So much for general description; now the cities are brought
into focus, beginning with Würzburg because "whoever is Bishop of this city holds the heart of Franconia in his possession."

> In our time Würzburg is the capital of Franconia. Among
> the ancients it has many names, Herbipolis, Peapolis, and
> Marcopolis. There is a theory that it is a Frankish founda-
> tion and did not exist in the time of Ptolemy.

This much is told of Würzburg in 1544, and with only the municipal escutcheon for an illustration. Six years later an elaborate municipal history and description takes up six pages,
not counting the initial feature, a seven-page catalogue of the
Bishops of Würzburg which had been submitted to the author

in 1548 by a collaborator. From St. Kilian, who is reckoned the
first to have occupied the episcopal seat, to Melchior Gutenberg,
the sixty-fourth, elected in September, 1544, the prelates are
named and briefly appraised. Next comes a long treatise on the
differing interpretations of Würzburg's name and of its origin
as a city. Then Münster describes its location and appearance:

> The city lies in a plain which is bordered on all sides by
> rolling hills and mountain knolls whose slopes bear vines
> and lovely orchards interspersed with meadows. The city
> is well protected by moats and ramparts as well as walls,
> towers, and other fortifications. It is a populous place and
> boasts many temples, monasteries and churches, though
> private residences, too, are splendidly built. Hidden canals
> and underground waterways carry off the city's sewage
> and this contributes not a little to the purity and whole-
> someness of her air.

The profile of Würzburg may be seen in a large, two-page xy-
lograph, and the Marienburg is singled out for special comment. The Würzburgers, he goes on, are mainly commercial
people, but that does not mean that they have no interest in
intellectual pursuits. Law, letters, and theology are all represented by outstanding scholars. A little color is added with a
description, expanded from ten lines in the 1544 edition, of the
ceremonies prescribed for the enthronement of a bishop. This
leads to a consideration of the municipal history of Würzburg,
first in ancient times and then, in a longer chapter, from the
middle of the eighth century to about 1500. It is no mere list
of official events. We hear about elections and councils, the
construction of important buildings, the opening of the municipal Gymnasium in 1402, and so on. Both versions of the Cosmography devote sections of varying length to other Franconian cities, Hennenberg, Wertheim and Bamberg in the
earlier work; Schweinfurt, Rotenburg, Wertheim, Frankfurt,
Hennenberg, and Bamberg in the later one. Münster does not
fail to note Frankfurt's importance as a commercial center
and its honorable role as the electoral seat for the choice of
the King of the Romans, the future Emperor. Splendid woodcuts make up for much that the descriptions lack in detail,
while the swift pacing of the narrative reminds us that much
else is to be seen in the land.
    Work on such a comprehensive scale could never really
cease, and Münster had no intention of allowing the 1550 edition
to remain the last one. New material was always being brought
to his attention, and there were other regions to be explored,
new informants to be utilized. Gaps had to be closed. To the

end of his life Münster was active in the furbishing of his major work. Hardly was the revised edition off the press when
he began to cast about for new contributions and ideas. "In the
meantime," he wrote to Vadian in December of 1550,

> I proceed with my work. I have my hands full with a num-
> ber of additions to the book suggested by many people who
> have been bombarding me with criticism since its publi-
> cation. I have come upon that fine description of Spain and
> Spanish cities which was printed two years ago. It is in
> Spanish, and is to Spain what my work is to Germany. [49]
> The Pomeranians are forwarding some material concern-
> ing their region and also some pictures of their cities.
> From Ulm I have also received something. The French
> have promised contributions. The Count Palatinate has
> already sent some descriptions and has promised more.
> Likewise the Strassburgers. I have also written to the
> King of Poland, to the rulers of Prussia and Mecklenburg,
> and to the magistrates of several German cities. I also
> expect something more from Italy. Some time ago I re-
> ceived material concerning Tunisia in Africa which the
> imperial troops captured not long since, [50] and I have had
> engravings made of these places. So you see, many people
> from various parts of the world have helped me out with
> material for my next edition, and this speeds my work and
> will enrich it greatly. If you know of something which I
> have not as yet included in the latest edition of the Cosmog-
> raphy do not fail to send it along no matter what its subject
> whether it concerns a city or a region, as long as you feel
> that it will be of interest to my readers. [51]

Concern for the interest of his readers was uppermost with
Münster, and, needless to say, the work had to appeal to all
sorts. In the chorography of Germany, Münster avoided as
much as he could an appeal to the sensational. But those who
read the book to marvel at strange and outlandish things were
rewarded by the Asian and African sections of the Cosmograph
which teem with monsters—human, half-human, and bestial—
with descriptions of tortures, revolting eating habits, and the
like. As Münster proceeds east from the Mediterranean, the
geographical accuracy of the text diminishes. The stress is
more and more on the fabulous and the anecdotal. Strabo, his
reliable guide, is left behind, and Münster is lured by Solinus
into a wonderland where fact and fancy are indistinguishable.
We can have no illusion whence came the popularity of the work

> As the wise philosopher [says] in his seventh boke of mo-
> ralls, our nature is suche throughe the combinacion of

> contrary thinges, that we cannot take continuall delectation
> or pleasure alwayes in one kinde of thinge, but naturallye
> wee are inclined and desire to be partakers of newes, of
> straunge and unaccustomed thinges, of variable and diverse
> matters which may breede some admiracion to any of oure
> sences.

This from Richard Eden's English abridgment of the Cosmography;[52] and among the many "straunge and unaccustomed
thinges" which the editor culls for inclusion in his epitome
are such delectables as "A monster borne nighe unto Wormes
in Germany in the yeare 1495," "A straunge historie of a king
devoured of Myce," "Of the Unicorne," "A Beare seking for
hony was the Cause of Delivering a man out of an hollow tree,"
and so forth. One hopes that German readers took at least
equal interest in Münster's expert representation of their
country and its territories.

   Much of all this meets us again in Johann Rauw's even bulkier Cosmographia. Münster himself had leaned somewhat on
Franck, but a true kinship both in form and substance bound
Rauw to the man he recognized as his master. Differences in
method have already been noted; Rauw is more matter-of-fact,
more frankly instructive, less flexible in his organization of
material. His catechistic method often makes for clarity, but
it is also monotonous. His lack of strong convictions, or his
ability to keep them out of his work—it would have been an un-
usual ability in the sixteenth century—deprives the book of
spirit, while his dependence on others, especially Münster,
leaves it little individuality. But his detailed account is none
the less valuable as a topographical-historical treatise. Indeed, it still makes a fine text for the study of German cultural
geography in the sixteenth century.
   Rauw's massive description of Germany follows his much
briefer surveys of England, Spain, and France, and is inter-
rupted by some chapters on Italy, for we must remember that
Rauw leads us around the body of a reclining woman whose
anatomy represents the map of Europe. Her head and chest
having been considered, we now follow the large artery which
has its source under her right breast. This is the Rhine, and
to the strip of Germany which lies west of that river Rauw now
turns. The remainder of Germany forms the lady's abdomen
and will be taken up later, after some attention has been given
to the right arm.
   First come the "Lowlands," by which Rauw means the cities
north of the point where the Main enters the Rhine, beginning
with Mainz.[53] It is Rauw's habit to locate places precisely,

giving the longitude and the latitude in degrees and minutes,
indicating the duration of the longest day, and relating the locality to the physical features of its environment. After Mainz
and the surrounding villages follow the cities to the north. The
Hunsrück is sighted to the west, then Trier, Coblentz, Bonn,
and finally Cologne come into view. There Rauw pauses briefly to record the essential geographic and historical statistics:
position on the map, original settlement by a tribe called Ubii,
the wooden bridge built by Caesar around which the ancient
town grew, the magnificent Cathedral and the nineteen parish
churches, thirteen monastic houses, and fourteen convents.
We also witness once again the procession of the Bishop of
Cologne, already reported by Sebastian Brant in his description of the Rhine valley. There is not enough time for local
history, but upon insistent prodding from his questioner Rauw
obliges with one story. The Bishops of Cologne, it seems, were
always at odds with the city over its political liberties, but all
attempts to wrest their rights from the burghers were defeated
by the community's determined love of freedom. Once, during
a period of bitter struggle, two priests attached to the Cathedral wheedled their way into the confidence of the Lord Mayor.
Pretending to honor him at a banquet they lured him into a hid
den chamber where the Bishop kept a half-starved lion for sin
ister purposes. Pushing the unsuspecting man into this room
the priests closed the door behind him, thinking they had seen
the last of him. But when the crazed animal rushed him, the
Mayor quickly slipped off his cloak, wrapped it about his arm,
and thrust it down the lion's throat, suffocating the beast. Thus
the Mayor survived, but the priests and the Bishop lived but a
brief while thereafter. [54]
   A survey of the Spanish Netherlands follows, and there is
enough leisure for an extended account of the Order of the
Golden Fleece. [55] Then Rauw retraces his steps and pursues
the upper course of the Rhine south of Mainz through Alsace,
where, incidentally, no mention of Franco-German contention
is made, and through Switzerland. In his account of the Swiss
wars for independence Rauw emphasizes the ferocity, not the
heroism, of the Swiss soldiers. His interest does not lie in
wars but in the affairs of the self-reliant cities of the Confederation: Basel, St. Gall, Zurich, and others. Each is described
in a little sketch, as is the country as a whole. One chapter
takes up "Animals of which little is known in our land," others
deal with plants found in the Alps, or with the mountains themselves, though Rauw cannot make his words approximate their
majesty. Nor do the small, crowded, rather awkward woodcuts
with which the printer Nikolaus Bassaeus illustrated the book

stimulate the imagination. The maps, too, are exceptionally
crude and difficult to make out.

In the initial pages of his next major section, on <u>Germania
Magna</u>, that central part of Germany which still lies within its
ancient boundaries,[56] Rauw displays his more skillful side.
A meticulous, carefully considered outline of the ethnic, linguistic, and geographical boundaries of Germany not only elu-
cidates the historical problem of a continental state without
clearly defined physical limits but introduces us to many of
Central Germany's most notable features. Here Rauw is pleased
to elaborate. At the mention of the Hercynian range, that great
forest which once covered most of Germany, the questioner interrupts. "I beg you to inform me," he says, "in some particulars about the situation of this forest and where it is called
the Thuringian forest, where the Bohemian forest, the Harz
forest, the Odenwald, and where the Black Forest."[57] Eager
as always to disentangle knotty geographical problems, Rauw
obliges.

Formerly, he begins, the Hercynian wood extended over all
of Germany, but now it has been lifted in places to make room
for towns and arable fields and orchards, so that modern Germany is second to no part of the world in comeliness. Conse-
quently, the extent of the forest is rather difficult to perceive.
But its topography is this:

> The forest begins near Halberstadt and occupies most of
> the land between the Elbe and the Weser in that latitude.
> ... In the west it turns south along the Weser, covering
> much of Hessen, and in this region it retains its ancient
> name, that is Harz forest.[58] Another section of this forest
> extends east from Thuringia and in the direction of Bohemia,
> and because its center is located in Thuringia it is there
> called the Thuringian forest. Its southeastern end divides
> into two parts; one descends due south to the Main and
> Franconia, the other part makes straight for the Elbe,
> dividing Meissen and Bohemia. For this reason it is re-
> ferred to as the Bohemian forest.
>
> Back in the west, crossing the Main near Mainz, you meet
> still another part of the Hercynian forest right between the
> Main and the Neckar. It is called the <u>Odenwald</u>.... This
> forest provides lumber for the entire Palatinate and part
> of the Rhineland. The logs are floated down the Neckar in-
> to the Rhine. These, however, are not fir trees as in the
> north but oaks, beeches, and birches. Continuing upstream
> along the Neckar, through Württemberg and Swabia, you

will see on your right still another section of the range,
the Black Forest. This is a rugged terrain, mountainous
and wintry,[59] but you also find marvelous grazing land
there. In fact, the peasants of the Black Forest raise such
fine animals that their meat exceeds Hungarian, Bohemian,
and Polish beef in quality. Timber from the Black Forest
supplies the whole Rhine valley as well as Swabia and
Württemberg, the city of Strassburg and all its environs.[60]

A reference to Celtis' authority on the Hercynian range (ninety
years after the publication of the Libri Amorum and the Germania generalis!) concludes the account of the forest which is
made much more explicit later in his survey of the particular
regions that comprise it.

When he has finished with the borders and the defining moun
tain ranges, Rauw concentrates on Germany's great rivers,
proceeding slowly along their courses and enumerating the
cities on the shores. To vary the pace a little, some historical chapters are now introduced: the origin of all Germans as
told by "Berosus"; a long paraphrase of Tacitus on the mores
of the ancient tribes; kings and emperors of medieval Germany
and some scattered events marking their reigns. But enough
has now been said, he concludes, about Germania magna in
general. It is time to take up each of its territorial divisions
in its particularity. What will be the order of exposition, asks
the questioner. Rauw answers:

> We shall start in upper Germany where the Rhine and
> Danube nearly meet and then proceed regularly from west
> to east and from south to north. First we shall locate the
> Duchy of Württemberg, containing a section of Bavaria
> and Swabia between the Danube and the Rhine, and other
> territories nearby. Going north from there we shall come
> to Franconia. Further north we shall reach Hessen. East
> of Hessen lies Thuringia, then comes Meissen, then Bo-
> hemia, Moravia, and Silesia, then as much of Poland as
> lies this side of the Vistula. North again of Hessen we
> find Westphalia and east of that land Saxony, then the Marc
> of Brandenburg. North of Westphalia lie Holland, Frisia,
> and east from there Mecklenburg and Pomerania. The
> northernmost countries are the region of Dittmarschen
> and the land of Denmark. . . . And there you have the divi-
> sions of Germania magna as we shall discover them.[61]

The pattern of the regional descriptions on which Rauw now
embarks varies little. He progresses through each territory
place by place, sketching with a minimum of lines each town's

appearance and character:

> Here you find also a noble city called Rotenburg, located
> on the south bank of the Tauber River, facing Swabia. It
> is a pleasant little place, but it is built high up in the hills
> and looks down on a deep valley where the Tauber has cut
> its bed. Rotenburg once was the seat of a line of Franconian
> Dukes, but when the last of them, Frederick, died in 1172
> the town came under the rule of the Empire. Rotenburg has
> an abundance of wine and fruit, but drinking water is a prob-
> lem because of the high elevation.... [62]

However, no attempt at organic municipal history is made;
events are merely recorded as in the annals. There follows a
chronological outline of the general political history of the entire region with emphasis on the territorial rulers, whose dy-
nasties are often commemorated in lengthy genealogical rosters.
Next comes an economic geography, a discussion of the region's
climate, condition of the soil, flora and fauna, products raised,
and activities carried on. The traits and customs of the local
populace are described in a chapter or two, and the section
here as always closes with a list of individual men of whom
the region is particularly proud.

Nearly three hundred pages are given to this description of
Germany's territorial divisions, not including those outside the
confines of the Rhine-Danube heartland. The newer German
territories beyond the Danube comprise a further section; then
two more long historical chapters conclude the German part
of the Cosmographia, one a list of the principalities and duchies
of the Empire and the other a history of the Christian Church
under the German emperors. There is much closely observed
detail in these pages, often more than is found in Münster. But
there can be no serious question of which is the better description. Rauw's minutiae overwhelm us, while Münster's details
focus our interest. Rauw succumbs to his material by including everything he knows. He cannot guide us to the significant.
Münster is discriminating in the choices he makes, and by se-
lecting his details critically he renders a sharper picture of
each place.

The personal differences between the three cosmographers
and their distinct methods of handling their material should
not obscure the similarity of structure, content, and disposition which marks the great cosmographies. Franck's work
must obviously be judged by its own standard, but even it ad-
heres to the externals of the cosmographical type. In interests,

matters of taste, methods of research and presentation, and
in ultimate conclusions, all three works have a great deal in
common.

There is, above all, a universality of approach and a broad-
mindedness which distinguishes the cosmographies from most
of the more strictly regional writings. Their moderation in
voicing national sentiments has already been noted; in matters
of religion, too, they managed to remain cool in an age in whic
tempers were easily inflamed. To turn out an approved versio
of Münster's Cosmography for Catholic readers, the censors
had only to ink over a few lines of text and paste in an occa-
ional strip of paper.[63] All three writers were also astonish-
ingly free of prejudices toward non-Christian religions. Both
Franck and Münster wrote understanding accounts of Moham-
medanism, and the ways of Turks, Mongols, and even the sav-
age inhabitants of South America are examined with sympathy
Rauw uses strong words only in describing "the loathsome
sect called Anabaptists." Luther is mentioned in no more than
a paragraph in any of the volumes.[64]

It is the same with the folkways of the world, whose depiction makes such rich freight for all three books. There are
evident peculiarities among them, even queerness bound to
cause headshaking, but no judgment is passed, and it is made
explicitly clear that all men are the children of one God. Ther
are even some tentative beginnings of what might be called coi
parative anthropology. The carnival frolics of Franconians re
mind Franck of the Lupercalia of pagan antiquity, and their
Christmas dances around wooden images of the Christ child
of the Roman Saturnalia.[65] Münster makes an elaborate comparison of Spanish and French traits which penetrates beyond
physical appearance, institutions, and occupations, into the
private home, the kitchen, even the marriage bed.[66] But the
ever present implication is that our minds should remain oper
to the ways of peoples everywhere. What may be strange to us
is natural to others, or, as Franck more pithily puts it, "We
must not think all Jews, Turks, and Pagans are fools and sav-
ages, for we find habits as queer as theirs right in our own
back yard."[67]

If the cosmographers draw a general lesson from the vast
scene they survey, it is this equality of all under God. They
marvel at the infinite variety of earthly phenomena, and no
careful reader of their works, nor a casual page-turner, not
even one who has time only to glance at the illustrations, can
fail to be impressed by the endless manifoldness of a world
in which astonishment need never cease and learning never
end. But under this diversity they sense a harmony and unity

which relates all things to the Creator. Nothing, they know, is
steady in human affairs. "What God has made endures, what
man does passes with him."[68] Human history is a sequence of
ups and downs in which all things wax and wane like man himself, who is "born small and insignificant onto this earth, and
then he grows and becomes a person but also ages and declines
from day to day until he falls prostrate to the ground."[69] In
this organic analogy there was at least the comfort of meaning for those who were despondent over the fate of the Empire.[70] To Münster it seemed at times a source of despair.
"Thus it goes," he reflects sadly,

> up and down, it's the truth. Nothing lasts which is in man's
> power and nothing under the sun is permanent. Kingdoms
> and duchies decline and rise again. One city is destroyed
> while another is founded. Whole populations are shifted
> from one country to another. Here a land is desolated,
> there another suddenly loses its fertility. So widely does
> the world veer from side to side that no one is able to tell
> it, and what is worse is that we crumble with the crumbling
> world and are destroyed in its destruction.[71]

But, as has been noted earlier, thoughts of Doomsday were
a matter of temperament. To Münster's constitution they were
not natural, though an occasional bout of despair was doubt-
less brought on by the jolt of a political or confessional calamity. He did not consciously seek an inner meaning in history.
His Cosmographia has a moral but it does not have a philosophy. "God has it in His power to make all the elements obey
Him," he wrote,[72] and that was his and his colleagues' answer
to the "whys" of the universe. What really impresses us in
the cosmographies, as indeed in all writings of German humanism, is not any profundity of thought but the extraordinary
scope of interests and the genuine eagerness to learn which
these men brought to their labors. They meant to be polyhis-
tors in the true sense, excluding nothing from their vision and
permitting little to escape their notice. No conceivable element
of civilization was considered irrelevant to the cosmographer's
task. But to bring all such matters within the range of their
understanding would have been scarcely possible, even for better men than Franck, Münster, and Rauw. They themselves
must have been sadly aware of their shortcomings. Faced
with the magnitude of the undertaking and their own limitations,
they became collectors rather than discoverers; they gathered
and compiled, incorporating what was available and leaving
gaps where nothing could be found.

There was no shame in this. "What can we properly claim

as our own," Solinus had asked, "when the diligence of men in former times has left nothing untouched unto our own day?"[73] With this thought, the cosmographers were in complete agreement. In the final analysis we must take much of their will for some of the deed. We can appreciate the cosmographies as ingenious descriptions of Germany and other parts of the world but we should not forget that the aims of their authors had been higher. Their hopes, at least, enclosed all of nature and all of man's experience between the covers of a stout book.

7

The Chorographies and their Readers

JF BY CHANCE we might locate somewhere a patient and inquisitive reader whose curiosity had carried him through the works of Kantzow, of Fabri and Brant, of Stumpf, Guler von Weineck, and Münster and Rauw, he would surely say, if we queried him, that there was now little to be added to these volumes. Germany was as thoroughly described as the fact-finding techniques of the age permitted and the attractiveness of her landscape merited. Through the dedicated labors of many men, Germany's tradition and character had been revealed. Her ancient roots and her living likeness had been told in words and pictures and maps to instruct and ennoble the minds of fellow men.

The topographical-historical books contained such riches that it would take half a century to digest them. The fat volumes which the variety of approaches and versatility of interests now demanded from even a local chorographer could hardly be excelled. What was needed now was not a new series of mighty tomes like Guler's and Rauw's, but lighter, more carefully edited fare. That was the conclusion of one cosmographer, Matthias Quad, at the very end of the century, when a terminal point in the development of the chorography seems to have been reached.[1] Quad knew the literature of his field better than most, and he must have been aware that his wish had already become deed. His own <u>Cosmographical Handbook</u> is a miniature cosmography, so identical in aim and method with the major works that it seems drawn to scale. Its expressed purpose was to teach the principles of the craft, and in this effort Quad was following a tradition. Rudolf Agricola's little treatise on the curriculum, the fountainhead of humanist education in Germany, gave as early as 1484 an approving nod in the direction of chorography.[2] Johann Cochlaeus, master of St. Lawrence School at Nuremberg, also held that geographical matters should be part of every educational program. "Let them please remember," he said, speaking of some who might object, "that the entire subject matter of this science can be perceived by the senses and that learning will come easily to students if the instructor explains everything carefully and uses his maps for visual demonstration"[3] The "Concise Description of Germany" which Cochlaeus appended to his textbook edition of Pomponius Mela is a primer for such teaching. It is also, like Quad's treatise, but eighty-seven years before it, a small-scale chorography, casting swift glances at the past and modern history of Germany, at institutions and folkways, at the pleasant appearance and bounty of her lands and her proud cities. When read with Cochlaeus' introductory syllabuses to general geography[4] it provides not only formal but stimulating instruction. In his six years of teaching, Cochlaeus must have drilled the rudiments of geography into many minds which later turned with pleasure to the art of chorography. His influence, at Nuremberg at least, was abiding. So was Vadian's at Vienna and St. Gall[5] and Michael Neander's at the celebrated school at Ilfeld. Neander's Cosmography, his own text for his lecture in geography,[6] assumes many of the tenets of chorographical writing as they had been stated by the greater masters. Topography and chronology, Neander asserts, are the two eyes through which we apprehend our world and, to change the metaphor, the keys which open the locks to all knowledge. They are our first steps in the learning process. His book is a chorography of the world in small format, but here again, Germany receives most favored attention.[7] Brevity is demanded by the purpose, but every feature of the chorographic form is there, clearly indicated though sparsely documented. In an especially comprehensive bibliographical section Neander lists the sources from which works such as his are compiled, partly to secure his own authority but perhaps also to suggest some further reading for his students' leisure hours.

When the gap between scholarship and textbooks has been closed, when the principles of chorography have been embraced by elementary works, we are justified in concluding that their acceptance has become universal. The step from informal to formal teaching was, of course, a natural one. The moving spirits of the genre had always aimed at the opening of new horizons to their readers. Man's mind, they assumed, was as capable of expansion as the world is large. At the end of the century there was no one whose life was so rushed or so leisurely, no one whose knowledge was so rudimentary or whose capacity for learning was so great, that he could not have found a chorography to suit his taste.

COSMOGRAPHIA,
Das ist:

Ein schöne, richtige vnd volkomliche

Beschreibung deß Göttlichen Geschöpffs /

Himmels vnd der Erden / beydes der Himmlischen vnd Jrdischen Kugel/ Wie die Himmlische in jre Circulos vnd Sphæras, vnd die Jrdische in jhre Theil/ Europam, Asiam vnd Aphricam, beneben Americam, vnd ein jedes Theil widerumb in seine vornemliche Königreiche vnd Landschafften dispescieret vnd getheilet wirdt.

Item / Was für vorneme Berge / Wasser / Stätte vnd dergleichen / in jeder Landschafften befunden: Was von anfang für Völcker dieselbigen bewohnet / Auch was für Sitten / Gebräuche vnd Religion sie gehabt: Deßgleichen was für Regenten von anfang biß auff diese gegenwertige Zeit / vber solche Länder regieret haben.

Sampt ingesprengten schönen / herrlichen vnd nützlichen Historien / an welchem Ort / vnd zu welcher Zeit dieselbigen geschehen seynd / Auch mit sehr schönen Figuren / Kupfferstücken / vnd Landtaffeln gezieret vnd geschmücket.

Alles fein richtig vnd ordentlich / vnd damit es dem Leser desto anmütiger seyn möchte / in richtige Fragen vnd Antwort gestellet / zum fleissigsten beschrieben / vnd in Truck gegeben / Durch

Den Ehrwirdigen vnd Wolgelährten Herrn Johann Rauwen
Meimbressensem, Pfarrherrn zu Wetter in Hessen.

Mit sonderlichen Röm. Keys. Maj. Privilegien vnd Freyheiten / auff zehen Jahr nicht nachzutrucken / begnadet.

Getruckt zu Franckfort am Mayn / durch Nicolaum Basssæum.

M. D. XCVII.

Title page of Johann Rauw's Cosmographia (Frankfurt, 1597).

"If you follow attentively the deeds, events, and objects which are mentioned in this book you will think that they have all come alive," boasted an advertising broadside of around 1500.[8] But no extravagant claims were needed to sell chorographic works. They were immensely popular throughout the century.[9] Every device known to the printer's trade was used to make the form as attractive as its content. Ease of scanning and of locating references was assured by the use of varying types of heads and subheads, by excellent indexes and detailed tables of contents. Careful attention was given to marginal summaries of long paragraphs.[10] Running heads at the top of each page "enable the reader to grasp at a glance what he is looking at."[11] Condensations and epitomes of the bulkier works placed at least the gist of the chorographies in the hands of those who did not have the purchase price or the time to expend upon the originals.

As books were now produced for a particular market, such digests found a ready outlet. Brevity, as some of our writers often observed, became a virtue in the trade. Cochlaeus, though his description of Germany is held to the barest minimum, still apologizes for its length,[12] and Quad sympathizes with the common man who might find his distance from the volumes of the great cosmographers increased by their size. "So large and fat have they become that they are too dear for some, too dense for others, and too heavy for any of us to carry. No one could get through one of these books in a year!"[13] Many publishers felt as did Quad, that to re-edit or translate the long works "would have been tediouse to my selfe, superfluouse to the reader, and very chargeable to the byer."[14] While the learned thought of expanding Münster and of translating Stumpf into Latin,[15] the condensations multiplied as the genre became ever more popular. Though the epitomizers rarely caught the substance of the works they reduced, their compendiums at least reached a wider circle of readers, none of them scholars but many of them perhaps men of affairs, or even of toil, to whom it made sense that

> You need not any longer now
> Peruse great tomes with furrowed brow;
> You save yourself much strain, and may
> Employ your time another way.[16]

But a great many people had little better use for their leisure moments than to lose themselves in the wonders of the world as they were revealed in the great descriptive works. And they were handsome volumes to look at, these chorographies and cosmographies, with their heavy beveled and sometimes em-

bossed boards, their title pages either neat and geometric
with curt Latin type or all curves and curlicues of interlaced
Gothic characters, with likely as not a line or two in red, and
the title winding its way down the page, describing as fully as
space permitted just what the book contained. On the heavy
but supple leaves inside, the print was crowded, but the narrative unfolded rapidly, and much of it was told in pictures —
woodcuts in square and rectangular frames which formed
patterns on the page and refreshed the eye.

To us, as we look at them today, these frames are little windows into the sixteenth century. We cannot fail to notice how
close these woodcuts are to the spirit of the works they illustrate. Canons of aesthetics were not involved in their conception; there is not much elegance in them, and only the best,
the products of a Hans Leonhard Schauffelin, a Burgkmair, or
a Wolgemuth, are in any sense works of art. Like the writers,
the artisans who engraved their wood blocks in the shops of
the printers experienced nature and life directly and with a
matter-of-fact naïveté. Their purpose was to give visual expression to the words of the author, to illustrate as plainly as
possible the essentials of the story he told. They were not
themselves creative artists, and to criticize them for lack of
aesthetic feeling or perfection of form is to miss the point.
The object of the artisan was to summarize the essence of a
description or of an incident. Landscapes are not idealized,
nor are they topographically exact. They are shown in epitom-
they are stylized. A tree is stem and crown. A craggy rock
represents the Alpine summits. Distant mountains are shaded
molehills, as they are on maps. The human figure is crudely
sketched, anatomy barely indicated. But the use of artistic
shorthand stops there. Details of costuming, of furnishings,
of utensils and implements are painstakingly exact. Streets,
rows of houses, public buildings, fortifications, and suburban
structures are precisely drawn. The surrounding landscape is
suggested in general outline, but the city itself is rendered
with photographic realism.

We know how a draftsman went about the depiction of a city
If a free conception was desired, he took up a position on a
neighboring hill and drew the architectural features which
struck his eye: towers and churches, the town hall, the bridge
These are exaggerated in size; the rest shrinks into a few roof houses. But this method was soon abandoned in favor of a
more exact one. The draftsman, with the aid of his assistants
now surveyed, measured, and sketched the length and breadth
of the town, its walls, streets, and houses, and then retired to
his studio to reconstruct the profile from the drawings and

figures. The Swiss artist Hans Aspers, for example, when commissioned to furnish a drawing of Solothurn, first portrayed
the city "in the simplest possible manner, as one looks from
far at a town and sees only the highest towers, the most prominent houses, walls, and roofs." But as he reflected on the antiquity and fame of the municipality he decided to do instead
a close profile. He and his two helpers therefore walked about
the city, measuring every detail of its plan and structures, and
these notes he took to Zurich, where the drawing was completed. [17]

The depictions which resulted from this method were both
ground plan and prospect because the measurements and
sketches made at various stations in the city resulted in mul-
tiple points of view. But they were always true representations. [18] The city spreads out before us in a broad sweep, each
quarter, each block of houses given equal weight. A citizen
would have no difficulty in recognizing the familiar ramparts,
the bell tower, the public gardens, his own residence if it stood
in an exposed place. After Stumpf's and Münster's great works,
with their many fine double pages of German cities, had found
a public, it was no longer possible to fake municipal drawings [19] or, as in Hartmann Schedel's Chronicle of 1493, to pass
off half the view of Magdeburg as the city of Paris. [20] When
Matthew Merian, in the next century, planned his sumptuous
volumes on the cities of Germany, he needed to devise no new
method for their representation.

More numerous in these volumes than city profiles and occasional drawings of natural settings are inset cuts depicting
incidents or individuals mentioned in the text. For the illustration of historical personalities, standard heads had to suffice for all but the most prominent contemporaries, a firm
visage with set chin for leaders of men, an observing eye on
an astrolabe for a mathematician or world traveler, a brooding mien for philosophers, religious reformers, and poets.
The reader is soon reconciled to recognizing in "Gutenberg"
the same face he studied a while back as "Albertus Magnus"
and before that as "Ptolemaeus." Infinitely more varied are
the visual comments on narrative portions of the text. Econ-
omy, of course, dictated that illustrations serve many needs,
and we find stock cuts used over and over again. But verisi-
militude and a feeling for the spirit of the narrative were also
important. That is why Stumpf's printer, Christoph Froschauer,
asked him to let the artist see the manuscript for which he was
to execute the blocks, "so that he, the artist, may read it himself, the better to be able to illustrate it." [21]

Illustrations were employed mainly to provide a respite for

eyes and mind fatigued with reading, and to add emphasis. In
the more lavish works there are few pages without woodcuts.
Individuals are shown, of course, and so are the climactic
events: coronations, sieges and sacks of fortified towns, effects of a pestilence. Other cuts illustrate in the proper sense
The printing press, animals and plants, a thatched hut in Africa, the court dress of a noble Spanish lady, and the loin
cloth of an East Indian islander are shown. The Rhine bridge
at Strassburg, a trawler fishing out of Stralsund, the ruins of
an ancient fortification, the fearful aspect of an upper Alpine
peak—these provide documentation for descriptive passages.
The scene in the courtyard at Canossa adds accent to that unhappy tale. By the middle of the century the reading public had
come to expect abundance and variety of visual attractions,[22]
and the natural competition among publishers tended to encourage the production of more and more lavish books as the
century progressed.

But public eagerness for visual excitement was capable of
exploitation, and nowhere was this more apparent than in the
growing tendency of publishers to cater to their public's taste
for the sensational and the gruesome. With what anticipation
a reader must have turned page 1049 of Münster's Cosmographia on which he had just learned of an especially refined
form of punishment devised by Alexander for a Bactrian usurp
er, to find it all illustrated on the reverse side! What deliciou
shudders he must have felt as he followed the true story of a
double axe murder perpetrated at Basel in 1565 and now spun
out over two full folio pages by Christian Wurstisen![23] How
it must have pleased at least some of the purchasers of the
one-volume edition of Stumpf's work to see that though the
number of woodcuts had been cut down drastically from the
larger first edition to save expense, nearly all the drawings
of slaughter, arson, and torture were still in place! Münster's
books bristle with descriptions of battles, and the documentar
views of carnage abound in lances that pierce chests, bodies
mangled under the hooves of charging horses, hands, legs, and
heads severed by swords swung wildly in the heat of hand-to-
hand combat. The effect of firearms is also convincingly dem
onstrated, though Münster, on another page, indignantly reject
the allegation that it was the Germans who invented them.[24] T
reports of the conquests of the New World intensified this mo
bid taste, just as the marvels of Mandeville had left their mar
on earlier geographical books. We need only thumb through
the consecutive editions of the new descriptions of America
and its inhabitants to realize the hold which accounts of barbarities had on readers. Hans Staden's experiences among the

"wild, naked, and ferocious cannibals" are illustrated at first
by crude woodcuts which showed much, but also left a good
deal for the mind to wonder about. In later editions of the work
these are made more and more gruesomely realistic until, in
De Bry's <u>Voyages</u> of 1600, in which Staden's text is included,
the copper engravings are so explicit as to leave absolutely
nothing to the imagination.

And then there are the monsters, those awesome inventions
of fertile imaginations, of which every chorographic work carries its share. Sebastian Münster, a rational soul, had never
beheld any such creatures and did not really think they existed.
"The ancients tell of such <u>monstra</u>, but I have never found a
reliable person who has seen one," he writes.[25] Yet there they
are, ten or twelve grotesque freaks tumbling down the page—
dragons breathing fire and lashing their tails, griffins and
werewolves, headless men, creatures with ears dragging on
the ground behind them or resting in the shade of one gigantic
foot.[26] The author did not believe in them, but the reader got
to see them anyway.

Such fascination with the abnormal is, of course, but a per-
version of a very real and absorbing concern with cultural
comparisons. The customs of groups of men in Germany and
in foreign countries were forever a source of interest, not
only for their queerness, but for the common or disparate
traditions they reflected and for what they revealed about geographic and climatic influences on minds and instincts of
peoples. The essence of men, the chorographers believed, is
revealed in their habits. Clothing, funeral celebrations, and
bridal songs are concrete expressions of the character of a
people. If we hear that the sartorial elegance of Frenchmen
takes a different direction each year while female fashions
change hardly at all,[27] we have surely learned something about
the French. If we can prove that the pithy, masculine speech
of the Germans is due to the northern latitude of their country
which "strengthens the breath," while "inhabitants of more
southerly climes, whose internal heat is low, are accustomed
to mild and mellifluous pronunciation,"[28] are we not then
able to make further observations regarding distinctions between the two peoples? Can we not also draw general conclusions about the influence of climate?

The man who made it possible for chorographic writers to
draw such conclusions was Johann Boemus of the little town
of Aub, near Würzburg. In 1520, Boemus published a concise
volume on <u>The Customs, Institutions, and Fashions of All
Peoples</u>,[29] which served the entire century as a generous
source of ethnological information. Boemus' own summing up

was that of the cosmographical writers: God has given each
man a life to lead. God has also given to each man a task to
perform. It is the responsibility of every member of the human race to respect the way of life of his fellow and, in turn,
to be content with his own lot.[30] The weight of this judgment
rests on the evidence which Boemus presents in his book, none
of it brought to light by himself but material which "famous
writers have confusedly and separately treated in their commentaries," and which he has now "collected and digested so
as to make of all subjects one book."[31]

   This is a modest statement. Boemus is far more than the
compiler he makes himself out to be. His conviction about the
responsibility of men to themselves and to each other arises
from his insight into their ways of life. In his book he compares the customs of different peoples and those of the same
people at different times, ranging over the whole inhabited
earth before coming to Germany.[32] Here the patchwork of territorial mores is an evident delight to him. Nothing is without
interest—the special cloth woven in Swabia whose warp is lin-
en and whose woof silk; the diet of Saxon infants, not pap or
cereal but stronger stuff, pre-chewed by their nurses ("that
sort of food makes the Saxons so sturdy," he comments); and
the Lenten frolics of Franconian youths, with an effigy of death
and a fiery cart wheel. But the chorographic writers who read
and excerpted Boemus received more from him than the data
he had collected. His careful judgments suggested an approach
and his thoroughness a method. His importance to them is not
always acknowledged—lifting the material of others was a
carefree process, and a line between borrowing and plagia-
rism could hardly be drawn—but his influence is easily established. Many writers quote him verbatim, while others
draw on him freely. His cheerful and judicious observations
meet us again and again as we follow the literature through
the century, and his diverting style set a high standard of exposition.

   Good description, of course, was a quality much to be prized
Lively prose, aptness of characterization, and vividness of detail made a success of the chorographic attempt; when these
were absent the result was less than stimulating. No one would
claim that the topographical-historical writers, as a group,
were notable stylists. Many were without skill in the use of
words, and others aimed at nothing more than transmission
of facts. But not a few knew the power of forthrightness and
were adept at evocative description. These men, especially
when they dealt with matters close to their hearts, and most
notably when they wrote in German, leave a strong impression

with the reader. The pithiness of Aventinus' style, the high coloration of Guler's scenic descriptions, the four-square integrity of Stumpf's comments on the historical scene—these belong with the best writing produced in the German language in early modern times, and are not unfit to be read while the sound of Luther's vigorous prose rings in one's ears.[33]

Ethnological studies depended on deft presentation. Even more did impressions of the natural scene rest upon the skill with which a visual image could be translated into language. More than precise expression was required, for the vision of a landscape could arise only from words which carried,in addition to exact meaning, the secondary qualities of sight and sound. The German humanists, to be sure, had a model for their descriptive writing in Enea Silvio's ingenious vignettes. But how was Enea's personal style to be assimilated? It had become a convention of chorography to invoke the physical attractions of one's land, but this practice quickly stiffened into a formal obligation in which the writer took his theme from stock adjectives and in which a genuine sense of beauty need play no role at all. Nor would Dürer's admonition that "the more exactly you imitate nature and life the better and more artful will your work turn out"[34] guarantee success. It was not a matter of copying reality but of communicating its sensation.

Was scenic beauty not a concern of the German chorographers? Of one group it may be confidently stated that it was not. The humanists of the old _Germania illustrata_ school had been too preoccupied with antiquarian researches and political assertions to mark the charms of nature. Celtis' descriptions of the Carpathians, the Neckar, and other abodes of his itinerant life were acute and often nicely put, but his views of forests and rivers and storms on the North Sea were engulfed in nature mysticism and given to epic statement. There are exceptions, of course, but ordinarily it is size or antiquity or historical association which moves the men of his school to rapture. It seems that a real appreciation of the natural setting and a more than rudimentary talent for suggesting it to the distant reader were present in only one group of writers, the Swiss. What the striking character of the Swiss landscape contributed to this collective talent must remain a conjecture. Striking scenery was certainly not absent in the north. But it is a fact that in Kantzow's picturesque descriptions, in Albinus' precise sketches of the eastern mining country, and in Cuspinian's views of the Danube valley, there is little or no revelation of the living beauty of the natural setting.

Page upon page of Guler von Weineck's superb _Raetia_ should

be reproduced here to show how extraordinarily vivid scenic
description could be. Not only is Guler's book a masterful re-
creation of a country's culture, but his descriptive skill is
so great that the vision he conjures up before the mind's eye
is full of substance and life. This is almost as true of other
Swiss chorographers. In Münster's descriptions of Alpine
glaciers and of the falls at Schaffhausen, nature is seen to
possess a reality independent of the spectator. Wurstisen's
view of the surroundings of Basel holds a joy of experience
rarely found in the writings of the northern chorographers.
Even such a bibliophile and antiquary as Conrad Gesner, who
in his forty-nine years published twenty-seven volumes and
left eighteen others unfinished, showed that life-long occupation with dead things need not dull one's senses to the beauties
of nature. In the dedicatory letter to one of his many works,[35]
Gesner speaks glowingly of his feelings for the majestic scenery of the Alps:

> I have determined for the future...each year to ascend a
> few mountains, or at least one,[36] when the vegetation is
> flourishing, partly to become acquainted with the latter,
> partly for the sake of suitable bodily exercise and the de-
> light of the spirit. For how great the pleasure, how great,
> think you, are the joys of the spirit, touched as is fit it
> should be, in wondering at the mighty mass of mountains
> while gazing upon their immensity and, as it were, in lift-
> ing one's head above the clouds! In some way or other the
> mind is overturned by their dizzying height and is caught
> up in contemplation of the Supreme Architect.[37]

When, some years later, he ascended the notorious Mount
Pilatus (the same peak which Vadian and three other Swiss
men of letters had scaled in 1518 in order to dispel a popular
superstition that Pontius Pilate lurked above the waters of a
shallow lake just below the summit), he set down a careful record of the climb and of the plant and animal life he observed
along the route of approach.[38] But we are more impressed by
the lonely dignity of the mountain itself as he conveys it to us.
He has a sense of color and of form, an ear for the song of
birds and for the momentous silence of the vast spaces around
him. Each of his senses reaches out for impressions of the Alpine heights, and in his agitation he felt compelled then and
there to plan a large volume on the majesty of the Alps. It was
never written, but his few extant descriptive passages go far
to suggest the beauty of the mountainous land in which he lived.
    The ordinary chorographic writer, however, felt that his
craft demanded precision rather than imagination. He avoided

no labor to achieve accuracy and integrity of statement, and sought to develop an expository style at once sober and communicative. It is this fusion of sound workmanship and popular appeal which most distinguishes the topographical-historical genre. An attractive, even diverting form was never allowed to drain the substance of its solidity, while no subject was considered so arcane that it could not be simply stated. Esoterics were avoided, not merely for the sake of the reading public, but because those German humanists who were most active in the genre lacked the intellectual subtlety to grapple with questions of theology and philosophy.[39] The scientific aspects of their craft had already been simplified for them. The rest was description.

A lack of depth and intellectual sophistication will be only too obvious to a reader who comes to these authors from the literature of the Italian renaissance. Political analysis, for example, is hardly to be found. The form of their works presented German writers with innumerable opportunities to study and compare the constitutions, the governments of their territories and cities. Describe them they did; that was part of their task. But they were not tempted to organize their comments into statements of political theory. Not one of the sixteenth-century writers rose above Felix Fabri's informative but uncritical sketch of the municipal government of Ulm. Most of these men were, of course, preoccupied with the religious developments of their age. Vadian, Stumpf, Pirckheimer, Münster, to say nothing of Franck and Aventinus, could see none but confessional links in the chain of causes and effects. Had they lived a century before their time they might well, like the Florentine historians, have examined their political institutions with greater insight. As it was, analysis and interpretation were trained on matters not directly related to the theme of chorography.

But here, too, our authors reflect the temper of the environment in which they lived. Their strengths as well as their weaknesses were those of the time. An unmistakable bond of comradeship united writers and readers of the chorographies. Figuratively and literally, they spoke the same language. That is why the most effective volumes were those written in German; Kantzow, Brant, Stumpf, Münster, Guler speak with a stronger voice than Krantz and Cuspinian.

Before the sixteenth century was half over, the prejudice of Celtis and his group against the use of German[40] had all but vanished. It was still a source of vexation that books written in the mother tongue remained closed to the learned world at large, but to many it seemed a disgrace that so little knowledge

of history and geography had been brought to those ignorant
of Latin.[41] From the days of Rudolf Agricola, who urged the
scholar to practice expressing himself in the vernacular,[42]
there had been many who regarded German as a fit vehicle
for serious thought. Others harbored a sentimental attachment
to the language of their infancy. Felix Fabri speaks with fervor, though in Latin, of his regard for "the noblest, most distinguished, most humane of tongues,"[43] and Wimpheling could
wax vehement on the kind of German who denies his native
speech.[44] The chorographic writers were far from this denial.
Though some were less practiced in German than they were
in Latin,[45] and all had acquired their professional competence
in the learned tongue, they were unashamed to employ the vernacular when the purpose was right. Theirs was "plain and
earthy speech, not the stilted style of the chancery,"[46] and it
was the force of this speech which drew the reader into the
chorographer's orbit and held him there until the lore of the
book could weave its own invisible ties to bind him captive.
The nature of the material and the tone of presentation are in-
separable, and it is in this consonance that the chorographies
attain that unity which makes the best of them almost works
of art.

But was it only the spell of the wide world and its denizens
which brought men and women of the sixteenth century to the
brimming pages of these books? The fascination was, of course
in what was written there of the places and peoples and animals
and things in this world. But beyond the excitement of all this,
beyond the color and variety which the chorographic form held
these books breathe an assertive spirit and speak with such
buoyancy that they are a joy to the heart as they are a pleasure
to the mind. The occasional resignation of a Münster was not
everyone's reaction to the age. Münster's dark despair, the
causes of which are not hard to find, reflects a temperament
less balanced by hope and trust than the constitutions of his
colleagues; and even Münster did not often surrender to his
despondent moods.

To most of their authors the chorographies were proof of
the vitality of existence, and expression of the hope with which
life eternally returns. Their eyes were not closed to the dis-
tress of their century, but they could see bright spots through
the gloom. Was theirs not the age in which Gutenberg and
Regiomontanus and Peurbach had placed knowledge on a surer
foundation?[47] Had not the art of medicine made enormous progress with a Paracelsus? Could not all languages now be studie
with ease? Were not painting and sculpture at their summit?
And did not their skill in the practical arts, of which former

generations had been wholly ignorant, make men masters over their environment?[48] All this seemed to suggest that a new Golden Age was only a step away,[49] and this Golden Age would be one whose blessings every individual, wise or simple, might reap. For learning was now so well assimilated that knowledge was within the grasp of every man:

> By the grace of God the liberal arts and useful skills have now scaled such heights—and still they wax, we all can see it—and so many clever, learned, and experienced scholars have studied and collected them that what in former days even the experts could not master, can in our time be understood by plain ordinary and scarcely half-learned men. There will come a time when none of the secrets of nature will be out of the reach of the human mind.[50]

The optimism of the humanist community was founded on this faith in the never-ending advance of the human spirit. With simple conviction these men saw it as God's high purpose that the achievements of the mind were to be the key to all problems, the answer to all enigmas. And that Golden Age which they thought they could see in the near future was the triumph of the intellect over ignorance and confusion. But here was a conflict and, perhaps, a contradiction. The ethical orientation of the German humanists, one of their very strong directive forces, had its fixed anchorage in the past, in the pristine existence of the Germanic tribes in a natural state. There, under the oaks of the German forests, as once before in the Eden of Genesis, had existed another age of perfection, "a time when the world was still golden and men kept faith,"[51] another Golden Age. Its scenes of idyllic contentment were vivid in the minds of the men of the century,[52] and a description of it might be found in the opening chapters of almost any cosmographic book:

> And in the Golden Age men lived in such quiet and lovely contemplation that strife and argument were not even known to them. For then mankind cared about wisdom and the useful arts, lived honestly and without affectation, and decided all matters not through might or law but in justice and decency.[53]

In its simplicity and harmony this ancient age of the Book of Genesis and the <u>Germania</u> seemed indeed ideal to many men, and their own world, by contrast, appeared crass and callous. Who, having once suffered the affronts of his fellow man, would not nostalgically look back to an era when men were

true to themselves and kind to one another? But it was an uneasy thought that such purity had depended on the absence of
those very attainments of the intellect whose advance was at
present heralding a new and more fortunate time. If man was
once pristinely good it was the exercise of his reason which
had corrupted his innocence, and in the expansion of this very
same faculty the humanists now saw their brightest hopes for
the future.

Few writers came to struggle with this logical perplexity,
and those who did could not free their discussions of internal
contradictions. Boemus and Münster both argued the dignity
of life under a primitive order,

> when men lived simply, even crudely, when they had no
> use for minted coins, for professions and commerce, but
> bartered this for that and requited one act of kindness with
> another. No one owned anything that he could call his pro-
> perty; earth and water were free as the air and the sky
> are free. No one then strove for earthly riches, for each
> was satisfied with what nature accorded him: to find a soft
> spot under a shady tree to serve him and his wife and dear
> children as refuge, to obtain honest nourishment from the
> fruits of the field and the milk of the animals, to clothe
> their nakedness with the broad leaves of trees.... [54]

But this paradise did not last. For some reason the fertility
of the soil gave out, animals began to maraud and "men from
foreign lands" [55] disturbed the peace. Then was the soil appor-
tioned, plots given to heads of households, while men gathered
in cities, built walls and moats, and elected governors over
themselves to keep law and order. [56] This happened, we are
given to understand, through necessity. The blissful life in the
Cockayne of the woods of Germany was reluctantly relinquished

But as soon as its abandonment has been told, our authors
shift their point of view. It is suddenly the future, no longer
the golden past, that draws their eager gaze, and this is how
the past is remembered:

> Laying aside all crude barbarism and beastly cruelty, ab-
> staining from mutual slaughter, from devouring human
> flesh, from rape and robbery, from incestuous mating of
> children with parents ... and from many more such prac-
> tices, they now applied their reason and skill to rehabili-
> tate the earth. [57]

Where was that "quiet and lovely contemplation," we wonder,
while all this was going on! It is hidden in silence from now
on, but Boemus is not disturbed by the logical flaw. He reports

that from that moment the earth once again became fertile,
everywhere the landscape blossomed out in unsuspected beauty. Habitations adorned the valleys, towers capped mountain
tops, water was pumped into towns, dams were built to re-
strain streams, bridges to span them. It was not long before
earth once again resembled that garden from which our first
parents had been ejected.[58] Arts and sciences were discovered
and brought each to its perfection by clever men. A truly
blessed life was inaugurated, and if the religious divisions of
the century which Satan. in his jealousy of man's good fortune,
has now aroused,[59] do not compel men to destroy one another,
the good life, Boemus thinks, will never end.[60]

But the deeper questions raised by the backward glance into
a long-departed age were not to be silenced. Had its moral
blamelessness no lesson for the present? Was there among
its guileless ways no corrective for modern ills? Could the
moral degeneration which Aventinus, Franck, Stumpf, and
Münster found in their surveys of country and people in their
own time, be avoided by eyes lifted to look into the future?
Could voices raised in a joyous greeting to the New Age drown
out the undertone of greed and perfidy to which the calamities
which beset their generation were due?[61] No German humanist
was insensitive to the implications of these challenges. They
would not, could not, evade the moral responsibility which
their understanding of the past imposed on them. Their age
needed "a second Tacitus" to draw a fresh moral order from
the strength and wholesomeness of Germanic antiquity. In some
way the ethics of the ancestors must be combined with the cultural sensitivity for which the humanists strove. The mores
maiores must be infused into the studia humanitatis, and the
new culture must not only be brilliant, but good.

It was in the hope of the realization of this lofty aim that
the chorographers invited their readers to be in good spirits.
Their own pleas for rectitude and industry, they knew well,
would not go far in turning the minds and hearts of their compatriots. But the real message they conveyed to their readers
was one of good cheer. Here was their country, favored beyond measure by God and nature, peopled with a race of ancient virtue, and lovingly built up by sturdy and capable men.
And as they saw this Germany spread out in the panoramic
view of the chorographies, and contemplated its material and
spiritual riches, the future, though seen from a time of ten-
sion, must have seemed bright with promise.

Appendix, Notes, Bibliographical Remarks, and Index

Abbreviations

ADB   Allgemeine deutsche Biographie

Bibl. d. lit. Ver. St.   Bibliothek des literarischen
                             Vereins in Stuttgart

HZ   Historische Zeitschrift

Qu. schw. Gesch.   Quellen zur schweizer Geschichte

Appendix

1. STRABO ON GERMANY

Geography, VII, 1, ii—v; 2, i—iv
Horace Leonard Jones, ed. & tr.
Loeb Library Edition.

Now the parts beyond the Rhenus, immediately after the country of the Celti, slope towards the east and are occupied by the Germans, who, though they vary slightly from the Celtic stock in that they are wilder, taller, and have yellower hair, are in all other respects similar, for in build, habits, and modes of life they are such as I have said the Celti are. And I also think that it was for this reason that the Romans assigned to them the name "Germani," as though they wished to indicate thereby that they were "genuine" Galatae, for in the language of the Romans "germani" means "genuine."

The first parts of this country are those that are next to the Rhenus, beginning at its source and extending as far as its outlet; and this stretch of river land taken as a whole is approximately the breadth of the country on its western side.... After the people who live along the river come the other tribes that live between the Rhenus and the river Albis [Elbe], which latter flows approximately parallel to the former, towards the ocean, and traverses no less territory than the former. Between the two are other navigable rivers also (among them the Amasias [Ems] on which Drusus won a naval victory over the Bructeri), which likewise flow from the south towards the north and the ocean; for the country is elevated towards the south and forms a mountain chain that connects with the Alps; and in truth some declare that they actually are a part of the Alps, both because of their aforesaid position and of the fact that they produce the same timber; however the country in this region does not rise to a sufficient height for that. Here,

too, is the Hercynian Forest [Black Forest, Harz, woods of
Westphalia and Nassau], and also the tribes of the Suevi, some
of which dwell inside the forest, as, for instance, the tribes
of the Coldui, in whose territory is Boihaemum, the domain
of Marabodus, the place whither he caused to migrate, not only
several other peoples, but in particular the Marcomanni, his
fellow-tribesmen;...However, while some of the tribes of the
Suevi dwell inside the forest, as I was saying, others dwell out
side of it, and have a common boundary with the Getae....It
is a common characteristic of all the peoples in this part of
the world that they migrate with ease, because of the meagre-
ness of their livelihood and because they do not till the soil or
even store up food, but live in small huts that are merely temporary structures; and they live for the most part off their
flocks, as the Nomads do, so that, in imitation of the Nomads,
they load their household belongings on their wagons and with
their beasts turn whithersoever they think best. But other German tribes are still more indigent. I mean the Cherusci, the
Chatti, the Gamabrivii, and the Chattuarii, and also, near the
ocean, the Sugambri, the Chaubi, the Bructeri, and the Cimbri,
and also the Cauci, the Caulci, the Camsiani, and several others. Both the Visurgis [Weser] and the Lupias [Lippe] rivers
run in the same direction as the Amasias, the Lupias being
about 600 stadia distant from the Rhenus and flowing through
the country of the Lesser Bructeri. Germany has also the Sala
river [Thuringian Saale]; and it was between the Salas and
the Rhenus that Drusus Germanicus, while he was successfully
carrying on the war, came to his end.

. . . .

These tribes have become known through their wars with the
Romans, in which they would either yield and then later revolt
again, or else quit their settlements; and they would have been
better known if Augustus had allowed his generals to cross the
Albis in pursuit of those who emigrated thither. But as a matter of fact he supposed that he could conduct the war in hand
more successfully if he should hold off from those outside the
Albis, who were living in peace, and should not incite them to
make common cause with the others in their enmity against
him....In dealing with these peoples distrust has been a great
advantage, whereas those who have been trusted have done the
greatest harm, as, for instance, the Cherusci and their subjects, in whose country three Roman legions, with their general Quintilius Varus, were destroyed by ambush in violation
of the treaty.

. . . .

The Hercynian Forest is not only rather dense, but also has large trees, and comprises a large circuit within regions that are fortified by nature; in the center of it, however, lies a country (of which I have already spoken) that is capable of affording an excellent livelihood. And near it are the sources of both the Ister and the Rhenus, as also the lake [Lake Constance, Bodensee] between the two sources, and the marshes [the Untersee] into which the Rhenus spreads. The perimeter of the lake is more than 300 stadia, while the passage across it is nearly 200. [Now the length is 46.5 miles (from Bregenz to Stein am Rhein) and the greatest width 10.5 miles.] There is also an island in it which Tiberius used as a base of operations in his naval battle with the Vindelici. This lake is south of the sources of the Ister, as is also the Hercynian Forest, so that necessarily, in going from Celtica to the Hercynian Forest, one first crosses the lake and then the Ister, and from there one advances through more passable regions—plateaux—to the forest. Tiberius had proceeded only a day's journey from the lake when he saw the sources of the Ister. The country of the Raeti adjoins the lake for only a short distance, whereas that of the Helvetii and the Vindelici, and also the desert of the Boii, adjoin the greater part of it. All the peoples as far as the Pannonii, but more especially the Helvetii and the Vindelici, inhabit plateaux. But the countries of the Raeti and the Norici extend as far as the passes over the Alps and verge toward Italy, a part of it bordering on the country of the Insubri and a part on that of the Carni and the regions about Aquileia. And there is also another large forest, Gabreta [Bohemian Forest]; it is on this side of the territory of the Suevi, whereas the Hercynian Forest, which is also held by them, is on the far side.
. . . .

Of the Germans, as I have said, those towards the north extend along the ocean; and beginning at the outlets of the Rhenus, they are known as far as the Albis; and of these the best known are the Sugambri and the Cimbri; but those parts of the country beyond the Albis that are near the ocean are wholly unknown to us. For of the men of earlier times I know of no one who has made this voyage along the coast to the eastern parts that extend as far as the mouth of the Caspian Sea; and the Romans have not yet advanced into the parts that are beyond the Albis; and likewise no one has made the journey by land either. However, it is clear from the "climata"[1] and the parallel distances

---

[1]Hipparchus took as a basis of calculation for latitudes and longitudes a principal parallel of latitude through the Pillars

that if one travels longitudinally toward the east, one encount-
ers the regions that are about the Borysthenes and that are to
the north of the Pontus; but what is beyond Germany and what
beyond the countries which are next after Germany—whether
one should say the Bastarnae, as most writers suspect, or say
that others lie in between, either the Iazyges, or the Roxolani,
or certain other of the wagon dwellers—it is not easy to say;
nor yet whether they extend as far as the ocean along its entire length, or whether any part is uninhabitable by reason of
the cold or other cause, or whether even a different race of
people, succeeding to the Germans, is situated between the
sea and the eastern Germans.

2. SENECA ON THE GERMANS AND GERMANY

> De Providentia, 4. (Dialogues, Book I.) This
> work circulated in the 15th and 16th centuries
> under the title De gubernatione mundi. Cf.
> Seneca, Opera moralia et epistolae (Naples,
> Matthias of Olmütz,1475) Hain-Copinger No.
> 14590, no signatures on leaves.

(This passage occurs in a treatise opening with the question:
Is the world governed by a providence, and if so, why do the
good suffer so many afflictions? Seneca justifies the existence
of evil by pointing to the salutary effects of hardship on those
who have learned to resist it. Life is a battle, and good men
steady themselves by inuring their natures to hardship. The
Germans are introduced as an example of a whole tribe to
which insecurity and privation are normal existence.)

   Consider the peoples beyond the limits of the Roman empire. I speak of the Germans and of all those vagrant tribes
whom one meets around the Danube. Living on sterile soil,
they must bear a perpetual winter and a gloomy sky. A mere
thatched roof protects them from rain. They walk about on
swampy ground hardened to ice by the cold. They nourish
themselves on the wild beasts which they hunt in the forests.
Are they unhappy? No, there is no unhappiness in that which

---

of Hercules and the Gulf of Issus, and a principal meridian
through Alexandria. He then drew parallels of latitude throug
various well-known places, and thus formed belts of latitude
which he called climata. By means of the solstitial day he determined the width of each clima, differences of latitude, and
so on. But Strabo uses the term primarily in reference to the
parallels of latitude themselves.

has become natural through habit; what has been begun in necessity soon becomes pleasure. They have no shelter and no
home other than the place where fatigue forces them down
each night. Their most common food must first be procured
by the labor of their hands. They are exposed to the intem-
perance of a frightful climate and have no clothing to protect
their bodies. Thus, what you would regard as misery is the
natural way of life of many peoples.

3. PLINY ON GERMANY

Natural History, IV, 13-15. tr. H. Rackham
Loeb Library Edition.

The whole of the sea-coast as far as the German river Scheldt
is inhabited by races the extent of whose territories it is impossible to state, so unlimited is the disagreement among the
writers who report about them. The Greek writers and some
of our own have given the coast of Germany as measuring
2,500 miles, while Agrippa makes the length of Germany including Raetia and Noricum 686 miles and the breadth 248
miles, whereas the breadth of Raetia alone almost exceeds
that figure; though to be sure it was only conquered about the
time of Agrippa's death—for Germany was explored many years
after, and that not fully. If one may be allowed to conjecture,
the coast will be found to be not much shorter than the Greek
idea of it and the length given by Agrippa.

There are five German races: the Vandals, who include the
Burgudiones, Varinnae, Charini and Gutones; the second race
the Inguaeones, including Cimbri, Teutoni and the tribes of the
Chauci; nearest to the Rhine the Istiaeones, including the
Sicambri; inland the Hermiones, including the Suebi, Her-
munduri, Chatti and Cherusci; and the fifth section the Peucini,
and the Basternae who march with the Dacians above mentioned.
Notable rivers that flow into the Ocean are the Gutalus [Oder],
the Visculus or Vistula, the Elbe, the Weser, the Ems, the
Rhine and the Meuse. In the interior stretches the Hercynian
range of mountains, which is inferior to none in grandeur. In
the Rhine itself, the most notable island is that of the Batavi
and Cannenefates, which is almost 100 miles in length, and
others are those of the Frisii, Chauci, Frisiavones, Sturii and
Marsacii, which lie between Briel and Vlieland. The latter
give their names to the mouth into which the Rhine divides,
discharging itself on the north into the lakes there and on the
west into the river Meuse, while at the middle mouth between
these two it keeps a small channel for its own name.

4. POMPONIUS MELA ON GERMANY

The de situ orbis was written about the middle of the first century A.D. The section
on Germany occurs in Book III, Chapter 3.

Germany is bounded in the west by the Rhine from its mouth
to the Alps, in the south by this same range, in the east by the
Sarmatian nation, in the north by the Ocean. Germany is inhabited by a hardy and robust people who find in war an outlet
for their natural ferocity and in strenuous exercise an employ
ment for the vigor of their bodies. They take pleasure in brav-
ing the cold and go about naked until the age of puberty (which
comes late to them). When they have reached manhood they
cover themselves with a skin or a garment made of the bark
of trees, this even in the severest time of winter. Swimming
is more than exercise with them, it is their passion. They
make war against all their neighbors for no reason other than
caprice, not to subjugate their enemies nor to extend their ter
ritory (for about this they care little), but only to have no othe
people nearby. They know no law but force, and no scruples
prevent them from engaging in brigandage; they are kind only
to their guests and charitable only to those who plead with the
for mercy. Their manner of living is crude and barbarous; the
even eat raw the flesh of their cattle and of wild beasts, being
content, when the meat is no longer fresh, to beat it with hands
and feet without even removing the skin.

The land is made impassable by a great many rivers, mountains, forests, and swamps.... Germany's greatest forests are
the Hercynian, and some others which have names too, but
since the former covers an area of a sixty days' journey it is
the most renowned of them all. The highest mountains are the
Taunus and the Rheticon, others have names we cannot express in our language. The most famous rivers are the Danub
and the Rhone which pass through other countries, the Main
and the Lupial [the Neckar, according to Vadian (Pomponius
Mela, 97 verso)] which flow into the Rhine, the Amisius [Ems
the Weser, and the Elbe which pour their waters into the Ocea

Notes

CHAPTER 1

1 Leonhard Rauwolff, <u>Aigentliche beschreibung der Raiss</u>, <u>so er vor diser Zeit gegen Auffgang inn die Morgenländer</u> ... <u>selbs vol-bracht</u> (Lauingen, 1582), ii recto.

2 <u>Chronica, durch Magistrum Johan Carion vleissig zusamen ge-zogen</u>, ... (Wittenberg, 1532), 169 recto.

3 Bartolomäus Küstler, <u>Eyn schön hübsch lesen von etlichen inss-len die so in kurtzen zyten funden synd</u> ... (Strassburg, 1497).

4 <u>Warhaftig Historia und beschreibung</u> ... <u>der wilden</u>, <u>nacketen, grimmigen Menschfresser</u> ... <u>in der newen Welt</u>. First edition, 1556.

5 On these collections see Max Böhme, <u>Die grossen samm-lungen des 16. Jahrhunderts</u> (Strassburg, 1904).

6 Konrad Peutinger compiled volumes of digests of voyages to Af-rica cand the West and East Indies. Erich König, <u>Peutingerstu-dien</u> (Freiburg i.B., 1914), p. 60.

7 Johann Kollauer to Celtis, May 4, 1503. Konrad Celtis, <u>Brief-wechsel</u>, ed. Hans Rupprich (Munich, 1934), No. 295.

8 <u>Pomponii Melae Hispani, Libri de situ orbis tres, adiectis Ioachimi Vadiani Helvetii in eosdem scholiis</u> ... (Vienna, 1518), 8 recto. Doubt on the reliability of the ancients is also expressed throughout the "Loca aliquot ex Pomponianis commentariis re-petita," <u>Pomponius Mela Commentaries</u>, 2nd. ed. (Basel, 1522), Aal recto ff.

9 <u>Weltbuch, spiegel und bildtniss des gantzen Erdtbodens</u> (Tübing-en, 1534), a iii verso.

10 Endorsement of Johann Rauw's <u>Cosmographia</u> (Frankfurt, 1597), unnumbered leaf 5 verso. The faculty was Protestant.

11 <u>Evagatorium in terrae sanctae, Arabiae et Egypti peregrinationem</u>, ed. K. D. Hassler, <u>Bibl. d. lit. Ver. St.</u>, II–IV (1843–49), I, 3.

12 <u>Libri odarum quattuor</u>, ed. F. Pindter, <u>Bibliotheca scriptorum medii recentisque aevorum</u> (Leipzig, 1937), I,'13. This edition will from now on be cited as Celtis, <u>Odes</u>.

13 <u>Petri Apiani Cosmographia</u> (Antwerp, 1533), p. 1.

14 <u>Henrici Glareani, poetae laureati, De Geographia liber unus</u>

(Basel, 1527), A 1 and A 2.

15 Abraham Ortelius, Theatrum orbis terrarum (Antwerp, 1570), A iiii.

16 Georg Braun and Franz Hogenberg, Civitates orbis terrarum (Cologne, 1572–1618), I, c recto.

17 Peter Albinus, Commentarius novus de Mysnia, oder Newe Meys nische Chronika (Wittenberg, 1580), p. 1.

18 In his De ritu, situ, moribus, et conditione Germaniae, descriptio, usually called Germania, the famous letter to the chancellor of the Archbishop of Mainz. I use Opera (Basel, 1571). The Germania is on pp. 1034–86, the passage quoted on p. 1052.

19 See bibliographical essay.

20 I use the edition in Schardius redivivus (Giessen, 1673), I, 95–104. It would be altogether impossible to give here a quantitative impression of humanist patriotism. I have selected example that appear to me characteristic.

21 Ibid., folios 11–101.

22 Soliloquium Wimphelingii pro pace Christianorum et pro Helveciis, ut resipiscant (1505), quoted in Joseph Knepper, Nationaler Gedanke und Kaiseridee bei den elsässischen Humanisten (Freiburg i.B., 1898), pp. 30–32.

23 Matthäus Gabathuler (ed.), Joachim Vadian: Lateinische Reden (St. Gall, 1953), p. 63.

24 Pomponius Mela (1518), 96 recto.

25 Albert Krantz, Wandalia (Cologne, 1519), XI, 26.

26 Schweizerchronik, i a and b, quoted in Hans Müller, "Der Geschichtschreiber Johann Stumpf...," Schweizer Studien zur Geschichtswissenschaft, N.F. (Zurich, 1945), p. 131.

27 Konrad Peutingers Briefwechsel, ed. Erich König (Munich, 1923) pp. 34–35.

28 Jakob Wimpheling, Epitoma rerum Germanicarum... (Strassbur 1505), preface.

29 Johann Guler von Weineck, Raetia (Zurich, 1616), iii verso.

30 Saxonia (Cologne, 1520), a ii verso. Again, I, 16. Similarly Willibald Pirckheimer, Germaniae ex variis scriptoribus perbrevis explicatio (Nuremberg, 1530), dedication. Similarly, Peter Albinus, Newe Meysnische Chronika (Wittenberg, 1580), p. 70.

31 Konrad Celtis in his Ingolstadt address. See below.

32 Orbis breviarium (Florence, 1493), fi recto–fii verso.

33 Saxonia, IV, 20, 25; Wandalia, IX, 3; XII, 34; Ecclesiastica Historia, sive Metropolis (Basel, 1548), IV, 20; V, 2; IX, 32.

34 These adjectives are used by Felix Fabri, Descriptio Sueviae, Qu. schw. Gesch., VI (1884), 134.

35 Joh.Antonii Campani Epistolae, ed. J. B. Mencken (Leipzig, 1707). My references are to this edition.

36 Ibid., p. 334.

37 Ibid., p. 352.

38 Ibid., pp. 356–57.

39 _Ibid._, p. 353.
40 _Ibid._, p. 402.
41 This complaint is heard often. An early statement occurs in
   Felix Fabri's _Historia Suevorum_. I use Melchior Goldast's edition in _Suevicarum rerum scriptores_ (Frankfurt, 1605), p. 121.
42 Preface by Kaspar Brusch to Book I of Aventinus' _Chronika vom
   Ursprung, Herkomen und Taten der uralten Teutschen; Johann
   Turmairs genannt Aventinus Sämmtliche Werke_ (Munich, 1880),
   p. 301. From now on cited as _Aventinus_.
43 Sebastian Franck, _Weltbuch_, 22 recto. Franck quotes Pirckheimer,
   Germaniae ... perbrevis explicatio (Nuremberg, 1530), A 2.
44 Sebastian Franck, _Chronicon Germaniae, Chronica des gantzen
   teutschen lands_ ... (Frankfurt, 1538), 279 recto.
45 Thomas Kantzow, _Ursprunk und Geschicht der Pomern_ ... , ed.
   Georg Gaebel (Stettin, 1897), Book V, p. 135.
46 Joachim Wagner, _Nationale Strömungen in Deutschland am Ausgange des Mittelalters_ (Weida in Thüringen, 1929), p. 9 and passim.
47 Kantzow, _Ursprunk und Geschicht_ ... , I, 304. The statement is
   a commonplace in humanist historiography.
48 Johann Boemus, _Omnium gentium mores_ ... (Augsburg, 1520),
   61 verso. Sebastian Franck, _Weltbuch_, 53 recto, quotes the same
   saying with a variation.
49 _Narrenschiff_ (1494), "Überhebung der hochfart," No. 92, p. 88,
   in the edition by F. Zarncke (Leipzig, 1854).
50 See bibliographical essay.
51 Hartmann Schedel, _Liber cronicarum cum figuris et ymagibus_
   (Nuremberg, 1493), 267 recto. This appears to be a free quota-
   tion of a passage from Enea's _Germania_ in _Opera_, p. 1046.
52 Heinrich Bebel (on the indigenousness of the German race),
   "Quod Germani sunt indigenae," _Schardius redivivus_, I, 105–7;
   Johann Cuspinian (on the truthfulness of Enea's _History of
   Frederick III_), _Austria_ ... (Frankfurt, 1601), p. 8.
53 _Liber cronicarum_. The _Europa_ begins on folio 267 verso.
54 See note 51.
55 _Wandalia_, I, chapter 4.
56 _Omnium gentium mores_, iv recto.
57 Christian Wurstisen, _Bassler Chronik_ (Basel, 1580), 657–65.
   The description of Basel is in Enea's letter to Giuliano de'
   Cesarini, "Der Briefwechsel des Enea Silvio Piccolomini," ed.
   Rudolf Wolkan, I, No. 16 (_Fontes rerum Austriacarum_, LXI,
   pp. 28–38).
58 _Methodus ad facilem historiarium cognitionem_ (Paris, 1572),
   p. 606.
59 See note 18.
60 I take the passage from Albert Werminghoff, _Nationalkirchliche
   Bestrebungen im deutschen Mittelalter_ (Stuttgart, 1810), p. 106.
   Enea repeats the charge; _Opera_, p. 1036.
61 _Asia_ was written in 1461; _Europa_ had been completed in 1458.

62 Cosmographia, Pii Papae ... (Paris, 1509), i verso.
63 Cosmographia, preface to Europa, 87 recto and 91 verso.
64 Georg Voigt, Enea Silvio de'Piccolomini (Berlin, 1856–63) II, 305.
65 Europa, chapter 20, 104 verso–105 recto.
66 Ibid., chapter 31, 114 verso.
67 Ibid., 116 recto.
68 Guarino of Verona's translation was completed in 1454 but not printed until 1471. Several Greek manuscripts had been circulating in Italy since the 1420's. On Strabo manuscripts, see W. Aly in Paulys Realenzyclopädie, VII (1931), 151–55. Enea seems to have been the first modern writer to make prominent use of Strabo.
69 Commentaries, Book IV. I use Pii Secundi Pontificis Max. Commentarii; Rerum memorabilium, quae temporibus suis contigerunt ... (Rome, 1584), pp. 201–2. The English translation is by Florence Alden Gragg in Smith College Studies in History, XXX (1947), 337–38.
70 From the 1434 letter to Giuliano de'Cesarini; see note 57. This is the description taken over by Wurstisen in his Bassler Chron
71 Commentaries, Book IX, 396 ff. English translation by Florence Alden Gragg in loc. cit., XXXV (1951), 569 ff.
72 Albrecht von Bonstetten in a dedicatory letter to Archduke Sigismund of Austria, dated Einsideln, 1492. Albert Büchi (ed.), "Albrecht von Bonstetten, Briefe und ausgewählte Schriften," Qu. schw. Gesch. XIII (1893), 127.
73 On Biondo, see the introduction by Bartolomeo Nogara to his edtion of Biondo's Scritti inediti e rari (Rome, 1927).
74 Pii Secundi ... Commentarii (Rome, 1584), XI, 310.
75 Ibid.
76 In Opera (Basel, 1571), pp. 144–281.
77 I use the Froben edition of Biondo's works (Basel, 1531), p. 217
78 Italiae illustratae libri VIII. I use the editio princeps (Rome, 1474), unnumbered folio 20.
79 This slighting reference to the German tribes nettled the German humanists. See Celtis' Ingolstadt speech below.
80 Italiae illustratae libri VIII, 20 recto and verso.
81 For an example, compare Schedel on Siena, Liber cronicarum, 80 recto and verso, to Biondo, 37 recto–38 recto in the 1474 edtion. The German version of Schedel's Chronicle is a faithful translation.
82 Krantz, Saxonia, VIII, 22.
83 Liber cronicarum, 246 recto.
84 On Celtis, see bibliographical essay.
85 "Settled" can have only a relative meaning in reference to Celti Cf. the letter from Erasmus Australis, 1494, Briefwechsel, No. 83, asking Celtis to stop his roaming about "which is more due to your irresponsibility and the instability of your character than to necessity."

86 He remained until 1497 when he transferred to Vienna.
87 Text of the speech in Hans Rupprich (ed.), Humanismus und Renaissance in den deutschen Städten und an den Universitäten (Leipzig, 1935), pp. 226–38. Also Leonard Forster, Selections from Conrad Celtis (Cambridge, 1948), pp. 36–65, from whose English translation I quote.
88 On the difference of opinion which existed on this point, see chapter 2.
89 The reference is to Biondo and Sabellicus.
90 History was, of course, a recognized part of the studia humanitatis.
91 Briefwechsel, No. 17.
92 De formando studio epistola of 1484. I use ed. in Philippi Melanchthonis de rhetorica libri tres ... (Cologne, 1525).
93 Odes, IV, 5.
94 For a fine discussion of this project see Paul Joachimsen, Geschichtsauffassung und Geschichtsschreibung in Deutschland unter dem Einfluss des Humanismus (Leipzig and Berlin, 1910), pp: 155–67.
95 Joseph Aschbach, Geschichte der Wiener Universität, II, 218, and Georg Leidinger, "Zur Geschichte der Entstehung von Aventins 'Germania illustrata,' " Sitzb. d. Bayer. Akad. d. Wiss., Phil.-hist. Abt., Jahrg. 1935, Heft 3, p. 6.
96 The Vita Celtis by the Sodalitas litteraria Rhenana refers to it among the works "oratione pedestri." The vita is contained in Conradi Celtis Protucii ... libri Odarum quatuor (Strassburg, 1513), b 3 verso.
97 A chronological list of Celtis' publications may be found in Joseph Aschbach, op. cit., pp. 230–70.
98 Quattuor libri amorum, ed. F. Pindter, Bibliotheca medii recentisque aevorum (Leipzig, 1934), from now on cited as Amores.
99 Dedication to Maximilian, Briefwechsel, No. 275.
100 See the critical edition by F. Pindter, published with the Amores.
101 Albert Werminghoff (ed.), Conrad Celtis und sein Buch über Nürnberg (Freiburg i. B., 1921). This is a critical edition.
102 Nuremberg, 1501; Briefwechsel, No. 267.
103 Ibid., No. 275. Also No. 258.
104 Ibid., No. 306.
105 Ibid., No. 242.
106 Ibid., No. 248.
107 Ibid., No. 269.
108 Ibid., No. 329. The work in question was never published. Peutinger had named it Imperatorum Augustorum et tyrannorum quorundam Romani imperii brevis gestorum annotatio. Its sources were coins, inscriptions, and narrative sources. Cf. König, Peutingerstudien, pp. 43–60, where the manuscript is described.
109 Plate in Ludwig Geiger, Renaissance und Humanismus (Berlin, 1882), p. 459.

110 Cosmographia Pomponii Melae: Authoris nitidissimi Tribus
     libris digesta: parvo quodam Compendio Joannis Coclei No-
     rici adaucta, quo Geographiae principia generaliter compre-
     henduntur, Brevis ... Germaniae descriptio ... (Nuremberg,
     1512). See Karl Langosch, "Zur Germania des Johannes
     Cochlaeus," Liber Floridus: Mittellateinische Studien, Paul
     Lehmann gewidmet (Munich, 1950), pp. 373-84.
111 Cosmographia ... "Peroratio ad Germaniam," L ii recto.
112 Aventinus, I, 643-46. Also Briefwechsel des Beatus Rhenanus,
     ed. Adalbert Horawitz and Karl Hartfelder (Leipzig, 1886), pp.
     345-46.
113 Rhenanus to Michael Hummelberg, December, 1525. Aventinus,
     VI, 88, note 1.
114 Ibid., I, 646, and Rhenanus, Briefwechsel, No. 254.
115 Aventinus to Rhenanus. Rhenanus, Briefwechsel, No. 409.
116 Indiculus Germaniae illustratae, Aventinus, VI, 60-71. On this
     Indiculus cf. Georg Leidinger, "Über ein wiedergefundenes
     Schriftchen Aventins," Sitzb. d. k.-bayer. Akad. d. Wiss.,
     philos.-philol.-hist. Kl. (1913), pp. 17-33. Leidinger prints a
     variant of the document which he included in Volume VI of
     Aventinus' works.
117 Germania illustrata, Aventinus, VI, 73-75.
118 Ibid., VI, 72-164.
119 Cosmographia: Beschreibung aller Lender durch Sebastianum
     Munsterum ... (Basel, 1544), Preface, unnumbered folio a v
     verso.
120 Erklerung des newen Instruments der Sunnen. ... Item ein ver-
     manung Sebastiani Münster an alle liebhaber der künstenn, im
     hilff zu thun zu warer und rechter beschreybung Teutscher
     Nation (Oppenheim, 1528). I have not seen this work, but it is
     described in Viktor Hantzsch, "Sebastian Münster, Leben,
     Werk, wissenschaftliche Bedeutung," Abhandl. d. Königl.
     Sächs. Ges. d. Wiss., phil.-hist. Cl., XVIII (1899), 33 ff.
121 His Germaniae atque aliarum regionum ... descriptio was
     printed in Basel in 1530 to elucidate an edition of the so-called
     Cusanus map of Germany. It was designed to stimulate further
     interest in his project. I use ed. in Schardius redivivus, I, 238
     ff.
122 Cosmographia, a v verso.
123 Franck, Chronicon Germaniae, aa ii verso.

CHAPTER 2

1 The "twenty lost books of Pliny on Germany" (See Chapter 1,
   note 30) were claimed only to accuse contemporary foreigners
   of suppressing German history. They were not remembered
   when the classical writers were charged with neglect. On the
   subject of the picture of Germany among the classical writers,
   cf. Gerald Strauss, "The Image of Germany in the Sixteenth Century," The Germanic Review, XXXIV, No. 3 (1959).

2 Georg Braun and Franz Hogenberg, Civitates orbis terrarum (Cologne, 1572–1618),I, b recto.
3 Heinrich Bebel, Epitoma laudum Suevorum. I used ed. in Melchior Goldast, Rerum Suevicarum scriptores (Ulm, 1727), pp. 6–7.
4 Chronicon Germaniae . . . (Frankfurt, 1538), end of preface. The point was made before him by Willibald Pirckheimer, Germaniae . . . perbrevis explicatio (Nuremberg, 1530), A 3 recto, and originally by Enea Silvio, Europa, in Cosmographia (Paris, 1509), 116 recto.
5 Cosmographia (Basel, 1544), pp. 160–61.
6 Peter Albinus, Commentarius novus de Mysnia . . . (Wittenberg, 1580), p. 616.
7 Hartmann Schedel, Liber cronicarum (Nuremberg, 1493), 299 recto.
8 Franz Irenicus, Germaniae exegeseos volumina duodecim (Hagenau, 1518), 6 verso. Repeated by Willibald Pirckheimer, op. cit., A 3 recto.
9 Irenicus, op. cit., 195 verso–196 recto.
10 On the parts played by Poggio, Niccolò Niccoli, and Pier Candido Decembrio in transmitting the Hersfeld codex, see R. P. Robinson, The Germania of Tacitus: A Critical Edition (Middletown, Conn., 1935), pp. 1–14. For a discussion of the older view that Enoch of Ascoli brought the codex to Rome, see Ibid., pp. 351–56. Cf. also R. Sabbadini, Le scoperte dei codici Latini e Greci ne'secoli XIV e XV (Florence, 1905), I, 108–9, 140–41.
11 The manuscript of Tacitus' Germania seems to have come to Enea after 1455. Paul Joachimsen, "Tacitus im deutschen Humanismus," Neue Jahrbücher für das klassische Altertum, XXVII–XXVIII, Heft 10, pp. 701–2.
12 Germania, in Opera (Basel, 1571), p. 1050.
13 ADB, I (1875), 365–66.
14 Andreas Althamer, Commentaria Germaniae in P. Cornelii Taciti Equitis Rom. libellum de situ, moribus, et populis Germanorum (Nuremberg, 1536).
15 Ibid., pp. 1–44.
16 Althamer to Peutinger, Konrad Peutingers Briefwechsel, No. 221.
17 Only Tacitus, Strabo, and Ptolemy are quoted more often by German humanists than the pseudo-Berosus to whom the legend of this descent is ascribed. Annius (or Nannius) of Viterbo, its real author, was a Dominican who, in 1499, was made Master of the Vatican by Alexander VI, an office which gave him censorial powers over everything printed in Rome. The choice of Annius for this post seems questionable, for the year before he had published his De Commentariis antiquitatum which purported to be a collection of seventeen treatises by ancient writers, lost until "rediscovered" by Annius. The tenth item in this volume is the "lost" history of Berosus of Babylon. Berosus was a

third-century writer of a Greek treatise on the history of Bab-
ylonia, but the Berosus of Annius is a fiction. Annius' treatise
begins with Chaldaean ideas of the world before the flood, follows the colonization of the world by the sons of Noah (it is
here that "Tuisco," the fourth son and ancestor of all Germans,
makes his appearance) and gives a list of Babylonian kings.
Scholarly dispute on the genuineness of this "Berosus" extended into the nineteenth century, although most writers won-
dered only whether Annius had been duped himself or was guilty of fraud. The latter seems clearly the case. Annius is also
credited with burying an inscribed stone near Viterbo and then
arranging to have it discovered by workmen. The stone was to pro
that his hometown had been founded by Isis and Osiris two thousand years before the building of Rome by Romulus and Remus.
See J. A. Farrer, Literary Forgeries (London and New York,
1907), pp. 67-81, and Don Cameron Allen, The Legend of Noah:
Renaissance Rationalism in Art, Science, and Letters (Urbana,
Ill., 1949), where Noah's progeny, as seen by Renaissance writers, is traced. On "Berosus," see pp. 114-19.

18 Other Tacitus commentaries, of a different scope, include
Melanchthon's little work Vocabula regionum et gentium quae
recensentur in hoc libello Tacito, which is noted for its rejec-
tion of the Tuisco myth. A more extensive academic elaboration
of Tacitus by Jodocus Willich, a professor at the University of
Frankfurt on the Oder, is not significant. Both are in Schardius
redivivus,I, 38-81. On a few others, and on translations into Ger
man, cf. Paul Joachimsen, "Tacitus im deutschen Humanismus,"
713-14, and Die humanistische Geschichtschreibung in Deutschland, Die Anfänge: Sigismund Meisterlin (Bonn, 1895), p. 60.

19 The references of Strabo, Seneca, Pliny, and Pomponius Mela
to Germany will be found in the Appendix.

20 Letter of dedication to his student Konrad Grebel, Pomponii
Melae Hispani, Libri de situ orbis tres, adiectis Ioachimi
Vadiani Helvetii in eosdem scholiis... (Vienna, 1518), 133 rec-
to. From now on cited as Pomponius Mela.

21 Letter of dedication to Abbot Francis of St. Gall, Ibid., a 3 recto.

22 For Vadian's knowledge of the discoveries of his time, see his
discussion of the antipodes in Ibid., 3 recto-7 verso, and the
concluding letter to Rudolf Agricola, 124 verso.

23 Loca aliquot ex Pomponianis commentariis repetita in the second edition of Pomponius Mela (Basel, 1522), Aa 4 recto-Aa 5
recto, Dd 4 recto-Dd 4 verso.

24 Ibid., 94 verso-98 recto.

25 Ibid., 96 verso.

26 Ibid.

27 Two further editions appeared in 1522 (Basel) and 1530 (Paris).

28 Emil Arbenz (ed.), "Die Vadianische Briefsammlung der Stadt-
bibliothek St. Gallen," Mitt. z. vaterl. Gesch. herausgg. vom

hist. Ver. in St. Gallen, V, No. 961. The year was 1537.

9 Hagenau, 1518. For later republications by Irenicus' son Paul,
cf. Walter Steinhauser, "Eine deutsche Altertumskunde aus dem
Anfang des 16. Jahrhunderts," Ztschr. f. dtschs. Altert. u.
dtsche. Litt., LXVI (1929), 25-30.

0 Adalbert Horawitz in ADB, XIV (1881), 582-83, and in "Nationale
Geschichtschreibung im sechzehnten Jahrhunderte," HZ, XXV
(1871), 82-100; Joachimsen, Geschichtsauffassung, 169-83.

1 Willy Andreas, Deutschland vor der Reformation (Stuttgart and
Berlin, 1932), p. 538.

2 Exegesis, 196 recto.

3 Ibid., 8th unnumbered leaf following folio 230, recto and verso.

4 Humanist definitions of geography and its sister sciences are
discussed in Chapter 3.

5 Exegesis, 167 recto-169 verso.

6 Ibid., 180 verso-181 verso.

7 Ibid., 218 verso.

8 Kaspar Brusch to Mergel, Johann Georg Schellhorn (ed.), Amoe-
nitates literariae (Frankfurt and Leipzig, 1725), I, 288-89.

9 Rhenanus to Aventinus, Rhenanus, Briefwechsel, No. 243.

0 Brusch to Mergel, Schellhorn, op. cit., I, 288-89.

1 One example for many: Abraham Ortelius, in his Theatrum orbis terrarum (Antwerp, 1570), has little space for the descriptive paragraphs which introduce his maps. For the earlier writers on Germany from whom more information could be gathered,
he refers to Irenicus: "Plures Germaniae scriptores, quos nos
non vidimus, enumerat Franciscus Irenicus, lib. I, Cap. 2 exegeseos Germaniae." Fol. 13 recto.

2 Nuremberg, 1530. It was the first systematic work of its kind.

3 Claudi Ptolemaei Geographiae Ennarationes Libri Octo, Bili-
baldo Pirckheymero interprete ... (Strassburg, 1525). This was
the so-called fourth Strassburg edition. It contained twenty-
three modern maps in addition to the twenty-seven of Ptolemy.

4 Germaniae ... perbrevis explicatio, A 3 recto.

5 For example: Noricum—Land an der Ens (A 5 verso): "Noricum
incipit ab Aeno fluvio, protenditurque ad Ortum Panoniam usque
superiorem. A meridie autem terminatur monte Carvanca [Car-
norum], et Alpibus Noricis, ad Italiam usque. A Septentrionibus
aunt Danubio: nunc vero inhabitant occasum versus Bavari. Ad
ortum autem est provincia, quae Ens ex fluvii Anassi nomine
vocatur, et Austriae pars. Ad meridiem autem Styria....

Civitates in Norico

Pontes Oeni	Oeting (certum)	Bidaio	Laufen (coniectura)
Bedacum	Burckhausen (coni.)	Iuvavium	Saltzburg (certum)"

6 "Artobriga iam Veltenburg, monasterium supra Ratisponam.
Certissimum ex magnis aedificiorum ruinis." Ibid., A 5 verso.

7 Theatrum, 13 recto.

8 French edition (Antwerp, 1581), 24 recto.

9 Johann Boemus, Omnium gentium mores ... (Augsburg, 1520),

52 recto.

50 Johann Stumpf, Gemeiner loblicher Eydgnoschaft Stetten, Lande
    und Völckeren chronikwirdiger Thaaten Beschreibung. 2nd. ed.
    (Zurich, 1586), Map II.
51 De Germanorum prima origine, Moribus, institutis, legibus, et
    memorabilibus pace et bello gestis ... (Basel, 1539), I, 5.
52 His words, more apropos here, are: "Cuius Germaniae? Nampe
    eius quae linguae communione aut intra vetustos limites aut
    certe prope illustris est. Equidem cum Pannones, Noricos,
    Vindelicos, Rhetos, tum maxime Helvetios inter Germanos nu-
    mero, minus terrae fortasse natura, at animorum fide, con-
    stantia et fortitudine magis." Matthäus Galbathuler (ed.) Joachim
    Vadian: Lateinische Reden (St. Gall, 1953), p. 62.
53 Enchiridion Cosmographicum, dass ist, Ein Handtbüchlin, der
    gantzen Welt gelegenheit...begreiffende... (Cologne, 1599),
    p. 65. Again, Fasciculus geographicus (Cologne, 1608), Map 12.
54 Eydgnoschaft, 17 recto. The point was first made by Enea Silvio
    Germania, in Opera, p. 1051.
55 Wandalia (Cologne, 1519), V. A. Nordmann, "Die Wandalia des
    Albert Krantz," Annales Academiae Scientiarum Fennicae, Ser
    B, XXIX (1934), 53.
56 Johann Rauw, Cosmographia (Frankfurt, 1597), p. 333.
57 Ibid., pp. 334-36.
58 Heinrich Pantaleon, Prosopographiae heroum atque illustrium
    virorum totius Germaniae libri III (Basel, 1565), p. 1.
59 Even if the Swabian mile is indicated here, this is an underes-
    timate. For distance measurements in use in his time, cf. Rauw
    op. cit., pp. 127-28, but his explanations are far from clear.
    There are 111.3 km. to one equatorial degree. An equatorial de-
    gree was equal to 15 German and Bavarian miles (each 7,420.43
    m.), about 14.8 Bohemian and Prussian miles (each 7,498.5 m.),
    12.5 Baden miles (each 8,900 m.), and 12 Swabian miles (each
    9,275 m.). The Swiss "Wegstunde" was equal to 4,808 m. Cf.
    Richard Klimpert, Lexikon der Münzen, Masse, Gewichte, Zähl-
    arten und Zeitgrössen (Berlin, 1896), pp. 221-22. Most of the
    sixteenth-century geographers believed that there were four Ro
    man millia to one German mile; in actuality there are five.
60 Joachim Vadian, Pomponius Mela (Vienna, 1518), 96 recto.
61 Ulrich Hugwald (Mutius), op. cit., I, 4. "Germani—Brothers"
    seems to conflict with the impression of fratricidal strife con-
    veyed by Tacitus. There were a few other interpretations: "Ger
    manus—totus vir," taking the German "ger" as "gar" (Althamer
    and "German, he who craves to meet the enemy in personal com
    bat," that is, "gert des mans," (Aventinus).
62 Germania generalis, "De situ Germaniae et moribus in generali
    pp. 5-7. Tacitus, Germania, 2, regarded the Germans as ab-
    original and unmixed.
63 Germaniae antiquae libri III (Leiden, 1616), I, chapters four and
    five. The arguments for and against indigenousness are admir-

ably summed up and the relevant authorities listed, in the treatise "Quod Germani sunt indigenae," by Heinrich Bebel. I use ed. in Schardius redivivus, I, 105–7.

64 Beati Rhenani Selestadiensis Rerum Germanicarum Libri Tres. All my references are to the second edition, "ab ipso autore diligenter revisi et emendati," (Basel, 1551). A synopsis of it may be found in Joachimsen, Geschichtsauffassung, pp. 131–37.

65 Basel, 1519. I use ed. in Schardius redivivus, I, 70–76, where it is attributed to Glareanus.

66 Rerum Germanicarum Libri Tres, p. 3.

67 Rhenanus holds the theory of autochthony. Ibid., p. 2.

68 Ibid., pp. 161–70.

69 De gentium aliquot migrationibus, sedibus fixis, reliquiis linguarumque initiis et immutationibus ac dialectis libri XII (Vienna, 1557).

70 This chapter is not exhaustive in its discussion of humanist investigations of German antiquity. For other minor works, cf. Erich Schmidt, Deutsche Volkskunde im Zeitalter des Humanismus und der Reformation (Berlin, 1904), Friedrich Gotthelf, Das deutsche Altertum in den Anschauungen des sechzehnten und siebzehnten Jahrhunderts (Berlin, 1900), and Theobald Bieder, Geschichte der Germanenforschung, Part I (Leipzig and Berlin, 1921).

CHAPTER 3

1 Sebastian Münster, Cosmographia (Basel, 1544), ii verso.

2 Poem by Salomon Frenzel, a crowned poet, prefaced to Marx Welser's Chronica der Stadt Augsburg in its German edition (Frankfurt, 1595), unnumbered folio 4 recto. In its entirety the poem runs to 8 folio pages.

3 Sebastian Brant, Narrenschiff, "Of Experience in all Lands," tr. Edwin H. Zeydel, Columbia University Records of Civilization (New York, 1944), pp. 220-25.

4 Ibid.; Brant is quoting Pliny, Naturalis Historia, II, 1.

5 Ibid.

6 Ptolemy, Geography, I, 1. I use Edward Luther Stevenson (tr. and ed.), Geography of Claudius Ptolemy (New York, 1932).

7 Geography, I, 2.

8 Strabo, Geography, II, 5, 1. I use the Loeb Classical Library edition, Horace Leonard Jones (ed. and tr.) (London, etc., 1927–49).

9 Ibid., II, 5, 1.

10 Ibid.

11 Johann Cochlaeus, Cosmographia Pomponii Melae: parvo quodam Compendio Joannis Coclei Norici adaucta, quo Geographiae principia generaliter comprehenduntur ... (Nuremberg, 1512), F i recto–G iv recto.

12 Johann Rauw, Cosmographia (Frankfurt, 1597), Part I.

13 Based entirely on Ptolemy's Book I. Cosmographia, a v recto.

14 Epitome trium terrae partium Asiae, Africae et Europae com-
    pendiariam locorum descriptionem continens ... (Zurich, 1534).
15 Astronomicum Caesareum (Ingolstadt, 1540), "Apianus lectori,"
    A iii recto..
16 The various editions bear different titles. The first is Landshut,
    1524. I use Antwerp, 1540, "per Gemmam Phrysium...denuo
    restituta."
17 First published Antwerp, 1530. I use ed. Antwerp, 1547.
18 Ibid., pp. 137–39.
19 Ibid., p. 139.
20 Geography, I, 2.
21 Op. cit., pp. 70–75.
22 Ibid., p. 142.
23 Libellus de locorum describendorum ratione, appended to Gem-
    ma's edition of Apianus, Cosmographicus liber (Antwerp, 1533).
24 "De novo modo inveniendi longitudinem," Chapter 18 of his De
    principiis astronomiae of 1530. Cf. A. Pogo, "Gemma Frisius,
    his method of determining differences of longitude by trans-
    porting time pieces (1530), and his treatise on triangulation
    (1533)," Isis, XXII (February, 1935), 469–85.
25 An older volume less often mentioned in the literature is Johann
    Schöner, Loculentissima quaedam terrae totius descriptio cum
    multis utilissimis cosmographiae iniciis (Nuremberg, 1515).
    Like Apianus' book, it is addressed to the lay reader and offers
    both a general introduction to scientific geography and a brief
    description of the four continents.
26 Gemma, De principiis, p. 142.
27 The 1472 Venice edition sees him "non minus historicus quam
    Geographus atque philosophus." Strabonis Geographia, latine ex
    interpretatione Guarini Veronensis et Gregorii Typhernatis ...
    (Venice, 1472), Preface.
28 Münster relies on him throughout: see preface to the Cosmog-
    raphia, a ii verso, and countless quotes of the "hoch erfaren ma
    Strabo" (Ibid., 65 recto) in the text. For a sweeping statement
    of faith in Strabo, see the prefatory letter by Wolfgang Wissen-
    burg of Basel to a volume of geographical treatises published b
    Heinrich Petri, Dominici Marii Nigri...Geographiae Commen-
    tariorum Libri XI (Basel, 1557), ii recto.
29 Geography, I, 1, 1.
30 Letter to Rhenanus, December, 1525, Aventinus, I, 644–45.
31 In Chapter 2. Cf. Friedrich Gotthelf, Das deutsche Altertum
    (Berlin, 1900), and Paul Joachimsen, Geschichtsauffassung
    (Leipzig and Berlin, 1910), passim.
32 Vadian to Bullinger, May, 1545, Vadianische Briefsammlung,
    No. 1395.
33 "Rudimentaria in Gaeographiam Catechesis," Pomponius Mela
    (Vienna, 1518), C 3 verso.
34 Ptolemy, Geography, I, 2.
35 F. Pindter (ed.), Bibliotheca scriptorum medii recentisque

aevorum (Leipzig, 1937), III, 5 (hereafter referred to as Celtis, Odes); Epigrams, ed. Karl Hartfelder, IV, 12.

36 Civitates (Cologne, 1572−1618), III, A verso.

37 Albrecht Dürer, Tagebuch der Reise in die Niederlande, ed. Fritz Bergemann (Leipzig, 1933); Aventinus, "Hauskalender," Aventinus, I, 655−89; Johann Stumpf, "Reisebericht," ed. Hermann Escher, Qu. schw. Gesch., VI (1884).

38 Eydgnoschaft (1586), 605 verso. Münster, likewise, crossed the Valais in order to expand the section on the canton for the third edition of the Cosmographia. Cf. Cosmographia, p. 330.

39 Christian Wurstisen, Bassler Chronik (Basel, 1580), p. 33. The passage turned out to be an ancient aqueduct.

40 "Ehren Gedechtnus des . . . Herrn Joachim von Watt," pp. 16−17; appended to Beschreibung der eidgenössischen Stadt St. Gallen (St. Gall, 1683). The climb is a reference to the scaling of Mt. Fractis.

41 "In der Frembde macht man kundtschafft und freundtschafft zusammen," quoted by Martin Crusius in his commentaries on Heliodorus' Aethiopica (Frankfurt, 1584), p. 29.

42 Francis Bacon, Works, ed. Spedding, Ellis, and Heath (Boston, n. d.), XII, 137−40.

43 Leonhart Rauwolf, Aigentliche beschreibung der Raiss, so er vor diser Zeit gegen Auffgang inn die Morgenländer . . . selbs volbracht . . . (Lauingen, 1582). The second edition of 1583 contains a valuable appendix depicting the botanical specimens Rauwolf brought back with him.

44 Rerum Moscoviticarum Commentarii (Vienna, 1549).

45 Edited by A. F. Walther as Hans Georg Ernstingers Raisbuch, Bibl. d. lit. Ver. St., CXXXI (1877).

46 Evagatorium in terrae sanctae, Arabiae et Egypti peregrinat tionem, ed. K. D. Hassler, Bibl. d. lit. Ver. St., II−IV (1843−49).

47 Cogmographia, (1544), a v recto.

48 Weltbuch (Tübingen, 1534), 143 verso.

49 This was never published. See note 109, Chapter 1.

50 Originum ac Germanicarum antiquitatum libri, Leges videlicet Salicae, Allemannorum, Saxonum, Angliorum, Thuringorum, Burgundionum, . . . (Basel, 1557).

51 Decribed in Franz X. von Wegele, Geschichte der deutschen Historiographie (Munich and Leipzig, 1885), pp. 216-17.

52 Prosopographiae heroum atque illustrium virorum totius Germaniae libri III (Basel, 1565−66); German translation 1567−70.

53 Cosmographia, pp. 72−74.

54 Ibid., pp. 225−26.

55 Ibid., p. 226.

56 Many of these are published by Andreas Felix Oefele, Rerum Boicarum scriptores (Augsburg, 1763), II, 557−664.

57 Gemeiner loblicher Eydgnoschaft Stetten, Landen und Völckeren chronikwirdiger Thaaten Beschreibung (1548), I, 291 verso.

58 Ibid., II, 207 verso-208 recto. He is referring to Hieronymus
   Gebwiler, on whom see Chapter 6.
59 Geography, I, 1.
60 Petri Apiani Cosmographia (Antwerp, 1540), iii-iv.
61 Joachim Rheticus, Chorographia, tewsch, durch Georgium
   Joachimum Rheticum ... zusamengebracht und an den Tag geben,
   MDXLi. I use the edition of the manuscript by Franz Hipler,
   "Die Chorographie des Joachim Rheticus," Zeitschrift für Mathematik und Physik, Hist.-lit. Abt., XXI (1876), 125-50.
62 "Ioachimi Vadiani Helvetii Rudimentaria in Geographiam Catechesis," Pomponius Mela (Vienna, 1518), a 3 verso ff.
63 Lucien Gallois, Les géographes allemands de la Renaissance
   (Paris, 1890), p. 160.
64 Bonaventura Vulcanius, in writing to Abraham Ortelius in 1598,
   took issue with the title "Cosmographia" as used for a truly geo
   graphical work by Paulus Merula: "κόσμον enim appellatione et
   caelum et terra comprehenditur. Et video doctos viros nonnullos
   etiam in huius vocis usurpatione labi; qui te Cosmographum Re-
   gium vocant; cum sis meo quidem judicio Geographus." Abraham
   Ortelii Epistulae, p. 743.
65 Cosmographia, Preface, a iii recto.
66 "...gelegenheit und form des gantzen Erdtreichs und seiner
   Stück, dass ist, besonderer Landtschafften, Cosmographia
   (1598), a v recto.
67 There was nothing exclusively German about the cosmographical
   form as described by Münster. Cf. André Thevet, La Cosmographie universelle (Paris, 1575), I, a v recto: "Vous trouverez
   qu'en ce mien oeuvre ie me suis essaié de faire comme Solin
   en son livre nommé Polyhistor, ou non seulement il fait mention
   des païs et villes: mais aussi des animaux, maniere de vivre
   des habitans, et plusieurs autres choses singulieres; a fin que
   l'oeuvre composé de diverses matieres, puisse mieux recreer
   l'entendement humain, qui est semblable aux terres, qui de-
   mandent diversité, et mutation de semences."
68 Preface to the reader by Johann Rudolph Stumpf in the second
   edition of the Eydgnoschaft (Zurich, 1586), iiii verso.
69 Cosmographia (Frankfurt, 1597), iiii recto.
70 Civitates, III, A verso-B recto. Jean Bodin, in the Methodus, pp
   26-30, arrives at the same definition, but goes on to distinguish
   between chorographia, topographia, and gromatica (land survey-
   ing).
71 Franck, Weltbuch, 3 recto.
72 Rauw, Cosmographia, iiii verso.
73 Stumpf, Eydgnoschaft (1586), iiii verso.
74 "Cum enim ea sit animi humani dum in corpore est cognoscendi
   sors, ut nisi a sensibus profecta interior intellectus capere ne-
   queat, et quaecunque cogitare et imaginari solemus, ea omnia
   certis figuris atque imaginibus circumscribamus, ad ea demum
   cognoscenda quae terrae sunt, hoc est sedes hominum, primam

omnium Gaeographiam quae omnia picturae nobis beneficio in-
dicare solet, ipsa cognoscendi ratio desiderat." "Catechesis,"
Pomponius Mela, b 1 recto.

CHAPTER 4

1 Evagatorium in terrae sanctae, Arabiae et Egypti peregrinationem, ed. K. D. Hassler, Bibl. d. lit. Ver. St., II–IV (1843–49),
   III, 371.
2 "Germaniae inferioris urbium, et aliarum quae finitimae infe-
   riori Germaniae ... Catalogus," Rerum gestarum a Brabantiae
   Ducibus Historia (Antwerp, 1551), 101 verso–108 verso. It is
   also printed in the same author's Dialogi omnes Hadriani
   Barlandi (Paris, 1530). On Barlandus, see the monograph by
   Etienne Daxhelet, Adrien Barlandus, humaniste belge ... (Louvain, 1938).
3 Batavia, in Petrus Schrijver (ed.), Batavia illustrata (Leyden,
   1609), pp. 77–120.
4 Germaniae inferioris Historiae et loca aliquot declarata. I use
   the edition appended to Pirckheimer's Germaniae ... perbrevis
   explicatio (Frankfurt, 1532). It may also be found in Schrijver,
   op. cit., pp. 70–73, along with Noviomagus' Insignium locorum
   ac oppidorum Bataviae nomina.
5 Op. cit., pp. 170–232.
6 Rostock founded in 1418, Greifswald in 1456, Frankfurt on the
   Oder in 1506.
7 Peter Gerrit Thielen, Die Kultur am Hofe Herzog Albrechts von
   Preussen (1525–1568) (Göttingen, 1953), gives an interesting
   picture of the many intellectual and cultural concerns of the
   Duke.
8 Chorographia,tewsch, durch Georgium Joachimum Rheticum ...
   zusamengebracht ... , MDXLi. I use the edition of the manuscript by Franz Hipler, "Die Chorographie des Joachim
   Rheticus," Zeitschr. f. Mathematik u. Physik, Hist.-lit. Abt.,
   XXI (1876). The passage is from the dedication, pp. 133–36.
9 A bare description of Prussian geography, probably not known
   to Rheticus, may be found in Erasmus Stella, De Borussiae
   antiquitatibus libri duo (Basel, 1518). The whole work is only
   38 quarto pages in length.
10 For titles see Otto Krabbe, Die Universität Rostock (Rostock,
   1854), pp. 224–36.
11 David Chytraeus, Vandaliae et Saxoniae Alberti Cranzii Conti-
   nuatio ... (Wittenberg, 1586).
12 Edited by Georg Gaebel, "Des Thomas Kantzow Chronik von
   Pommern in niederdeutscher Mundart," Veröffentlichungen der
   hist. Komm. f. Pommern I, Heft 4 (Stettin, 1929). The references
   in the preceding paragraph are to pp. 1 and 2 of this edition.
13 Ursprunck und Geschicht der Pomern und Rhügianer, ed. Georg
   Gaebel, Des Thomas Kantzow Chronik von Pommern in hoch-

deutscher Mundart, Letzte Bearbeitung (Stettin, 1897); Erste
Bearbeitung (Stettin, 1898). I cite according to the final version,
by book and pages of the Gaebel edition of 1897.

14 Ursprunck und Geschicht, XIV, 407-8.

15 Ibid, 411-12.

16 Ibid., 413.

17 The manuscript of the final version breaks off before this description of cities, but the earlier High German version (Gaebel
edition of 1898, pp. 256-61), indicates the plan Kantzow would
have followed had he completed the manuscript.

18 J. J. Merlo (ed.), "Johann Haselberg und sein Lobgedicht auf die
Stadt Köln," Annalen d. hist. Ver. f. d. Niederrhein, XLIV
(1885), 152, 154.

19 Beschreibung etlicher Gelegenheit Teutschen lands an wasser,
berg, stetten, und grentzen, mit anzeygung der meilen und
strassen von statt zu statt, published by Caspar Hedio as an appendix to his Ein auserlessne Chronik... (Strassburg, 1539). I
use ed. Strassburg, 1549. Cf. Konrad Varrentrapp, "Sebastian
Brants Beschreibung von Deutschland," Zeitschr. f. d. Gesch. d.
Oberrheins, N. F., XI (1896), 288-308.

20 Beschreibung etlicher Gelegenheit, p. 48.

21 Ibid., pp. 15-16.

22 Ibid., pp. 49-56.

23 Cf. what Vadian writes about those who give first place to authorities in the study of geography: "Catechesis" in Pomponius
Mela (1518), C 3 verso.

24 Tractatus de Civitate Ulmensi, de eius origine, ordine, regimine
de civibus eius et statu, Preface, p. 1. All my references are to
the edition by Veesenmeyer in Bibl. d. lit. Ver. St., CLXXXVI
(1889).

25 Descriptio Sueviae, ed. in part by Hermann Escher, Qu. z. schw
Gesch., VI (1884), 109-229, and in extenso by Melchior Goldast
in his Suevicarum rerum scriptores (Frankfurt, 1605). I cite according to the Escher edition.

26 Ibid., p. 117.

27 Ibid., p. 120.

28 Hans Kohn, The Idea of Nationalism (New York, 1944), p. 138.

29 See the analysis of the sources of the patriotism of Wimpheling,
Gebwiler, Brant, and Rhenanus by Hedwig Riess, Motive des
patriotischen Stolzes bei den deutschen Humanisten (Berlin,
1934), Chapter 3.

30 Methodus, p. 538.

31 Germania Jacobi Wimpffelingi ad Rempublicam Argentinensem
(Strassburg, 1501).

32 Epitoma rerum Germanicarum (Strassburg, 1505).

33 Ibid., Chapter 67.

34 An exaggeration. The tower is 440 feet high. But Giovanni Botero
too, regarded the Strassburg cathedral as "l'ottavo miracolo del
mondo." Le relationi universali (Venice, 1597), I, 76.

35 Panegyris Carolina, cum eiusdem notis, in quibus Alsatia et Argentoratum brevi descriptione illustrantur (Strassburg, 1641), pp. 12-16.

36 Cosmographia (Basel, 1544), p. 307.

37 For the sympathy which this dispute struck among the German humanists, see Konrad Peutinger's Sermones convivales (first printed 1506) and the letters and poems to Peutinger from many of the literary notables of his time contained in the edition of this work in Schardius redivivus I, 200-13.

38 Beati Rhenani...Rerum Germanicarum libri tres (Basel, 1551), pp. 161-70. See Chapter 2.

39 Cf. Hans Heckel, Geschichte der deutschen Literatur in Schlesien (Breslau, 1929), I, 76 ff.

40 Laurentius Corvinus, Geographia ostendens omnes regiones terrae habitabiles, diversa hominum genera, diversis moribus et conditionibus viventes, annumerans diversa animalia in diversis provinciis, insulas, maria, flumina, et montes, et plurima scitu dignissima. First edition, Basel, 1496. I use ed. Basel, 1557 bound with Dominicus Marius Niger, Geographiae commentariorum Libri XI, pp. 593-672. On Corvinus (Lorenz Rabe), see the monograph of Ludwig Bauch, "Laurentius Corvinus, der Breslauer Stadtschreiber und Humanist," Zeitschr. d. Ver. f. Gesch. u. Alt. Schlesiens, XVII (1883).

41 Corvinus, op. cit., p. 621.

42 On a few other titles see Heckel, op. cit., I, 94-108.

43 Commentarius novus de Mysnia oder Newe Meysnische Chronica (first edition Wittenberg, 1580).

44 Ibid., pp. 617 ff.

45 It is entitled Meissnische Land und Berg Chronica (Dresden, 1589).

46 Meissnische Bergchronica, dated 1590.

47 Pp. 430-37.

48 Bergchronica, iii verso-iv recto. Cf. Georg Agricola, De re metallica libri XII (Basel, 1556), 3 ff. Agricola's entire first book is an answer to the various critics of mining operations. An interesting reflection of the contemporary concern with the ethics of mining may be found in Paul Schneevogel (Niavis), Iudicium Iovis in valle amoenitatis habitum, written about 1495. (I use ed. in Hans Rupprich, Humanismus und Renaissance in den deutschen Städten und an den Universitäten (Leipzig, 1935), pp. 239-67.

49 Meissnische Land und Berg Chronica, ii recto.

50 Celtis, Norimberga, Chapter 3, in the Werminghoff edition (Freiburg, 1921), p. 39; Johann Rauw, Cosmographia (Frankfurt, 1597), pp. 337-38; Münster, Cosmographia (1544), v recto, pp. 501-2.

51 Evagatorium in terrae sanctae, Arabiae et Egypti peregrinationem, ed. Konrad Dietrich Hassler, in Bibl. d. lit. Ver. St., II-IV (1843-49).

52 Evagatorium, III, 371.
53 See note 25.
54 Op. cit., Preface, p. 1.
55 Ibid., p. 14.
56 Ibid., p. 4, for Fabri's plan of the seven divisions. Ibid., p. 209, for his farewell to the reader.
57 Albert Werminghoff (ed.), Conrad Celtis und sein Buch über Nürnberg (Freiburg i. B., 1921), a critical edition of the Norimberga. The manuscript was not published until 1502.
58 Hans Rosenplüt's poem on Nuremberg of 1447; Georg Lochner (ed.), Der Lobspruch von Nürnberg des Hans Rosenplüt (Nuremberg, 1854), p. 6.
59 Kuntz Hass, poem on Nuremberg; K. A. Barack (ed.), Zeitschr. f. dtsche. Kulturgech., III (1858), 376-405.
60 On these poems see Joseph Neff, Helius Eobanus Hesse: Norimberga illustrata (Berlin, 1896), Introduction.
61 Cf. William Hammer, Latin and German Encomia of Cities (Chicago, 1937), especially the "Index of Cities Praised," pp. 75-78.
62 Turcograeciae libri octo... (Basel, 1584) and Germanograeciae libri sex (Basel, 1585). Both volumes were compiled to keep the west informed of the progress of the Greek lands and Greek culture under Turkish rule.
63 Annales Suevici. I use the German translation by Johann Jakob Moser, Martin Crusii... Schwäbische Chronik (Frankfurt, 1733).
64 Ibid., Preface by Moser; I,c2 verso.
65 Contained in the Turcograecia and Germanograecia.
66 Schwäbische Chronik, II, 408-10.
67 See his letter to Beatus Rhenanus of December, 1525. I cite all Aventinus references according to the critical edition of his works by the K. Akademie der Wissenschaften, Johannes Turmairs genannt Aventinus Sämmtliche Werke, 6 vols. (Munich, 1880-1908). The reference is to I, 643-46.
68 Annales Ducum Boiariae, I, 2, Aventinus, II, 36-41, in Latin, and Bayerische Chronik, Book I, Ibid., IV, 35-42, in German.
69 In a letter to Beatus Rhenanus of November, 1525. Aventinus, I, 646, and Beatus Rhenanus, Briefwechsel, No. 246, p. 346.
70 Aventinus, IV, 38.
71 Declaratio Tabulae sive descriptionis Bavariae, printed in Oberbayerisches Archiv für vaterländische Geschichte, XXXIX (1880).
72 Letter from Philip Apianus to Duke Albrecht, printed by Carl Prantl, Geschichte der Ludwig-Maximilians-Universität in Ingolstadt (Munich, 1872), II, 259-60.
73 Declaratio Tabulae, 221-22.
74 Heinrich Ulmann, Kaiser Maximilian I, I, 206.
75 See the description by Konrad Peutinger of his own part in these researches, Briefwechsel, p. 65. See also the documents in Joseph Aschbach, Geschichte der Wiener Universität, II, 378-81.
76 Pomponius Mela (1518), 97 verso.

77 The topographical descriptions of Suntheim have come down to us only in fragments. These are printed as noted. The Vallis Danubio has been published by Franz Pfeiffer in Jahrb. f. vaterl. Gesch. (Vienna, 1861). The passage is on p. 291.

78 Julius Hartmann (ed.), Württembergische Vierteljahrsschrift für Landesgeschichte, VII (1884), 127.

79 The genealogical studies pertaining to the houses of Bavaria, the Palatinate, Baden, Württemberg, Brandenburg, Pomerania, Thuringia, and Hesse are printed in Andreas Felix Oefele, Rerum Boicarum scriptores (Augsburg, 1763), II, 557-644. The geographical notes are included.

80 Aschbach, op. cit., II, 289.

81 Austria Ioannis Cuspiniani. First edition by Caspar Brusch (Basel, 1553). I use ed. Frankfurt, 1601.

82 Austria, p. 71, and Cuspinian to Bernhard von Cles, Briefwechsel, p. 174.

83 Austria, p. 55.

84 Hirschfogel's plan may be seen in facsimile in Albert Camesina (ed.), Plan der Stadt Wien vom Jahre 1547 (Vienna, 1863).

CHAPTER 5

1 From the description of the battle of Grandson in the Kronika von der loblichen Eydtgnoschaft... of the Lucerne chronicler Petermann Etterlin (Basel, 1507), 89 verso-91 recto.

2 In the dedication to his Superioris Germaniae Confoederationis Descriptio, ed. Albert Büchi, Qu. schw. Gesch., XIII (1893), 113-14. The dedication is dated Einsiedeln, 1478.

3 Ibid., pp. 226-28.

4 Heinrich Bullinger, Historia gemeiner loblicher Eydgnoschaft, quoted in Hans Georg Wirz, "Heinrich Bullingers erste Schweizerchronik," Nova Turicensia (Zurich, 1911), p. 254.

5 Erasmus to Johannes Sapidus, October, 1515, from Basel. P. S. Allen (ed.),Opus Epistolarum Des. Erasmi... II (Oxford, 1910), No. 364.

6 Superioris Germaniae Confoederationis Descriptio, completed in 1479, the German version in 1485. Both in Qu. schw. Gesch., XIII (1893), 219-67.

7 Albert Büchi, Albrecht von Bonstetten (Munich, 1889), p. 18.

8 Descriptio, p. 264 in German, p. 246 in Latin

9 De situ Confoederatorum Descriptio, ed. Georg von Wyss, Qu. schw. Gesch. VI (1884), 1. Two versions, Latin and German, are included in this edition.

10 Ibid., p. 4.

11 Ibid., p. 37. Cf. long descriptions of Bern and Zurich, and somewhat lesser ones of Lucerne, Zug, and Solothurn.

12 A. Bodmer, "Die Familie von Watt, Geschichte eines St. Gallischen Bürgergeschlechtes," Mitt. z. vaterl. Gesch. herausgg. v. hist. Ver. d. Kant. St. Gallen, XXXVII (1936), Heft 2. The en-

tire literature on Vadian is discussed by his most recent and
best biographer, Werner Näf, Vadian und seine Stadt St. Gallen,
I (St. Gall, 1944), 3-12.

13 Cf. Vadian's enthusiastic characterization of Celtis in his De
Poetica, in Celtis, Briefwechsel, 616 ff.

14 Vadianische Briefsammlung,VI, p. 414. This was in 1545.

15 This is the purpose of Vadian's Diarium (in Ernst Götzinger
[ed.], Deutsche historische Schriften, III, 227-528), recorded in
the years 1529-33 when the struggle between town and monastery foreshadowed an important historical transition.

16 All published by Götzinger.

17 Vadian to Bullinger, Vadianische Briefsammlung, VI, No. 1395.

18 Götzinger (ed.), op. cit., II, 418-29.

19 Otto Fridolin Fritzsche, Glarean, sein Leben und seine Schriften
(Frauenfeld, 1890).

20 Rudolf Wackernagel, Geschichte der Stadt Basel, III, 151-52.

21 Henrici Glareani, poetae laureati, De Geographia liber unus. I
use ed. Freiburg, 1536. The preface is dated 1529.

22 Helvetiae descriptio et in laudatissimum Helvetiorum foedus
panegyricum ... (Basel, 1514). It has been edited by Werner Näf,
Beschreibung der Schweiz, Lob der dreizehn Orte (St. Gall,
1948).

23 Henrici Loriti Glareani Descriptio Helvetiae ... cum Commentariis Oswaldi Myconii, ed. Conrad Orellus (Zurich, 1737), pp.
5-7.

24 See note 23.

25 Myconius to Vadian, 1518, Vadianische Briefsammlung, II, Nos.
137, 138.

26 Adolf Gasser, Die territoriale Entwicklung der schweizerischen
Eidgenossenschaft (Aarau, n. d.), pp. 133-37.

27 De prisca ac vera Alpina Raetia. I use ed. in Schardius redivivus
I, 269-303. Tschudi's German title was Die uralt warhafftig Al-
pisch Rhetia. He himself did not publish it. It was edited by
Münster in Basel in 1538 along with Münster's own Latin translation.

28 Glareanus, in a letter to Johannes Aal, July, 1538, refers to the
excellence of this map. E. Tatarinoff (ed.), "Die Briefe Glareans
an Johannes Aal...," Mitt. d. solothurnischen Ver., II (1895),
Heft 3, p. 9.

29 Johann Guler von Weineck, Raetia: Das ist, aussführliche und
wahrhaffte Beschreibung der dreyen loblichen Grawen Bündten
und anderer Raetischen Völcker ... (Zurich, 1616), iiii recto
and verso.

30 Ulrici Campelli Raetiae Alpestris topographica descriptio. Not
published until the modern edition by C. J. Kind (ed.), Qu. schw.
Gesch., VII (1884).

31 Campell's ambitions for his Raetia are known to us from his
nine letters to Josias Simler, 1570-75. Zentralbibliothek Zurich
Ms. F 57, folios 28 recto-36 recto. The numbering of the leaves

does not correspond to the dates of the letters.
32 Ibid., November, 1570, folio 30 recto and verso.
33 Ibid., January, 1574, folio 28 recto.
34 It was completed late in 1573. Ibid., folio 28 recto.
35 Ibid., May, 1573, folio 35 recto and verso.
36 Ibid., folio 28 recto.
37 Ibid., folio 33 recto.
38 ADB., X (1879), 115–18. Georg Leonhardi's Ritter Johannes
    Guler von Weineck (Bern, 1863) is an insipid life.
39 Raetia, 182 verso–183 recto.
40 Ibid., Book XI, 163 recto–167 recto.
41 Guler gives essentially the same etymological information as
    Stumpf, but in greater detail. Cf. Eydgnoschaft (1586), 571 verso.
42 See note 59, Chapter 2, on distance measurements.
43 Stumpf, Eydgnoschaft (1586), 571 verso, gives the same informa-
    tion and quotations, but also supplies references: Georgics, II,
    and Suetonius.
44 A sharp contrast to this picture of peace and prosperity is of-
    fered by what Willibald Pirckheimer had seen when, a little over
    a century before, he had crossed the valley in the service of
    Maximilian during the Swiss-Habsburg wars of 1499. No pas-
    sage I know conveys a more heart-rending impression of the
    suffering and waste of war:

> I passed through a large village which had been burned to the
> ground. Two old women, herding about forty boys and girls
> before them, met me on the road. All were emaciated and
> deathly pale of face, a gruesome sight to behold. I inquired
> of the crones where they were leading their pitiful charges.
> "You shall see presently," was the reply. The children had
> by now reached the meadow. There they squatted and began
> to graze among the grasses and herbs, like cattle, except
> that they tore them not with their mouths but with their hands.
> ... I stood stunned and speechless. "Now do you see," one of
> the women spoke, "where I have led these wretches, who
> would be better off had they never been born? Their fathers
> fell before the sword, their mothers succumbed to hunger,
> their belongings became the booty of the enemy, their houses
> the victims of flames." "Having seen and heard this," Pirck-
> heimer concludes, "I could not suppress tears while I be-
> wailed the piteous fate of man and cursed the fury of war."

    De bello Elvetico, Book II, Chapter 4, in Opera (Goldast) (1610).
    A fine critical edition is Karl Rück (ed.), Willibald Pirckheimers
    Schweizerkrieg (Munich, 1895). The passage occurs on p. 98.
45 Thomas Schöpf, Inclytae Bernatum Urbis, cum omni ditionis
    suae agro et provinciis, Delineatio chorographica, in W. A. B.
    Coolidge, Josias Simler et les origines de l'Alpinisme (Gre-
    noble, 1904), Appendices, 249–63. Quotation from p. 252.
46 Seven letters from Pierre Pithou to Simler, 1570–72, Zentral-

bibliothek Zurich Ms. F 60.
47 In 1574. Both edited by W. A. B. Coolidge, Josias Simler ...
   (Grenoble, 1904).
48 Vallesiae Descriptio, in ibid., p. 6.
49 De Alpibus Commentarius, preface, in ibid., p. 32.
50 Vallesiae Descriptio, ibid., p. 12.
51 De Alpibus Commentarius, in ibid., p. 32.
52 Ibid., p. 56.
53 Bassler Chronik (Basel, 1580), p. iv.
54 Ibid., p. 14.
55 Josias Simler, Vallesiae Descriptio, preface in Coolidge, op. cit
   p. 8.
56 Gemeiner loblicher Eydgnoschaft Stetten, Landen und Völckeren
   chronikwirdiger Thaaten Beschreibung. I use both the first edition (Zurich, 1548, in two volumes), and the second edition (Zurich, 1586, in one volume), the latter augmented by Johann
   Rudolph Stumpf.
57 Eduard Fueter, Geschichte der neueren Historiographie (Munich
   and Berlin, 1936), p. 208.
58 See Attilio Bonomo, Johannes Stumpf, der Reformator und Geschichtschreiber (Genoa, 1923) for Stumpf's brief autobiography.
59 Catalogus Bibliothecae Stumphianae, in Gustav Muller, Die
   Quellen zur Beschreibung des Zürich- und Aargaus in Johannes
   Stumpfs Schweizerchronik (Zurich, 1916), p. 37.
60 R. Luginbühl, "Heinrich Brennwalds Schweizerchronik," Qu.
   schw. Gesch., N. F., I₁ (1908) and I₂ (1910). Hans Müller, "Der
   Geschichtschreiber Johann Stumpf," Schweizer Studien zur Geschichtswissenschaft, N. F., VIII (1945), 14–25.
61 Eydgnoschaft (1548), I, 114 verso.
62 It is worth a note, in this connection, that Stumpf tried hard, in
   the preface to the Eydgnoschaft, to demonstrate that the beginning of Swiss independence did not result from a flouting of lawfu
   authority, but rather from the re-establishment of traditional
   liberties. Ibid. (1586), iii verso.
63 Methodus, p. 606.
64 Georg von Wyss, Geschichte der Historiographie in der Schweiz,
   p. 195.
65 The letters and documents pertaining to Stumpf's biography
   have been collected by Attilio Bonomo in two typescript volumes
   at the Zentralbibliothek in Zurich: Mss. Z. I. 103 and 103 a. I
   shall cite them as Bonomo, followed by the page number. The
   pagination of the two volumes is consecutive. On the history of
   Stumpf's Eydgnoschaft, cf. Gerald Strauss, "The Production of
   Johann Stumpf's Description of the Swiss Confederation," Me-
   dievalia et Humanistica, XII (1958), 104–22.
66 Vadianische Briefsammlung, VI, 334.
67 Stumpf to Vadian, January, 1547, Vadianische Briefsammlung,
   VI, 588–89.
68 Tschudi's protest in a letter to Johann Friess, December 1547,

Bonomo, pp. 297-98. Vadian's draft reply in <u>Vadianische Brief</u>-<u>sammlung</u>, VII, 139 ff.

69 Bonomo, p. 296.

70 A full alphabetical list of authors, ancient and modern, who have been consulted or who participated occurs at the beginning of the book. The prefaces to Books XI and XII (<u>Eydgnoschaft</u> [1586], 605 verso and 636 verso, respectively) express the author's gratitude to those who have personally assisted him by sending material. Cf. also Hans Müller, <u>op</u>. <u>cit</u>., pp. 35-49, where the collaborators are named and their contributions listed.

71 <u>Vadianische Briefsammlung</u>, VI, 433.

72 <u>Eydgnoschaft</u> (1586), iii recto and verso. He feels that all German history and geography have been similarly ignored. <u>Ibid</u>., 21 verso.

73 <u>Ibid</u>., 563 recto.

74 <u>Ibid</u>., 226 recto and verso.

75 <u>Ibid</u>., ii recto.

76 Stumpf's outline in Ernst Götzinger (ed.), <u>Vadian: deutsche his</u>-<u>torische Schriften</u>, II, xxxvi-lvi. Vadian's treatise in <u>ibid</u>., volumes I-II.

77 <u>Eydgnoschaft</u> (1586), 331 recto.

78 Bonomo, p. 223. But see the letter of Nicolaus Brieffer of December, 1542, <u>ibid</u>., pp. 169-73. The scheme of the work seems then still to have been fluid. Preliminary work for the <u>Description</u> must have dated back some twenty years.

79 "Reisebericht aus dem Jahre 1544," ed. Hermann Escher, <u>Qu</u>. <u>schw</u>. <u>Gesch</u>., VI (1884). Stumpf traveled with a group, but does not identify the other members.

80 Cf. note 59, Chapter 2, on distance measurements.

81 <u>Eydgnoschaft</u> (1548), I, ii recto.

82 Ruthardt Oehme, "Die kartographische Bedeutung der Landtafeln des Johannes Stumpf," <u>Otto Glauning zum 60. Geburtstag</u> (Leipzig, 1938), pp. 53-59. Leo Weisz (ed.), <u>Die Landkarten des Johann Stumpf</u> (Bern, 1942), and Paul Leemann-van Elck, <u>Der Buch</u>-<u>schmuck der Stumpfschen Chronik</u> (Bern, 1935).

83 Most of these are not included in the 1586 edition. In maps, type, and every other detail of presentation the two-volume 1548 edition is far more lavish.

84 The 1586 edition has an additional chapter at the end of this book, listing events from 1546 to 1586.

85 <u>Eydgnoschaft</u> (1586), 645 verso-646 recto.

86 <u>Ibid</u>., 555 verso-563 recto.

87 <u>Ibid</u>., 556 recto.

88 <u>Ibid</u>., 687 recto. Illustration in 1548 ed., II, 425.

89 <u>Ibid</u>., (1586), 410 recto and 448 verso.

90 Bonomo, pp. 230, 245, 296; <u>Vadianische Briefsammlung</u>, VI, 334, 414 ff., 420, 433, 439 ff., 586, 602.

91 These are dated 1547. The general edition is dated 1548.

92 Bonomo, pp. 651-52.

93 Vadianische Briefsammlung, VI, 688.
94 Ibid., VII, 152.
95 Tschudi to Friess, December, 1547, Bonomo, pp. 297–98.
96 Stumpf to Bullinger, December, 1549, ibid., pp. 365–66.
97 Ibid., p. 320 b.
98 Cf. Tschudi's favorable judgment of the book as a whole in the same letter in which he objects to the theological observations, ibid. p. 298.
99 See the "Preface to the Reader" by Johann Wolff, printer of the third (1606) edition, unnumbered leaf 6 recto and verso.

CHAPTER 6

1 Methodus, p. 603; also p. 111. André Thevet, who had great respect for Münster, also thought his book mainly pertinent to Germany: La Cosmographie universelle (Paris, 1575), II, 930 verso.
2 Cosmographia (Basel, 1544), a v verso.
3 Ibid., a iiii verso.
4 Cosmographia (Frankfurt, 1597), p. 346.
5 Chronicon Germaniae (Frankfurt, 1538), 81 verso.
6 The one just cited from Pirckheimer's Germaniae ... perbrevis explicatio (Nuremberg, 1530), A3–A4.
7 Weltbuch (Tübingen, 1534), 23 recto.
8 Chronica, Zeitbuch und Geschichtsbibel von Anbegyn biss in diss gegenwärtig MDXXXI jar ... (Strassburg, 1531), Preface, ii recto.
9 See note 8.
10 Weltbuch, Preface, iiii recto. See the sympathetic study of Franck as a representative of a freer direction in German protestantism in Karl Hagen, Deutschlands literarische und religiöse Verhältnisse im Reformationszeitalter ..., 2nd ed. (Frankfurt, 1868), III, 314–96, and also Will-Erich Peuckert, Sebastian Franck, ein deutscher Sucher (Munich, 1943). For a recent discussion of Franck's ideas of toleration see "Friedensidee und Toleranzgedanke bei Paracelsus und den Spiritualisten: II, Franck und Weigel," Archiv für Reformationsgeschichte, XLVII (1956), Heft 2, pp. 180–200.
11 Weltbuch; spiegel und bildtniss des gantzen Erdtbodens (Tübingen, 1534).
12 Ibid., 3 recto.
13 Ibid., a ii verso.
14 Preface to the second part of Kaspar Hedio's Ein auserlessne Chronik von Anfang der Welt biss auf das Jahr ... 1543 ... (Strassburg, 1549), dd iii verso.
15 Cosmographia (1544), iv verso.
16 Ibid., p. 17.
17 Cosmographia, iiii recto.
18 Ibid., ii verso.
19 Ibid., ii verso, quoting Psalm 105, verse 2.

20 Full title: Cosmographia, das ist Ein schöne, richtige und volkom-
   liche Beschreibung dess Göttlichen Geschöpffs, Himmels und der
   Erden, beydes der Himmlischen und Irdischen Kugel.
21 Ibid.
22 Ibid., unnumbered leaf 6 verso.
23 I use two editions, the first German one, Cosmographia:Beschrei-
   bung aller Lender durch Sebastianum Munsterum, in welcher
   begriffen aller Völcker, Herrschafften, Stetten, und namhafftiger
   flecken herkommen...durch die gantze Welt, und fürnemlich
   Teutscher Nation... (Basel, 1544), and the greatly enlarged
   third edition,Cosmographiae universalis Libri VI... (Basel,
   1550). The latter is the second Latin edition, but the third one
   of the work itself; the German edition of 1545 was slightly augmented. The 1550 edition was the last on which Münster himself
   worked. He died of the plague in 1552. Other editions continued
   to appear until 1650: see S. Vögelin, "Sebastian Münsters Cos-
   mographey," Basler Jahrbuch (1882), pp. 118-26, and Viktor
   Hantzsch, "Sebastian Münster, Leben, Werk, wissenschaftliche
   Bedeutung," Abhandl. d. kgl. sächs. Ges. d. Wiss., phil.-hist.
   Cl., XVIII (1899), 153-57. Hantzsch's study is still by far the
   best on Münster's life and work.
24 Cosmographia (1544), v recto, for Münster's own list of places
   he observed personally.
25 Ibid., Münster goes on to give a list of his helpers. Cf. Hantzsch,
   op. cit., pp 63-65, for their identities. No correspondence pertaining to the immediate origin of the Cosmographia seems to
   have survived.
26 Cosmosgraphia (1544), p. 138, Preface to Book III. Similarly,
   a ii verso.
27 Chronicon Germaniae, last line of title.
28 Weltbuch, iii recto. Franck was not consistent in this position.
29 Cosmographia (1544), iii recto.
30 Among the "Geographistorici universales," Methodus, p. 591.
   Also p. 109.
31 Dedication to King Gustav I of Sweden, Cosmographia (1544), a
   ii recto.
32 "Austeilung und Entwerfung des gantzen Erdtbodens, erstlich
   etwas im gemein," Weltbuch, vi recto-aii verso.
33 Ibid., 2 verso.
34 Weltbuch, 7 recto and verso.
35 Franck's Book II, Münster's Book II, Rauw's Part II.
36 Cosmographia, p. 224.
37 Weltbuch, 42 verso. German women suffer a special denuncia-
   tion, ibid., 47 recto.
38 Ibid., 49 verso.
39 Ibid., 52 recto-53 verso.
40 Ibid., 97 verso-122 verso.
41 Germaniae atque aliarum regionum quae ad imperium usque
   Constantinopolitanum protenduntur descriptio, per Sebastianum

Munsterum ex historicis atque cosmographis, pro Tabula
Nicolai Cusae intelligenda excerpta (Basel, 1530). I use ed. in
Schardius redivivus, I, 238–58.

42 Cosmographei: Mappa Europae, Eygentlich fürgebildet, auss-
gelegt, unnd beschribenn..., durch Sebastianum Munsterum an
tag geben (Frankfurt, 1537). I have not seen this work, but it is
described in Viktor Hantzsch, op. cit., pp. 39–41, and in greater
detail in Vögelin, op. cit., pp. 113–16.

43 Bonomo, p. 225 (see note 65, Chapter 5).

44 Münster to Konrad Pellican, February, 1544, ibid., p. 237.

45 For the artists see Hantzsch, op. cit., pp. 65–67, and G. K.
Nagler, Die Monogrammisten. The cuts of the earlier edition
must have come from the files, because we find them in so
many of Petri's books.

46 Cosmographia (1544), p. 138.

47 Ibid., p. 205.

48 Ibid., pp. 451–57; Cosmographia (1550), pp. 650–78.

49 This must be the Libro de las grandezas y cosas memorables
de España by the Seville cosmographer Pedro de Medina. It first
appeared in Seville in 1543 and was reissued in 1545, 1546, 1548,
1549, and eight more times up to 1616.

50 A reference to the victory over Khairedding and the capture of
Tunis by Charles V in 1535.

51 Vadianische Briefsammlung, VI, No. 1727.

52 A Briefe Collection and compendious extract of straunge and
memorable thinges, gathered oute of the Cosmogravhye of
Sebastian Münster (London, 1572), unnumbered page 1, Preface.

53 Cosmographia, pp. 178 ff.

54 Ibid. pp. 182–83.

55 Ibid., pp. 183–209.

56 Ibid., pp. 230 ff.

57 Ibid., p. 337.

58 The extent of the Harz is somewhat exaggerated in Rauw's account.

59 What Rauw writes of the Black Forest here is taken directly
from Münster, Cosmographia (1544), pp. 501–2.

60 Cosmographia, pp. 337–38.

61 Ibid., p. 357.

62 Ibid., p. 395.

63 Vögelin, op. cit., p. 122.

64 Münster (1544), p. 483; Rauw, p. 729.

65 Weltbuch, 50 verso.

66 Cosmographia (1544), pp. 46–48.

67 Weltbuch, 50 verso.

68 Münster, Cosmographia (1544), p. 17.

69 Ibid., p. 18.

70 The political events of the twenty years or so previous to the
publication of the Cosmographia hardly justified optimism. The
Turks were in Belgrade in 1521, defeated the last Jagellon at

Mohacs, besieged Vienna in 1529, occupied Croatia in 1537, and
took Ofen (Buda) in 1541. In 1542 an imperial army under the
Elector Joachim II of Brandenburg, sent to relieve Hungary, re-
fused to storm Ofen and retreated. At the same time the power
struggle between Charles V and Francis I reached an uneasy
truce (the Peace of Crespy) in September, 1544. The internal
affairs of the Empire could give rise to no higher hopes. The uprising of the Knights under Sickingen in 1522 had been suppressed,
but only by the efforts of the territorial rulers. The ineffectual
role of the central government was glaringly apparent, and the
new Reichsregiment, forced on an unwilling Charles V by the
Estates in 1521, was abolished by the same Estates in 1524. The
terrible destruction wrought in the Black Forest, Franconia, and
Thuringia by the great peasant uprising of 1524–25 must have
still been fresh in many minds. Meanwhile, there seemed to be
cause for despair in the splits developing among the Protestants,
and in the impending civil war.

71 Cosmographia (1544), p. 17.
72 Ibid., p. 161.
73 C. Julius Solinus, Collectanea rerum memorabilium, ed. Theodor
Mommsen (Berlin, 1895), dedicatory letter, p. 2.

CHAPTER 7

1 Matthias Quad, Enchiridion Cosmographicum, dass ist, Ein
Handtbüchlin, der gantzen Welt gelegenheit...begreiffende ...
(Cologne, 1599), a 2 recto. Quad, an active scholar and copper
engraver (ADB, XXVII [1888], 1–2) flourished in Cologne,
where all his works were published, in the last half of the sixteenth century.
2 Rudolf Agricola, De formando studio epistola. The letter was re-
printed frequently after 1484. I use ed. in Philippi Melanchthonis
de rhetorica libri tres ... (Cologne, 1525), E iii recto.
3 Johann Cochlaeus, Cosmographia Pomponii Melae ... (Nuremberg, 1512), E vi verso, in a letter to Pirckheimer.
4 Meteorologia Aristotelis ... commentarioque Ioannis Cochlaei
Norici declarata ... (Nuremberg, 1512), in spite of its title a
geographical treatise; De quinque zonis Terrae, Compendium
Io. Coclei Norici in Geographiam introductorium x capitibus
conflatum, contained in his Pomponius Mela, F i recto–G iv recto. This work explains the sphericity of the earth, the zones,
continents, and climates, and defines terms frequently used,
such as "nation," "people," "mountain," "hill," etc.
5 See his Epitome trium terrae partium Asiae, Africae et Europae
compendiariam locorum descriptionem continens ... (Zurich,
1534), a textbook similar to Cochlaeus'.
6 Orbis terrae partium succincta explicatio, seu simplex enume-
ratio, written in 1582, first published Leipzig, 1583. I use ed.
Leipzig, 1586.
7 Germany, in 83 leaves, takes up more space than all the conti-

nents together.

8 Cited in Oscar Hase, Die Koberger (Leipzig, 1885), p. 304. The reference is to Schedel, Liber cronicarum (Nuremberg, 1493).

9 A study of the catalogues of the Frankfurt book fairs reveals that from the middle of the sixteenth century, when these lists began to be published, to about 1600, the topographical-historical works enjoyed a lively sale. After 1600 the topographical-historical category, called Libri historici, politici, et geographic showed a marked increase in the number of political titles and an abrupt decrease in topographical volumes. There are two compilations of catalogues for the sixteenth century: Collectio in unum corpus, omnium librorum...qui in nundinis Franco-furtensibus ab anno 1564 usque ad nundinas Autumnales anni 1592, partim novi, partim nova forma, et diversis in locis editi, venales extiterunt... (Frankfurt, 1592) and Elenchus, seu Index generalis, in quo continentur libri omnes qui ultimo seculi 1500 lustro, post annum 1593 usque ad annum 1600 in S. Romano Imper et vicinis regionibus novi auctive prodierunt... (Leipzig, 1600). For the years after 1600 I consulted the semiannual catalogues published by the Rathskanzlei in Frankfurt.

10 Ulrich Campell conferred with his mentor Josias Simler on this point and drew up a statement of details to be observed by the printer in setting the marginal notes to Campell's Raetia. Campell to Simler, May, 1573, Zentralbibliothek Zurich Ms. F 57, folio 35 verso.

11 Johann Rauw, Cosmographia (Frankfurt, 1597), unnumbered folio 6 verso.

12 Cosmographia Pomponii Melae, L ii recto.

13 Quad, Enchiridion Cosmographicum, a 2 recto.

14 From the preface to Richard Eden's English condensation of Münster, Cosmographia: A Briefe Collection and compendious extract of straunge and memorable thinges... (London, 1572), unnumbered third page.

15 This was one of the projects of Josias Simler. Cf. his Vallesiae Descriptio, preface. I use ed. Leiden, 1633, a 2 verso.

16 Matthias Quad, Die Jahr Blum (Cologne, 1595), A ii. This is a résumé of world history, in sprightly verse.

17 Joseph Zemp, Die schweizerischen Bilderchroniken und ihre Architekturdarstellungen (Zurich, 1897), p. 207, quoting from a letter by the magistrates of Solothurn in commendation of Aspers' effort.

18 Ibid., pp. 211-12, has a list of city views in Stumpf and Münster which are accurate in every detail.

19 As in Münster's 1544 edition.

20 Liber cronicarum, 179 verso-180 recto for Magdeburg; 39 recto for "Paris."

21 Zentralbibliothek Zurich Ms. N 351 b, folio 87 recto.

22 Ulrich Campell, writing to Josias Simler, mentions his fear that prospective readers will expect more of his projected Raetia than he can offer in illustrations and maps. Campell to

Simler, September, 1571, Zentralbibliothek Zurich Ms. F 57, folio 35 verso.

23 Bassler Chronik (Basel, 1580), pp. 645–47.

24 Cosmographia (1544), p. 333.

25 Ibid., pp. 628–29.

26 The stranger creatures were always associated with the most exotic part of the world. Monsters which, in the earlier editions, are said to have their habitat in India are transferred to America in the 1627 edition.

27 Johann Boemus, Omnium gentium mores ... (Augsburg, 1520), 74 recto and verso.

28 Guler von Weineck, Raetia (Zurich, 1616), 9 verso.

29 Omnium gentium mores, leges, et ritus, ex multis clarissimis rerum scriptoribus ... nuper collectos ... (Augsburg, 1520).

30 Ibid., 80 verso.

31 Ibid., iv recto.

32 Ibid., Book III, Chapters 12 ff.

33 For a contrast see the choice examples of contemporary "Kanzlei-deutsch" collected by Georg Steinhausen in his Geschichte des deutschen Briefes (Berlin, 1889), I, 119–25.

34 From Dürer's manuscript notes for a planned theoretical work on human anatomy. Dürers schriftlicher Nachlass, eds. K. Lange and F. Fuhse (Halle, 1893), p. 249.

35 "Epistola ad Jacobum Avienum de montium admiratione," preceding the Libellus de lacte et operibus lactariis (Zurich, 1543), A_2 recto.

36 Gesner carried this resolution into practice. Cf. the preface to his Descriptio Montis Fracti, bound with the Commentariolus de raris et admirandis herbis quae ... Lunariae nominantur (Zurich, 1555), p. 44, where he refers to his practice of an annual ascent.

37 Translation by H. B. D. Soulé in an edition of the Libellus for the Grabhorn Press (San Francisco, 1937), p. 5.

38 Descriptio Montis Fracti, p. 52. Gesner includes in his little treatise Vadian's account of this ascent. Ibid., pp. 55–60.

39 Vadian must be excepted from this generalization.

40 See his "Ad Sigismundum Fusilium de his quod futurus philo-sophus scire debat," Odes (1513), I, 11; (Pindter ed. [Leipzig, 1937], p. 15), and "Ad Apollinem repertorem poetices ut ab Italis ad Germanos veniat," Odes (1513), IV, 5; (Pindter ed., p. 127). Celtis was felicitated by his comtemporaries for having "chased the barbarous tongue from our land"; Hieronymus of Croaria to Celtis in 1500, Celtis, Briefwechsel, No. 237.

41 Johann Stumpf, Eydgnoschaft (1548), I, 2 verso.

42 Op. cit., E iii verso.

43 Evagatorium in terrae sanctae, Arabiae et Egypti peregrinationem, ed. K. D. Hassler, Bibl. d. lit. Ver. St., II–IV (1843–49), III, 449.

44 Germania (Strassburg, 1501), Preface.

45 Cuspinian: "... dan ich vil mer geübt pin im latein dan im teutschen...." Cuspinian, Briefwechsel, No. 21.

46 Stumpf, Eydgnoschaft (1548), I, iiii recto.
47 Exchange of letters between Augustinus Moravus of Olmütz and
   Johannes Lucilius Santritter of Heilbronn in 1492, cited in Lynn
   Thorndike, A History of Magic and Experimental Science, V (New
   York, 1941), 334-35.
48 These assertions are made by Heinrich Pantaleon, Prosopographiae heroum atque illustrium virorum totius Germaniae
   libri III (Basel, 1565-66), III, A 3 recto.
49 Moravus and Santritter letters, loc. cit., p. 335. Pantaleon concludes the passage referred to above by congratulating Maximilian II on his good fortune to be ruling over a Golden Age.
   Pròspographia, III, A 3 recto.
50 Quad, Enchiridion Cosmographicum, a 2 recto.
51 Sebastian Münster, Cosmographia (Basel, 1544), p. 93.
52 Cf. the Aurei seculi imago (Antwerp, 1596) of Abraham Ortelius
   which, in ten drawings with brief comments, depicted as many
   scenes from the life of the ancient Germans.
53 Georg Braun and Franz Hogenberg, Civitates orbis terrarum
   (Cologne, 1572-1618), II, unnumbered folio 2 recto.
54 Münster, Cosmographia, iii verso. Taken almost verbatim from
   Boemus, Omnium gentium mores, iv recto.
55 Münster, Cosmographia, iii verso.
56 "Und oberkeiten erwalet, damit sie fridsamlichen bei einander
   leben möchten. . . . " Ibid. "Legesque sibi et magistratus, ut
   pacate et ipsi inter se viverent, eligere. . . ." Boemus, op. cit.,
   iv recto.
57 Ibid., iv recto.
58 Ibid., iv verso.
59 Ibid., v recto.
60 Johann Stumpf furnishes another example of this inconsistency.
   One can almost see him swell with pride as he describes a town
   growth to prosperity and the far-flung enterprises of its industr
   and commerce. Lindau on Lake Constance, for example, is "ein
   herrlich Emporium," and her busy artisans, merchants, and
   middlemen are shown to be altogether admirable. (Eydgnoschaft
   1548 ed., Book V, f. 51 recto.) On the other hand, when his subject is the Spartan virtues of the ancient Helvetians, his own
   society's wealth and comfort cannot even arouse his sympathy:
   "But nowadays people are no longer satisfied with the simple
   gifts of God which our forefathers enjoyed. Instead our towns,
   villages, highways, and inns are crammed to the rafters with
   businessmen and their imported wines, their alien delicacies,
   their spices, and other merchandise from abroad. . . . " (Ibid.,
   IV, f. 264 recto.)
61 The strongest statement of these questions is to be found in
   Aventinus' agonized Ein warnus und anzeigung der Ursach,
   warumb got der her dem Türken . . . so vil sigs wider uns
   Christen gebe . . . , Johann Turmairs genannt Aventinus
   Sämmtliche Werke I (Munich, 1880), 175, 183, 214-15.

Bibliographical Remarks

Everyone who studies the intellectual history of sixteenth-century Germany knows how welcome a comprehensive work on German humanism would be. But no such work exists. In the absence of a connected account, one may obtain a balanced view of the nature of the movement from the following : Georg Ellinger's article in Merker and Stammler's _Reallexikon der deutschen Literatur-beschichte_ I (1925–26), 525–72, ãnd more briefly in _Gebhardts Handbuch der deutschen Geschichte_, 7th ed. (1930–31), I, 549 ff. Paul Joachimsen, in "Der Humanismus und die Entwicklung des deutschen Geistes," _Deutsche Vierteljahresschrift für Literatur-wissenschaft und Geistesgeschichte_, VIII (1930), 419 ff., and "Re-naissance, Humanismus und Reformation," Zeitwende, II (1925), attempted a definition of the principles of German humanism. His views are augmented and complemented by Gerhard Ritter, "Die geschichtliche Bedeutung des deutschen Humanismus," _Historische Zeitschrift_, CXXVII (1922–23), 408–14; Rudolf Wolkan, "Über den Ursprung des Humanismus," _Zeitschrift für die österreichischen Gymnasien_, LXVII (1916), 241–68; and Hans Baron, "Zur Frage des Ursprungs des deutschen Humanismus und seiner religiösen Reformbestrebungen," HZ, CXXXII (1925), 413–46. Willy Andreas, _Deutschland vor der Reformation_ (1932) surveys the movement somewhat more drily than Joachimsen, being, as he writes, "einige Grade kühler gestimmt." The literary historian Josef Nadler presents his own interpretation of the character of German humanism in his _Literaturgeschichte des deutschen Volkes_, 4th ed. (1939), p. 226. The entire course of the conceptual discussion may be followed in Hans Rupprich, "Deutsche Literatur im Zeitalter des Humanismus und der Reformation," _Dtsche. Vierteljahresschr. f. Litwiss. u. Geistesgesch._, XVII(1939), Referatenheft, 83–133; Werner Näf, "Aus der Forschung zur Geschichte des deutschen Humanismus," _Schweizer Beiträge zur allgemeinen Geschichte_, II (1944), 211–30 (since Joachimsen); and, for the older literature, in the discussions by Joachimsen himself, Baron, and Ankwicz von Kleehoven in _Jahresberichte für deutsche Geschichte_, 1925–35.

There is no full account of the geographical interests of German humanists. One may mention only Viktor Hantzsch's brief attempt, "Die landeskundliche Literatur Deutschlands im Reformations-zeitalter," Deutsche Geschichtsblätter, I (1900), 18–22, 41–47; and Siegmund Günther, "Der Humanismus in seinem Einflusse auf die Entwicklung der Erdkunde," Geographische Zeitschrift 6. Jahr-gang (1900), 65 ff., besides Lucien Gallois' not very satisfactory chapter in his Les géographes allemands de la Renaissance (1890). The historiographical accomplishments of German humanism, on the other hand, are admirably discussed by Paul Joachimsen, Ge-schichtsauffassung und Geschichtsschreibung in Deutschland unter dem Einfluss des Humanismus (1910); also by Emil Mencke-Glücke Die Geschichtschreibung der Reformation und Gegenreformation (1912). See in addition the very detailed Geschichte der deutschen Historiographie (1885) of Franz X. von Wegele. Friedrich Gotthelf, in Das deutsche Altertum in den Anschauungen des 16. und 17. Jahrhunderts (1900) and H. Dannenbauer, "Germanisches Altertum und deutsche Geschichtswissenschaft," Philosophie und Geschichte, LII (1935) deal with an important result of this historical research.

Humanist patriotism has been a touchy subject for German his-torians to handle. There is no systematic treatment. Joachim Wagner's Nationale Strömungen in Deutschland am Ausgange des Mittelalters (1929) reaches no farther than the reign of Frederick III, and Joachimsen added only a popular book, Vom deutschen Volk zum deutschen Staat, eine Geschichte des deutschen National-bewusstseins (1916), and a collection of excerpts, Der deutsche Staatsgedanke von seinen Anfängen bis auf Leibnitz und Friedrich den Grossen (1921), to the excellent comments on the subject in his Geschichtsauffassung. A rather thin volume by Hedwig Riess, Motive des patriotischen Stolzes bei den deutschen Humanisten (1934), may also be mentioned.

The person of the humanist has attracted the historian more often than has the movement. There are biographies of many in-dividuals, and reference to most of these has been made in the notes. Most are sketchy, and often they are also uncritical and, by now, rather old-fashioned. Werner Näf's splendid "life and times," Vadian und seine Stadt St. Gallen (Vol. I, 1944; Vol. II, 1957) stands as a rare example of what a biographical study of a German hu-manist should be. Konrad Celtis has had the lion's share of atten-tion. The most illuminating study of his career remains Friedrich von Bezold's "Konrad Celtis, 'der deutsche Erzhumanist,'" Aus Mittelalter und Renaissance, kulturgeschichtliche Studien (1918). A new book, in English, is Lewis Spitz, Conrad Celtis, The Ger-man Arch-Humanist (1957), where references to further Celtis studies may be found. Two other works which provide glimpses not only of individuals but also of the age are Max Herrmann, Albrecht von Eyb und die Frühzeit des deutschen Humanismus (1893) and W. A. B. Coolidge, Josias Simler et les origines de l'Alpinisme (1904).

The passage of elements of Italian culture to Germany has also

been traced through the careers of individuals. The most familiar
work is Georg Voigt's provocative Enea Silvio de' Piccolomini als
Papst Pius II und sein Zeitalter (1856–63), especially II, 342 ff.
See also Anton Weiss, Aeneas Silvio Piccolomini als Papst Pius
II, sein Leben und Einfluss auf die literarische Cultur Deutschlands (1897) and Wilhelm Wattenbach, "Peter Luder, der erste humanistische Lehrer in Heidelberg," Zeitschrift für die Geschichte
des Oberrheins, XXII (1869), 33–127. Also, Ludwig Geiger, "Be-
ziehungen zwischen Deutschland und Italien zur Zeit des Humanismus," Zeitschrift für deutsche Kulturgeschichte N.F. IV (1875),
104 ff., and the same author's general volume, Renaissance und
Humanismus in Italien und Deutschland (1882).

On the visual aspects of the topographical-historical volumes,
the following may be suggested. Maps and cartography: Leo Bagrow,
Die Geschichte der Kartographie (1951), Arthur Breusing, Leitfaden
durch das Wiegenalter der Kartographie bis zum Jahre 1600 mit
besonderer Berücksichtigung Deutschlands (1883), and Leo Weisz,
Die Landkarten des Johann Stumpf (1942). On Ortelius there is the
monograph by H. Wauwermans, Histoire de l'école cartographique
Belge et Anversoise du XVIe siècle (1895), but one should go directly to one of the many editions of Ortelius' Theatrum. Illustrations, xylography, and printing: Richard Muther, Die deutsche
Bücherillustration der Gothik und Frührenaissance (1884), Joseph
Zemp, Die schweizerischen Bilderchroniken und ihre Architektur-
Darstellungen (1897), and Paul Leehmann-van Elck, Der Buch-
schmuck der Stumpfschen Chronik (1935).

Histories of universities hold much interesting material on the
activities of humanist scholars in Germany. Specially mentioned
may be Joseph Aschbach, Geschichte der Wiener Universität
(1877), Carl Prantl, Geschichte der Ludwig-Maximilians-Universität in Ingolstadt (1872), and Gerhard Ritter, Die Heidelberger
Universität (1936). As for general volumes on the period, there
are too many to list even a representative collection of them, but
one should mention Willy Andreas' book on Germany before the
Reformation, already cited. Good bibliographical guides may be
found in Gebhardts Handbuch der deutschen Geschichte, 7th ed.
(1930–31), G. Wolf, Quellenkunde der deutschen Reformationsgeschichte (1915), Myron P. Gilmore, The World of Humanism
(1952), and, most complete and up-to-date, Karl Schottenloher,
Bibliographie zur deutschen Geschichte im Zeitalter der Glaubens-
spaltung, 2nd ed. (1956 ff.).

Index

Adda River, 99–100
Adula Alps, 93
Agricola, Georg, 73, 74
Agricola, Rudolf, 22, 135, 146
Albinus, Peter, 6, 111, 143; Newe Meysnische Chronica, 73–75
Alps, 144
Alsace, 10, 43, 44, 65; description, 69–72
Althamer, Andreas, 31–32, 35
Apianus, Peter, 6, 26, 56, 80, 117; Cosmographia, 48–50
Apianus, Philip, 75, 80–81
Aristotle, 89
Aspers, Hans, 139
Austria, 92; description, 81–85
Aventinus, Johann, 25–26, 27, 51, 52, 60, 79–80, 143, 145, 149

Bacon, Francis, 52, 115
Barlandus, Adrianus, 61
Basel, 13, 16, 43, 87, 108, 144; description, 66, 103
Bavaria: description, 79–81
Bebel, Heinrich, 7
Bern, 88
Berosus, 32, 130
Biondo, Flavio, 7, 17–19, 22; Italia Illustrata, 18–19, 104
Black Forest, 129–30
Bodin, Jean, 13, 69, 105, 111, 117
Boemus, Johann, 11, 12, 141–42, 148–49
Bohemia, 10, 11
Bonstetten, Albrecht von, 86, 87–88; quoted, 17
Brant, Sebastian, 8, 46, 111, 128, 135, 145; The Ship of Fools, 11, 12;
    Beschreibung etlicher gelegenheyt..., 65–67
Braun, Georg, 52, 58
Breitgau, 93
Brennwald, Heinrich, 104
Brieffer, Nicolaus, 105
Bruni, Leonardo, 7

Brusch, Caspar, 38, 93
Bry, Theodor de, 4
Bullinger, Heinrich, 87, 90, 105-6, 121
Burgkmair, Hans, 25, 138

Calendarium historicum, 53-54
Campano, Giovanni Antonio: letters on Germany, 9-10
Campell, Ulrich: Raetia, 93-94
Carion, Johann, 4
Cartography, 40, 80, 92, 94, 107, 118; and voyages of discovery, 6
Celtis, Konrad, 27, 28, 37, 42, 51-52, 72, 89, 90, 130, 143; interest
    in geography, 5, 6, 23-24; Ingolstadt address, 19-22; Germania
    Illustrata, 23-25; edits medieval sources, 23; interest in folk-
    lore, 23; Germania Generalis, 24; Norimberga, 24, 38, 77; edits
    Tacitus' Germania, 31
Charles V, Emperor of Germany, 4, 48, 70, 83
Chorography. See Topography
Chytraeus, David, 62
Clüver, Philip, 42, 44; Germania Antiqua, 31
Cochlaeus, Johann, 25, 47, 135-36, 137
Collimitius, Georg, 83
Cologne, 128; description, 65-67
Columbus, Christopher, 4
Constance, Lake of, 66, 87, 90
Corvinus, Lorenz, 72
Cosmography: definitions of, 55-59
Crusius, Martin, 78-79
Cuspinian, Johann, 89, 143, 145; Austria, 83-85

Danube River, 24, 40, 41, 119; description, 66, 67, 82, 84-85
Dürer, Albrecht, 52, 143

Eber, Paul, 53-54
Eden, Richard, 127
Elbe River, 24, 73
Enea Silvio de Piccolomini. See Piccolomini, Enea Silvio de
Erasmus, Desiderius, 87
Ercker, Lazarus, 74
Ernstinger, Georg, 52

Fabri, Felix, 6, 60, 135, 145, 146; Evagatorium, 52-53, 75-76; Des-
    criptio Sueviae, 67-69, 75-76; Tractatus de Civitate Ulmensi,
    76-77
Feyerabend, Sigmund, 4
Folkways: study of, 14, 23, 108, 141-42
Franck, Sebastian, 5, 12, 30, 53, 60, 111-33 passim, 145, 149; Chro-
    nicon Germaniae, 28; Weltbuch, 112-14, 119-20
Franconia, 11; description, 123-25
Frankfurt am Main, 125

Frederick III, Emperor of Germany, 19
Freiburg (Switzerland), 88–89
Frische Haff: description, 63
Frisia, 11
Froschauer, Christoph, 105, 139

Gebwiler, Hieronymus, 70–72
Gemma, Rainer (Frisius), 56, 117; De Principiis Astronomiae, 48–50
Genealogy, 54
Geneva, 87
Geography: and the German humanists, 6, 45-50; descriptive, 47–51, 54; definitions of, 55-59; in the academic curriculum, 91, 135–36
Germania Illustrata, 22–25, 28, 29, 39, 49, 51, 54, 143
Germanic Tribes, 11, 32, 36, 43, 84, 122, 144
Germany: constitutional reform, 3; peasant uprisings, 3; religious disputes, 3; nationalism, 7–11, 13; ignored by classical authors, 20, 29–30, 122; in antiquity, 29, 45, 47; comparison of ancient and modern, 31, 33–34, 40; geography, 32, 33, 37–38, 39–40; extent and boundaries, 33, 40–42, 61; customs, 34, 64; meaning of name, 42; description, 46, 49. See also Protestant Reformation
Gesner, Conrad, 144
Glareanus, Heinrich, 6, 26, 91–92
Grandson, Battle of, 86
Guillimann, Franz, 93
Guler von Weineck, Johann, 93, 107, 135, 143–44, 145; Raetia, 94–102
Gutenberg, Johann, 139, 146

Haselberg, Johann, 65
Hass, Kunz, 78
Herberstain, Siegmund von, 52
Hercynian Forest, 24, 32, 37, 129–30
Herodotus, 14, 118
Herold, Johann, 53
Historiography: local, 107–8, 123
History and Historiography, 50–52; as instruction, 11; need for, 20–21; concepts of, 34, 36, 51, 106, 133
Hogenberg, Franz, 52, 58
Hulsius, Levinus, 4
Humanists: interest in geography, 5, 6, 45–50, 55–59; and Middle Ages, 7, 21; attitude toward Italy, 7, 11–12; patriotism of, 7–11, 60, 65, 69; ethical precepts, 11, 147; reforming impulses, 11; travels by, 19, 2 3, 51–53, 54; as a community, 23, 27, 34, 53; historical scholarship, 29, 50–52, 54, 82; as teachers, 48, 116, 136; originality of, 53; and German language, 145–46
Hutten, Ulrich von, 60

Illustrations, 121, 137, 138—41
Ingolstadt, 19
Irenicus, Franz, 30, 43; _Exegesis Germaniae_, 34—39
Italy: alleged suppression of German records, 8—9; resentment by
  German humanists, 8—10; cultural influence on Germany, 60

Jungfrau, 102

Kantzow, Thomas, 62—65, 135, 143, 145
Krantz, Albert, 8, 9, 12, 40, 62, 145

Lazius, Wolfgang, 44
Lilius, Zacharias, 9
Livy, 30
Loriti, Heinrich. _See_ Glareanus, Heinrich
Low Countries: description, 61
Luther, Martin, 105, 115, 132, 143

Magdeburg, 37
Main River, 123, 124, 127
Manlius, Jacob, 54
Maps. _See_ Cartography
Maximilian I, Emperor of Germany, 3, 6, 7, 24, 54, 82, 83, 91
Mayr, Martin, 13, 31
Meissen: description, 73
Melanchthon, Philip, 53, 114
Merian, Matthew, 139
Morbenn: description, 94—96
Münster, Sebastian, 12, 26—28, 30, 53, 57, 60, 62, 71, 74, 93, 111—33
  passim, 135, 137, 139-49; _Cosmographia_, 27, 48, 54, 58, 75, 115-
  16, 120-27; edits Ptolemy's _Geography_, 34, 107; definitions of
  topography, 58
Mutius, Ulrich, 40
Myconius, Oswald, 91—92

Neander, Michael, 136
New World, 49, 121, 140
Niger, Franz, 93
Nuremberg, 113; description, 77—78

Oder River: description, 63—64
Ortelius, Abraham, 40

Palatinate, 11
Pantaleon, Heinrich, 54
Petri, Publishing Firm of, 103, 121
Peurbach, Johann, 146
Peutinger, Konrad, 8, 25, 26—27, 53

Piccolomini, Enea Silvio de, 9, 12, 13, 37, 55, 69, 88, 143; quoted,
    6–7; as geographer, 12–17; Cosmographia, 12, 13, 48; Germania,
    13, 31; on Germany, 14; study of folkways, 14; Commentaries,
    15–17
Pirckheimer, Willibald, 39–40, 61, 120, 145
Pithou, Pierre, 102
Pius II, Pope. See Piccolomini, Enea Silvio de
Pliny The Elder, 13, 30, 37, 57, 89, 109
Polybius, 30
Pomerania: description, 62–65
Pomponius Mela, 25, 32, 37, 47, 89, 90, 136
Printing, 24
Protestant Reformation, 90, 104, 105, 108, 110, 113, 115
Ptolemy (Claudius Ptolemaeus), 10, 14, 30, 39, 47, 48, 49, 55–56,
    61, 91, 93, 118, 139

Quad, Matthias, 40, 135, 137

Raetia, 32; description, 92–102
Rauw, Johann, 47, 58, 60, 111–33 passim, 135; Cosmographia, 41–42
    75, 115, 127–31
Rauwolf, Leonhart, 52; quoted, 3
Regiomontanus (Müller, Johannes), 146
Rhenanus, Beatus, 25, 42–44, 71
Rheticus, Joachim, 56, 61–62
Rhine River, 24, 26, 37, 40, 41, 65, 86, 87, 119, 123, 127–28; des-
    cription, 65–69
Rosenplüt, Hans, 77–78
Rothenburg, 131

Saale River, 73
St. Gall: description, 90, 108
Saxony, 11; mines and mining, 74–75
Scenic Description, 97–102, 103, 143–45
Schaffhausen, 68, 144
Schauffelin (Schäufelin), Hans Leonhard, 138
Schedel, Hartmann, 4, 12, 18–19, 109, 139
Schlettstadt, 43; description, 70
Schrijver, Petrus, 61
Silesia: description, 72
Simler, Josias, 93, 102–3
Solinus, Gaius Julius, 126, 134
Stabius, Johann, 54, 83
Staden, Hans, 4, 140–41
Strabo, 13, 14–15, 30, 32, 35, 37, 39, 47, 48, 50–51, 55, 57, 89, 93,
    126
Strassburg, 65, 67, 70, 113
Stumpf, Johann, 8, 40, 52, 54, 93, 111, 135, 137, 139, 140, 143, 145,
    149; Eydgnoschaft, 19, 104–10, 121; definitions of topography, 58

Stumpf, Johann Rudolf, 109–10
Suntheim, Ladislaus, 54, 82–83
Swabia, 11; description, 75–79, 119–20
Switzerland, 10, 11, 123; relationship to Holy Roman Empire, 7, 86–87; description, 86–110; patriotism, 87; military affairs, 87, 88, 92, 128; political development, 92, 100; scenic beauty, 143

Tacitus, 10, 37, 39, 42, 75, 122, 130, 149; Germania, 30–31, 42, 147
Tirol, 24
Topographies: appearance, 137–38; literary quality, 142–45; popularity of, 137–38
Topography: stimuli, 5–6, 10, 26–27; models, 12–17, 17–19; definitions of, 49, 55–59; interest of humanists in, 55–59; local and regional, 111–12
Tschudi, Aegidius (Gilg), 92–93, 105, 107, 110
Türst, Conrad, 88–89
Tuisco, 32. See also Berosus
Turgau: description, 90, 106
Turks, 3, 61, 107, 113, 116, 120, 132

Ulm: description, 76–77

Vadian, Joachim, 5, 7, 35, 40, 48, 51, 52, 58, 89–90, 91, 126, 136, 144, 145; Commentary on Pomponius Mela, 32–34; definitions of geography, 56–59; Catechesis, 56–57; collaboration with Stumpf, 90–91, 105–6, 109–10
Valais, 52; description, 102–3
Valtellina, 92; description, 97–102
Vespucci, Amerigo, 4
Vienna: description, 85
Virgil, 98
Vistula, 24
Voyages of Discovery, 3–4, 5; interest of humanists in, 5, 33

Watt, Joachim von. See Vadian, Joachim
Weineck, Guler von. See Guler von Weineck, Johann
Welser, Marcus, 93
Wimpheling, Jakob, 7, 60, 69–70, 146
Würzburg: description, 124–25
Wurstisen, Christian, 140, 144; Bassler Chronik, 103–4

Zurich, 105, 108, 110
Zwingli, Ulrich, 87, 105